EXPERT RESUMES for
Teachers and Educators

Wendy S. Enelow and
Louise M. Kursmark

jist®
Works

Expert Resumes for Teachers and Educators

© 2002 by Wendy S. Enelow and Louise M. Kursmark

Published by JIST Works, an imprint of JIST Publishing, Inc.
8902 Otis Avenue
Indianapolis, IN 46216-1033
Phone: 1-800-648-JIST   Fax: 1-800-JIST-FAX   E-mail: info@jist.com

Visit our Web site at **www.jist.com** for information on JIST, free job search information, book chapters, and ordering information on our many products!

See the back of this book for additional JIST titles and ordering information. Quantity discounts are available for JIST books. Please call our Sales Department at 1-800-648-5478 for a free catalog and more information.

Acquisitions and Development Editor: Lori Cates
Cover Designer: Katy Bodenmiller
Interior Designer: Trudy Coler
Page Layout Technicians: Trudy Coler and Aleata Howard
Indexer: Tina Trettin

Printed in the United States of America
06 05 04   9 8 7 6 5 4 3

Library of Congress Cataloging-in-Publication Data

Enelow, Wendy S.
 Expert resumes for teachers and educators / Wendy S. Enelow and Louise M. Kursmark.
   p. cm.
Includes index.
ISBN 1-56370-799-3
 1. Teachers—Employment. 2. Educators—Employment. 3. Resumes (Employment) 4. Cover letters. I. Kursmark, Louise. II. Title.

LB1780 . E64 2001
808'.06665—dc21

2001029995

ISBN 1-56370-799-3

CONTENTS AT A GLANCE

Resumes for Adjunct Faculty, Cooperative/Adult Education Teachers, Art Teachers, Computer Instructors, Dance Teachers, Distance-Learning Professionals, and E-Learning Specialists.

Resumes for Librarians/Interactive Media Directors, Media Educators, Substitute Teachers, School Social Workers, Admissions Counselors, Guidance Counselors, School Psychologists, School Volunteer Leaders, Technology Coordinators, and Aides/Program Coordinators.

Resumes for College and University Faculty, Adjunct Faculty, Clinical Instructors, and University Education Coordinators.

CVs for Secondary and University Educators, and International Educators.

Resumes for Assistant Principals, Principals, Athletic Directors, University Student Activities Directors, Public School Administrators, Superintendents of Schools, Campus Coordinators, Directors of Education, Educational Materials Coordinators, and Daycare Licensing Administrators.

Resumes for Corporate Training Managers, Training and Development Professionals, Corporate Trainers, Training Consultants, Executive Training and Development Professionals, Technical Trainers/Training Managers, Sales Trainers, Performance Technologists, Coaches/Mentors, and Software Trainers.

Where to go on the Web for help with your job search: general job search advice, education career information, resume key words, company and school information, interviewing tips, and salary information.

How to find professional resume writers in your area.

TABLE OF CONTENTS

ABOUT THIS BOOK

The profession of education and its related career paths are showing strong and steady growth, according to the U.S. Department of Labor's projections. Experts anticipate that this growth will continue through at least 2008.

What's more, education has changed. When we talk about education professionals, we're no longer referring to just classroom teachers. The specializations and sub-specializations of the education profession have grown phenomenally and now include the following:

- Pre-school, elementary, secondary, special education/remedial, gifted and talented, college and university, and proprietary school teachers

- School-based counselors, therapists, psychologists, and social workers

- Librarians, multimedia specialists, and research assistants

- School administrators, assistant principals, principals, college and university deans, and department chairpersons

- Education support professionals, including coaches, security officers, DARE officers, secretaries, clerks, and transportation staff

- Corporate training and development professionals, instructional technology designers, multimedia training developers, "stand-up" trainers, and training consultants

And the list continues. As an educator, you no longer have to look to the school system for employment opportunities. There is now a wealth of for-profit training companies, tens of thousands of companies that employ training professionals, and unlimited opportunities as a self-employed trainer and coach. What's more, there are thousands and thousands of positions with the more traditional school-based systems, colleges, and universities. What this means is that there are unlimited employment opportunities, and that's great news for you!

To take advantage of all of these opportunities, you must first develop a powerful, performance-based resume. To be a savvy and successful job seeker, you must know how to communicate your qualifications in a strong and effective written presentation. Sure, it's important to let employers know essential details, but a resume is more than just your job history and academic credentials. A winning resume is a concise yet comprehensive document that gives you a competitive edge in the job market. Creating such a powerful document is what this book is all about.

We'll explore the changes in resume presentation that have arisen over the past decade. In the past, resumes were almost always printed on paper and mailed. Today, e-mail has become the chosen method for resume distribution in many industries. In turn, many of the traditional methods for "typing" and presenting resumes have changed dramatically. This book will instruct you in the methods for preparing resumes for e-mail, scanning, and Web site posting, as well as the traditional printed resume.

By using *Expert Resumes for Teachers and Educators* as your professional guide, you will succeed in developing a powerful and effective resume that opens doors, gets interviews, and helps you land your next great opportunity!

INTRODUCTION

According to the U.S. Department of Labor's Bureau of Labor Statistics, the education professions are projected to show relatively strong and steady growth over the next seven years, through 2008. Some of the most interesting statistics anticipate growth for the following professions:

Profession	Percentage of Growth Through 2008
School Health Professionals	36.9%
Special Education Teachers	33.7%
School Counselors, Secondary School Teachers, College Faculty	22.6%
Administrative Support Personnel	19.9%
Pre-School, Kindergarten, Elementary School Teachers	11.5%
Education Administrators	11.5%
Librarians, Vocational Education Instructors	11.5%

These statistics and others clearly demonstrate that there is tremendous opportunity within the education professions. Not only is the number of positions increasing year after year, salaries are also moving upward, albeit at a slower rate of increase than the position growth rate.

What's more, the dramatic and rapid emergence of technology throughout all sectors of our lives has also impacted the field of education with a host of new professional opportunities. When you combine all of your options, you're presented with the following array of career opportunities:

- **Education professionals** (early-childhood education, primary, secondary, college, university, and for-profit training companies)

- **Educational services support professionals** (librarians and media specialists, coaches, teaching assistants, school counselors, and educational institution administrative staff)

- **Education management professionals** (school administrators, college and university deans, and school-based department chairpersons)

- **Corporate training professionals** (corporate trainers, technical trainers, training and development specialists, and training department managers)

- **Educational technology specialists** (educational software designers, Web-based instructional programmers, and distance-learning specialists)

To take advantage of these opportunities, you must be an educated job seeker. That means you must know what you want in your career, where the hiring action is, what qualifications and credentials you need to attain your desired career goals, and how best to market your qualifications. It is no longer enough to be a talented teacher, librarian, administrator, or training and development professional! Now, you must be a strategic marketer, able to package and promote your experience to take advantage of this wave of employment opportunity.

There's no doubt that the employment market has changed dramatically from only a few years ago. According to the U.S. Department of Labor (2000), you should expect to hold between 10 and 20 different jobs during your career. No longer is stability the status quo. Today, the norm is movement, onward and upward, in a fast-paced and intense employment market. And to stay on top of all the changes and opportunities, you must proactively control and manage your career.

Education Job Search Questions and Answers

Whether you're currently employed in the education field or looking to enter the profession for the first time, here's some practical advice:

HOW DO YOU ENTER THE EDUCATION PROFESSION?

As with any other industry or profession, your employment experience, education, and credentials are the keys to entry and long-term success. It is difficult to obtain a position in education without some related work experience, relevant education, or credentials. Here are a few pointers:

- **If you're just starting to plan and build your career,** consider a four-year degree in an education-related discipline or completion of a teaching certification program. Once you've earned your initial degree, you'll want to keep your sights focused on an advanced degree. Education is one of many professions where master's and doctoral degrees are virtually prerequisites for long-term career advancement.

- **If you're an educator, administrator, or other school-based professional** who wants to move forward in your career to a position of greater responsibility, leadership, and compensation, focus your resume on what you have achieved thus far in your career, your specific areas of expertise, your professional credentials and, most significantly, why you are a valuable resource.

- **If you're a classroom teacher or school administrator who wants to make a move into corporate training and development,** sell your knowledge and experience in order to "connect" yourself to T&D. Highlight the programs and courses you've designed, the instructional materials you've created, the training you've provided to other educational professionals, and more. Make the case that you're not an outsider, but rather an insider who has experience in organizational needs assessment, training, program design, and presentation. Link yourself to the new industry.

- **If you're a successful businessperson, technologist, manager, administrator, or the like,** but have no teaching or educational experience, focus your resume on your professional experiences and how they relate to the field of education. Who better to teach a business-management course than a business manager? Who better to manage the finances of a school board than an experienced CFO?

WHAT IS THE BEST RESUME STRATEGY IF YOU'RE ALREADY IN THE EDUCATION PROFESSION?

If you're already employed in the education field but are interested in moving onward and upward, remember one critical fact:

> Your resume is a marketing tool written to sell YOU!

If you're a classroom teacher, *sell* the fact that you've been instrumental in developing new course curricula and designing innovative instructional tools. If you're a school administrator, *sell* the new initiatives you've introduced to strengthen educational standards and build support throughout your local community. If you're a corporate training specialist, *sell* the fact that you conceived, developed, and led the corporation's first-ever multimedia training presentations.

When writing your resume, your challenge is to create a picture of knowledge, action, and results. In essence, you're stating "This is what I know, this is how I've used it, and this is how well I've performed." Success sells, so be sure to highlight yours. If you don't, no one else will.

WHERE ARE THE JOBS?

The jobs are everywhere—from major universities to small rural school districts; from government education lobbies to high school libraries; from the corporate giants of the world to local instructional technology companies.

- The jobs are in **classroom teaching,** at all levels and in all types of early-childhood, primary, secondary, and advanced educational institutions, both public and private.

- The jobs are in the **development** of new educational and instructional systems, methodologies, and protocols.

- The jobs are in the **design** of new courses, new curricula, new instructional materials, and other new teaching and learning resources.

- The jobs are in the **administration, funding, and management** of educational programs, systems, and facilities.

- The jobs are in the **educational support** professions (for example, librarians, coaches, teaching aides, and school counselors).

- The jobs are in the **design, engineering, marketing, and support** of instructional technologies, applications, and tools.

- The jobs are in **educational research, funding, and outreach** for both public and private research facilities, universities, and foundations.

- The jobs are in the **design and delivery** of corporate training and development programs.

In short, the jobs are everywhere.

How Do You Get the Jobs?

To answer this question, we need to review the basic principle underlying job search:

> Job search is marketing!

You have a product to sell—yourself—and the best way to sell it is to use all appropriate *marketing channels* just as you would for any other product.

Suppose you wanted to sell televisions. What would you do? You'd market your products using newspaper, magazine, and radio advertisements. You might develop a company Web site to build your e-business, and perhaps you'd hire a field sales representative to market to major retail chains. Each of these is a different *marketing channel* through which you're attempting to reach your audience.

The same is true for job search. You must use every marketing channel that's right for you. Unfortunately, there is no single formula. What's right for you depends on your specific career objectives—type of position, type of industry, geographic restrictions, salary requirements, and more.

Following are the most valuable marketing channels for a successful job search within the education industry. These are in order from most effective to least effective.

1. **Referrals.** There is nothing better than a personal referral to a company or institution, either in general or for a specific position. Referrals can open doors that, in most instances, would never be accessible any other way. If you know anyone who could possibly refer you to a specific organization, contact that person immediately and ask for assistance.

2. **Networking.** Networking is the backbone of every successful job search. Although you may consider it a task, it is essential that you network effectively with your professional colleagues and associates, past employers, past coworkers, suppliers, neighbors, bankers, and others who may know of opportunities that are right for you. Another good strategy is to attend meetings of professional associations in your area to make new contacts and expand your professional network. And particularly in today's nomadic job market—where you're likely to change jobs every few years—the best strategy is to keep your network "alive" even when you're *not* searching for a new position.

3. **Responses to newspaper, magazine, and periodical advertisements.** Although, as you'll read below, the opportunity to post job opportunities online has reduced the overall number of print advertisements, they still abound. Do not forget about this "tried and true" marketing strategy. If they've got the job and you have the qualifications, it's a perfect fit.

4. **Responses to online job postings.** One of the greatest advantages of the technology revolution is an employer's ability to post job announcements and a job seeker's ability to respond immediately via e-mail. It's a wonder! In most

(but not all) instances, these are bona fide opportunities, and it's well worth your while to spend time searching for and responding to appropriate postings. However, don't make the mistake of devoting *too* much time to searching the Internet. It can consume a huge amount of your time that you should spend on other job search efforts.

To expedite your search, here are some of the largest and most widely used online job posting sites—presented alphabetically, not necessarily in order of effectiveness or value (see the appendix for a more complete listing of job search Web sites):

www.careerbuilder.com

www.careermosaic.com

www.careerpath.com

www.dice.com

www.flipdog.com

www.hotjobs.com

www.monster.com

www.sixfigurejobs.com

www.wantedtechnologies.com

5. **Targeted e-mail campaigns (resumes and cover letters) to recruiters.** Recruiters have jobs, and you want one. It's pretty straightforward. The only catch is to find the "right" recruiters who have the "right" jobs. Therefore, you must devote the time and effort to prepare the "right" list of recruiters. There are many resources on the Internet where you can access information about recruiters (for a fee), sort that information by industry (education, training and development, software development, and so on), and then cross-reference with position specialization (teaching, training, administration, library services, and so on). This allows you to identify just the "right" recruiters who would be interested in a candidate with your qualifications. What's more, because these campaigns are transmitted electronically, they are easy and inexpensive to produce.

    When working with recruiters, it's important to realize that they *do not* work for you! Their clients are the hiring companies that pay their fees. They are not in business to "find a job" for you, but rather to fill a specific position with a qualified candidate, either you or someone else. To maximize your chances of finding a position through a recruiter or agency, don't rely on just one or two, but distribute your resume to many that meet your specific criteria.

6. **Online resume postings.** The Net is swarming with reasonably priced (if not free) Web sites where you can post your resume. It's quick, easy, and the only *passive* thing you can do in your search. All of the other marketing channels require action on your part. With online resume postings, once you've posted, you're done. You then just wait (and hope!) for some response.

7. **Targeted e-mail and print campaigns to employers.** Just as with campaigns to recruiters (see item 5 above), you must be extremely careful to select just the right employers that would be interested in a candidate with your qualifica-tions. The closer you stick to "where you belong" in relation to your specific

experience, the better your response rate will be. If you are targeting technology companies, you can also contact these employers via e-mail. If you are looking at employers outside the technology industries, which is extremely likely for most education professionals, we believe that print campaigns (paper and envelopes mailed the old-fashioned way) are a more suitable and effective presentation—particularly if you are an administrative or executive candidate.

8. **In-person "cold calls" to companies and recruiters.** We consider this the least effective and most time-consuming marketing strategy for education jobs. It is extremely difficult to just walk in the door and get in front of the right person, or any person who can take hiring action. You'll be much better off focusing your time and energy on other, more productive channels.

WHAT ABOUT OPPORTUNITIES IN CONSULTING AND CONTRACTING IN THE EDUCATION INDUSTRY?

Are you familiar with the term "free agent"? It's the latest buzz word for an independent contractor or consultant who moves from project to project and company to company as the work load dictates. If you are an education professional, this may be appropriate for you if you work in a corporate environment and specialize in the design, development, and delivery of corporate training programs.

According to a recent article in *Quality Progress* magazine (November 2000), 10 years ago less than 10 percent of the U.S. work force was employed as free agents. Currently, that number is greater than 20 percent and is expected to increase to 40 percent over the next 10 years. The demand for free agents is vast, and the market offers excellent career opportunities.

The reason for this growth is directly related to the manner in which companies are now hiring—or not hiring—their work forces. The opportunity now exists for companies to hire on a "per project" basis and avoid the costs associated with full-time permanent employees. Companies hire the staff they need just when they need them—and when they no longer need them, they're gone.

The newest revolution in online job search has risen in response to this demand: job-auction sites where employers bid on prospective employees. Individuals post their resumes and qualifications for review by prospective employers. The employers then competitively bid to hire or contract with each candidate. The two largest and most well-established job-auction Web sites are www.bid4geeks.com and www.freeagent.com. Check them out. They're quite interesting, particularly if you're pursuing a career in educational consulting or contracting.

Conclusion

Career opportunities abound within the education industries and professions today. What's more, it has never been easier to learn about and apply for jobs. Arm yourself with a powerful resume and cover letter, identify the most appropriate marketing channels, and start your search today. You're destined to reach the next rung on your career ladder.

PART I

Resume Writing, Strategy, and Formats

CHAPTER 1

Resume Writing Strategies for Education Professionals

If you're reading this book, chances are you've decided to make a career move. It may be because:

- You're graduating from college or a certification program and are ready to launch your professional career.

- You've just earned your graduate degree and are ready to make a step upward in your career.

- You're ready to leave your current position and move up the ladder to a higher-paying and more responsible position.

- You've decided on a career change and will be looking at opportunities in allied professions and industries.

- You're unhappy with your current school or employer, or its management/administrative team, and have decided to pursue opportunities elsewhere.

- You've been laid off, downsized, or otherwise left your position and must find a new one.

- You've completed a contract assignment and are looking for a new "free-agent" job or perhaps a permanent position.

- You're relocating to a new area and need to find a new job.

- You're returning to the work force after several years of unemployment or retirement.

- You're simply ready for a change.

There may even be other reasons for your job search besides these. However, no matter the reason, a powerful resume is an essential component of your search campaign. In fact, it is virtually impossible to conduct a search without a resume. It is your calling card that briefly, yet powerfully, communicates the skills, qualifications, experience, and value you bring to a prospective employer. It is the document that will open doors and generate interviews. It is the first thing people will learn about you when you forward it in response to an advertisement, and it is the last thing they'll remember when they're reviewing your qualifications after an interview.

Your resume is a sales document, and you are the product! You must identify the *features* (*what you know* and *what you can do*) and *benefits* (*how you can help an employer*) of that product, then communicate them in a concise and hard-hitting written presentation. Remind yourself over and over as you work your way through the resume process that you are writing marketing literature designed to sell a new product—YOU—into a new position.

Your resume can have tremendous power and a phenomenal impact on your job search. So don't take it lightly. Rather, devote the time, energy, and resources that are essential to developing a resume that is well-written, visually attractive, and effective in communicating *who* you are and *how* you want to be perceived.

The Most Critical Question: Resume or CV?

As an education professional, you have to ask yourself one critical question before you begin to even think about writing a single word of your resume:

> "Do you need a resume or do you need a curriculum vitae (CV)?"

As we've discussed, a resume is a sales and marketing tool, designed to entice a prospective employer to call you for an interview. It is a teaser, giving just enough information to establish you as a credible candidate. A resume focuses on the highlights of your career, your most notable achievements and contributions, your educational credentials, and more. Succinctly stated, it is your own personal career advertisement. It's usually one to two pages long, but if you've been in the work force for a long time and have extensive accomplishments, it is sometimes acceptable to use three pages.

A CV, on the other hand, is a less "aggressive" document. Obviously, just as with a resume, your objective is to sell yourself into a new position. However, the sell is more subtle, using your educational credentials, professional and teaching experience, research experience, publications, task forces, committees, and more to establish yourself as a qualified candidate. CVs, by their nature, tend to be longer documents, anywhere from two to three pages to as many as 10 or more pages. Length is *not* a consideration when preparing a CV.

As you look through all of the samples in chapters 4 through 12, you will note a dramatic difference in tone and style between resumes and CVs. However, for the purpose of this book, when we are referring to resumes, we are also, unless otherwise noted, referring to CVs.

If you're uncertain about whether to write a resume or a CV, the following table may guide your decision-making. However, there are no hard-and-fast rules, and resume writing is an art, not a science. Each decision is made based on the qualifications and experience of each candidate and that individual's career goals.

Profession	CV	Resume
Classroom teacher		X
College or university professor	X	X
Educational researcher/scientist	X	X
School administrator	X	X
College or university administrator	X	X
Guidance counselor		X
School psychologist	X	X
Librarian/media specialist		X
Corporate training professional		X

In deciding which format to use, consider the following:

- What is most accepted for your profession and the organizations you're targeting?

- Which format will better represent you and your qualifications?

- What will your competitors (those also vying for the position) use?

To add to the confusion, people in traditional CV fields such as medicine, law, and academia often use the term "CV" when referring to what is in fact a resume! We suggest you review the samples in chapters 4 through 12 and research your target institutions to find out the preferred format for your specific circumstances.

Resume Strategies

Following are the nine core strategies for writing effective and successful resumes.

RESUME STRATEGY #1: WHO ARE YOU AND HOW DO YOU WANT TO BE PERCEIVED?

Now that you've decided to look for a new position, the very first step is to identify your career interests, goals, and objectives. *This task is critical,* because it is the underlying foundation for *what* you will include in your resume, *how* you will include it, and *where* you will include it. You cannot write an effective resume without knowing, at least to some degree, what type or types of positions you will be seeking.

There are two concepts to consider here:

- **Who you are:** This relates to what you have done professionally and/or academically. Are you a teacher, school administrator, librarian, or corporate trainer? Are you an instructional media designer, curriculum developer, or education grant writer? Are you a recent graduate with a degree in elementary education, or do you have a master's in education administration? Who are you?

- **How you want to be perceived:** This relates to your current career objectives. If you're a teacher looking for a position as a departmental chairperson, don't focus solely on your teaching skills. Put an equal emphasis on designing curricula and instructional materials, training other educators, your public speaking and association leadership experience, and the like. If you're an administrator for a for-profit educational services company interested in a university administration position, highlight your experience in funding, program development, records management, grant writing, and other functions directly related to the administration of teaching programs and educational facilities.

The strategy, then, is to connect these two concepts by using the *who you are* information that ties directly to the *how you want to be perceived* message to determine what information to include in your resume. By following this strategy, you're painting a picture that allows a prospective employer to see you as you wish to be seen—as an individual with the qualifications for the type of position you are pursuing.

> **WARNING:** If you prepare a resume without first clearly identifying what your objectives are and how you want to be perceived, your resume will have no focus and no direction. Without the underlying knowledge of "This is what I want to be," you do not know what to highlight in your resume. In turn, the document becomes an historical overview of your career and not the sales document it is designed to be.

RESUME STRATEGY #2: Sell It to Me...Don't Tell It to Me

We've already established the fact that resume writing is sales. You are the product, and you must create a document that powerfully communicates the value of that product. One particularly effective strategy for accomplishing this is the "Sell It to Me...Don't Tell It to Me" strategy that impacts virtually every single word you write on your resume.

If you "tell it," you are simply stating facts. If you "sell it," you promote it, advertise it, and draw attention to it. Look at the difference in impact between these examples:

> **Tell It Strategy:** Participated in the development of a new curriculum for the English department.

> **Sell It Strategy:** Appointed to 3-person team charged with developing a new English curriculum for 2,000+ students, and for designing and producing all supporting instructional materials.

> **Tell It Strategy:** Responsible for $28 million annual operating budget for a 200,000-student school district.

Sell It Strategy: Managed $28 million annual operating budget for 200,000-student school district. Closed FY 99–00 at 10% under budget by renegotiating services contracts, repairing used equipment, and eliminating excess expenditures.

Tell It Strategy: Served as a Multimedia Specialist for students in grades 7–9.

Sell It Strategy: Designed and produced a host of multimedia presentations to enrich student learning experiences and heighten retention for an at-risk middle school population.

What's the difference between "telling it" and "selling it"? In a nutshell…

Telling It	*Selling It*
Describes features.	Describes benefits.
Tells what and how.	Sells why the "what" and "how" are important.
Details activities.	Includes results.
Focuses on what you did.	Details how what you did benefited your employer, department, team members, students, and so on.

RESUME STRATEGY #3: USE KEY WORDS

No matter what you read or who you talk to about job search, the concept of key words is sure to come up. Key words (or, as they were previously known, buzz words) are words and phrases specific to a particular industry or profession. For example, key words for education include *accreditation, classroom teaching, course design, instructional media, peer counseling, research, scholastic standards, standardized testing, student services, textbook review,* and many, many more.

When you use these words and phrases—in your resume, in your cover letter, or during an interview—you are communicating a very specific message. For example, when you include the words *"school administration"* in your resume, your reader will most likely assume that you have experience in budgeting, staffing, teacher training, facilities management, community outreach, emergency response, reporting and documentation, and more. As you can see, people will make inferences about your skills based on the use of just one or two individual words.

Here are a few other examples:

- When you use the words **multimedia instructional technology,** people will assume you have experience with programming, CD-ROM, graphic interfacing, the Internet, and more.

- When you mention **lifelong learning,** readers and listeners will infer that you have experience in the design and delivery of educational programs for children and adults throughout all phases of the growth, developing, and aging life cycle.

- By referencing **intercollegiate athletics** in your resume, you convey that you most likely have experience in coaching, competitive athletics, game play strategy, scheduling, equipment management, and team leadership.

- When you use the words **alumni relations,** most people will assume you are familiar with alumni communications, fund raising, marketing, event planning, and more.

Key words are also an integral component of the resume scanning process, whereby employers and recruiters electronically search resumes for specific terms to find candidates with the skills, qualifications, and credentials for their particular hiring needs. Although not nearly as prevalent in education as in other industries, particularly technology-related industries and large corporations with significant hiring activity, key-word scanning is increasing in popularity because of its ease and efficiency. Just like any other job seekers, education professionals must stay on top of the latest trends in hiring and employment.

In organizations where it has been implemented, electronic scanning has replaced the more traditional method of an actual person reading your resume (at least initially). Therefore, to some degree, the *only* thing that matters in this instance is that you have included the "right" key words to match the company's or the recruiter's needs. Without them, you will most certainly be passed over.

Of course, in virtually every instance your resume will be read at some point by human eyes, so it's not enough just to throw together a list of key words and leave it at that. In fact, it's not even necessary to include a separate paragraph called a "key word summary" on your resume. A better strategy is to incorporate key words naturally into the text within the appropriate sections of your resume.

Keep in mind, too, that key words are arbitrary; there is no defined set of key words for a classroom teacher, university professor, corporate trainer, librarian, or educational services administrator. Employers searching to fill these positions develop a list of terms that reflect the specifics they desire in a qualified candidate. These might be a combination of professional qualifications, skills, education, length of experience, and other easily defined criteria, along with "soft skills," such as leadership, problem-solving, and communication.

NOTE: Because of the complex and arbitrary nature of key-word selection, we cannot overemphasize how vital it is to be certain that *all* of the key words that represent your experience and knowledge are included in your resume!

How can you be sure that you are including all the key words and the right key words? Just by describing your work experience, achievements, credentials, publications, public speaking engagements, and the like, you will naturally include most of the terms that are important in your field. To cross-check what you've written, review online or print job postings for positions that are of interest to you. Look at the precise terms used in the ads and be sure you have included them in your resume (as appropriate to your skills and qualifications).

Another great benefit of today's technology revolution is our ability to find instant information, even information as specific as key words for the education and training industries. Refer to the appendix to find Web sites that have education key words. Remember also to scan a variety of job listings to pick up the "buzz words" and current terminology. These are outstanding resources.

RESUME STRATEGY #4: USE THE "BIG" AND SAVE THE "LITTLE"

When deciding what you want to include in your resume, try to focus on the "big" things—new programs, new curricula, reduced operating costs, improved profitability, major projects, improvements in student test results, and more. Give a good, broad-based picture of what you were responsible for and how well you did it. Here's an example:

> Senior-level Administrator with full responsibility for the strategic planning, development, budgeting, and leadership of Admissions, Financial Aid, Alumni Relations, and Career Development departments for a 13,000-student university. Manage $900,000 in annual operating and administrative budgets. Direct a staff of 42.

Then, save the "little" stuff—the details—for the interview. With this strategy, you will accomplish two things: You'll keep your resume readable and of a reasonable length (while still selling your achievements), and you'll have new and interesting information to share during the interview, rather than merely repeating what is already on your resume. Using the preceding example, when discussing this experience during an interview you could elaborate on your improvements in student admission and retention, improvements to the financial aid process, reductions in annual operating expenses, and increases in alumni giving.

RESUME STRATEGY #5: MAKE YOUR RESUME "INTERVIEWABLE"

One of your greatest challenges is to make your resume a useful interview tool. Once it's been determined that you meet the primary qualifications for a position (you've passed the key-word scanning test or initial review) and you are contacted for a telephone or in-person interview, your resume becomes all-important in leading and prompting your interviewer during your conversation.

Your job, then, is to make sure the resume leads the reader where you want to go and presents just the right organization, content, and appearance to stimulate a productive discussion. To improve the "interviewability" of your resume, consider these tactics:

- Make good use of Resume Strategy #4 ("Use the 'Big' and Save the 'Little'") to invite further discussion about your experiences.

- Be sure your greatest "selling points" are featured prominently, not buried within the resume.

- Conversely, don't devote lots of space and attention to areas of your background that are irrelevant or about which you feel less than positive; you'll only invite questions about things you really don't want to discuss.

- Make sure your resume is highly readable—this means plenty of white space, an adequate font size, and a logical flow from start to finish.

RESUME STRATEGY #6: ELIMINATE CONFUSION WITH STRUCTURE AND CONTEXT

Keep in mind that your resume will be read *very quickly* by hiring authorities! You may agonize over every word and spend hours working on content and design, but the average reader will skim quickly through your masterpiece and expect to pick up important facts in just a few seconds. Try to make it as easy as possible for readers to grasp the essential facts:

- **Be consistent:** For example, put job titles, company names, and dates in the same place for each position.

- **Make information easy to find** by clearly defining different sections of your resume with large, highly visible headings.

- **Define the context in which you worked** (for example, the organization, your department, the specific challenges you faced) before you start describing your activities and accomplishments.

RESUME STRATEGY #7: USE FUNCTION TO DEMONSTRATE ACHIEVEMENT

When you write a resume that focuses only on your job functions, it can be dry and uninteresting and will say very little about your unique activities and contributions. Consider the following example:

> Responsible for the design and development of all courses for grades 3–5.

Now, consider using that same function to demonstrate achievement and see what happens to the tone and energy of the sentence. It becomes alive and clearly communicates that you deliver results.

> Forged a major initiative to redesign and enhance all course curricula for grades 3–5. Partnered with public and private-sector organizations to identify the best practices in education and program design worldwide. Delivered 11 new curricula within the first year.

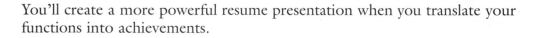

You'll create a more powerful resume presentation when you translate your functions into achievements.

RESUME STRATEGY #8: REMAIN IN THE REALM OF REALITY

We've already established that resume writing is sales. And, as any good salesperson does, one feels somewhat inclined to stretch the truth just a bit. However, be forewarned that you must stay within the realm of reality. Do not push your skills and qualifications outside the bounds of what is truthful. You never want to be in a position where you have to defend something that you've written on your resume. If that's the case, you'll lose the opportunity before you ever get started.

RESUME STRATEGY #9: BE CONFIDENT

You are unique. There is only one individual with the specific combination of employment experience, qualifications, achievements, and educational credentials that you have. In turn, this positions you as a unique commodity within the competitive job search market. To succeed, you must prepare a resume that is written to sell *you,* and highlight *your* qualifications and *your* success. If you can accomplish this, you will have won the job search game by generating interest, interviews, and offers.

There Are No Resume Writing Rules

One of the greatest challenges in resume writing is that there are no rules to the game. There are certain expectations about information that you will include: principally, your employment history and your educational qualifications. Beyond that, what you include is entirely dependent on you and what you have done in your career. What's more, you have tremendous flexibility in determining how to include the information you have selected. In chapter 2, you'll find a complete listing of each possible category you might include in your resume, the type of information in each category, preferred formats for presentation, and sample text you can edit and use.

Although there are no rules, there are a few standards to live by as you write your resume. The following sections discuss these standards in detail.

CONTENT STANDARDS

Content is, of course, the text that goes into your resume. Content standards regard the writing style you should use, items you should be sure to include, items you should avoid including, and the order and format in which you list your qualifications.

Writing Style

Always write in the first person, dropping the word "I" from the front of each sentence. This style gives your resume a more aggressive and more professional tone than the passive third-person voice. Here are some examples:

First Person:

> Manage a 12-person team in the design and market commercialization of next-generation instructional technology.

Third Person:

> Mr. Jones manages a team of 12 in the design and market commercialization of next-generation instructional technology.

By using the first-person voice, you are assuming "ownership" of that statement. You did such-and-such. When you use the third-person, "someone else" did it. Can you see the difference?

Stay Away From...

Try *not* to use phrases such as "responsible for" or "duties included." These words create a passive tone and style. Instead, use active verbs to describe what you did.

Compare these two ways of conveying the same information:

> Duties included the planning and daily operation of a university library servicing 20,000 undergraduate and graduate students at the University of Wisconsin. Administered $1.2 million annual budget.

Or

> Managed a $1.2 million university library servicing 20,000 undergraduate and graduate students at the University of Wisconsin. Redesigned purchasing systems, restructured physical layout, recruited and trained support staff, and increased student satisfaction ratings by 22%.

Resume Style

The traditional **chronological** resume lists experience in reverse-chronological order (starting with your current or most recent position). The **functional** style de-emphasizes the "where" and "when" of your career and instead groups similar experience, talents, and qualifications regardless of when they occurred.

Today, however, most resumes follow neither a strictly chronological nor strictly functional format; rather, they are an effective mixture of the two styles, usually known as a "combination" or "hybrid" format.

Like the chronological format, the hybrid format includes specifics about where you worked, when you worked there, and what your job titles were. Like a functional resume, a hybrid emphasizes your most relevant qualifications—perhaps within chronological job descriptions, in an expanded summary section, in several "career highlights" bullet points at the top of your resume, or in project summaries. Most of the examples in this book are hybrids and show a wide diversity of organizational formats that you can use as inspiration for designing your own resume.

Resume Formats

Resumes, principally career summaries and job descriptions, are most often written in a paragraph format, a bulleted format, or a combination of both. Following are three job descriptions, all very similar in content, yet presented in each of the three different formats. The advantages and disadvantages of each format are also addressed.

Paragraph Format

Fourth-Grade Teacher   1997 to 2001

Inner Harbor Magnet School, Baltimore City Schools, Baltimore, Maryland

Selected from a competitive field of 800 candidates for newly created teaching position. Solely responsible for developing curricula for all essential subjects, designing instructional tools and techniques, preparing classroom lectures, and evaluating student performance. Team-teach with remedial reading and remedial math teacher.

Provide significant input into the district's committee on "Setting 4th-Grade Benchmarks" for state curriculum. Designed and implemented multisensory reading program, a holistic approach that also involves writing and spelling. Program provides reinforcement via all learning modalities and ensures retention. Provided significant input into developing the school's first science fair. Encourage student participation to help them develop presentation skills through cooperative learning.

Advantages:

Requires the least amount of space on the page. Brief, succinct, and to the point.

Disadvantages:

Achievements get lost in the text of the second paragraph. They are not visually distinctive, nor do they stand alone to draw attention to them.

Bulleted Format

Fourth-Grade Teacher   1997 to 2001

Inner Harbor Magnet School, Baltimore City Schools, Baltimore, Maryland
- Selected from a competitive field of 800 candidates for newly created teaching position.

- Solely responsible for developing curricula for all essential subjects, designing instructional tools and techniques, preparing classroom lectures, and evaluating student performance.

- Team-teach with remedial reading and remedial math teacher.

- Provide significant input into the district's committee on "Setting 4th-Grade Benchmarks" for state curriculum.

- Designed and implemented multisensory reading program, a holistic approach that also involves writing and spelling. Program provides reinforcement via all learning modalities and ensures retention.

- Provided significant input into developing the school's first science fair. Encourage student participation to help them develop presentation skills through cooperative learning.

Advantages:

Quick and easy to peruse.

Disadvantages:

Responsibilities and achievements are lumped together with everything of equal value. In turn, the achievements get lost further down the list and are not immediately recognizable.

Combination Format

Fourth-Grade Teacher   1997 to 2001

Inner Harbor Magnet School, Baltimore City Schools, Baltimore, Maryland

Selected from a competitive field of 800 candidates for newly created teaching position. Solely responsible for developing curricula for all essential subjects, designing instructional tools and techniques, preparing classroom lectures, and evaluating student performance. Team-teach with remedial reading and remedial math teacher.

- Provide significant input into the district's committee on "Setting 4th-Grade Benchmarks" for state curriculum.

- Designed and implemented multisensory reading program, a holistic approach that also involves writing and spelling. Program provides reinforcement via all learning modalities and ensures retention.

- Provided significant input into developing the school's first science fair. Encourage student participation to help them develop presentation skills through cooperative learning.

Advantages:

Our recommended format. Clearly presents overall responsibilities in the introductory paragraph and then accentuates each achievement as a separate bullet.

Disadvantages:

If you don't have clearly identifiable accomplishments, this format is not effective. It also may shine a glaring light on the positions where your accomplishments were less notable.

E-Mail Address and URL

Be sure to include your e-mail address prominently at the top of your resume. As we all know, e-mail has become one of the most preferred methods of communication in job search.

We advise against using your employer's e-mail address on your resume. Not only does this present a negative impression to future employers, it will become useless once you make your next career move. And since your resume may exist in cyberspace long after you've completed your current job search, you don't want to direct interested parties to an obsolete e-mail address. Instead, obtain a private e-mail address that will be yours permanently. A free e-mail address from a provider such as Yahoo!, Hotmail, or NetZero is perfectly acceptable to use on your resume.

In addition to your e-mail address, if you have a URL (Web site) where you have posted your Web resume, be sure to also display that prominently at the top of your resume. For more information on Web resumes, refer to chapter 3.

PRESENTATION STANDARDS

Presentation is the way your resume looks. It includes the fonts you use, the paper you print it on, any graphics you might include, and how many pages your resume should be.

Typestyle (or Font)

Use a typestyle (font) that is clean, conservative, and easy to read. Stay away from anything that is too fancy, glitzy, curly, and the like. Here are a few recommended typestyles:

Tahoma	Times New Roman
Arial	Bookman
Krone	Book Antiqua
Soutane	Garamond
CG Omega	Century Schoolbook
Century Gothic	**Lucida Sans**
Gill Sans	**Verdana**

Other fonts that work well for resumes include Franklin Gothic, Myriad Roman, Helvetica, Univers, Palomino, Souvenir, and Fritz.

Although it is extremely popular, Times New Roman is our least preferred typestyle simply because it is overused. More than 90 percent of the resumes we see are typed in Times New Roman. Your goal is to create a competitive-distinctive document. To achieve that, we recommend an alternative typestyle.

Your choice of typestyle should be dictated by the content, format, and length of your resume. Some fonts look better than others at smaller or larger sizes; some have "bolder" boldface type; some require more white space to make them readable. Once you've written your resume, experiment with a few different typestyles to see which one best enhances your document.

Type Size

Readability is everything! If the type size is too small, your resume will be difficult to read and difficult to skim for essential information. Interestingly, a too-large type size, particularly for senior-level professionals, can also give a negative impression by conveying a juvenile or unprofessional image.

As a general rule, select type from 10 to 12 points in size. However, there's no hard-and-fast rule, and a lot depends on the typestyle you choose. Take a look at the following examples:

Very readable in 9-point Verdana:

Won the 1999 "Teacher of the Year" award in Montgomery, Alabama. Honored for innovative contributions to the classroom, students, and community, with auxiliary commendation for service to special-needs children.

Difficult to read in too-small 9-point Gill Sans:

Won the 1999 "Teacher of the Year" award in Montgomery, Alabama. Honored for innovative contributions to the classroom, students, and community, with auxiliary commendation for service to special-needs children.

Concise and readable in 12-point Times New Roman:

Training & Development Consultant specializing in the design, development, and presentation of multimedia corporate training programs for sales, marketing, and technology professionals.

A bit overwhelming in too-large 12-point Bookman Old Style:

Training & Development Consultant specializing in the design, development, and presentation of multimedia corporate training programs for sales, marketing, and technology professionals.

Type Enhancements

Bold, *italics,* underlining, and CAPITALIZATION are ideal to highlight certain words, phrases, achievements, projects, numbers, and other information to which you want to draw special attention. However, do not overuse these enhancements. If your resume becomes too cluttered, nothing stands out.

> **NOTE:** Resumes intended for electronic transmission and computer scanning have specific restrictions on typestyle, type size, and type enhancements. We discuss these details in chapter 3.

Page Length

For most industries and professions, including many of you in the education professions, the "one-to-two-page rule" for resume writing still holds true. Keep it short and succinct, giving just enough to entice your readers' interest. However, there are many instances when an education resume will be longer than two pages. For example:

- When you're really not writing a resume, but rather a curriculum vitae (as discussed earlier in this chapter) used by many university professors, researchers, school administrators, published authors, and others.

- You have an extensive list of publications, public-speaking engagements, volunteer experiences, and such that are relevant to the position for which you are applying.

- You have extensive educational training and numerous credentials/certifications, all of which are important to include.

- You have an extensive list of courses you've taught and it is necessary to include them all.

- You have an extensive list of "special projects" to include, such as new educational programs you've designed, curricula you've developed, instructional materials you've created, technology-based training innovations, research projects, and more.

- You have an extensive list of professional honors, awards, and commendations. This list is tremendously valuable in validating your credibility and distinguishing you from the competition.

If you create a resume that's longer than two pages, make it more reader-friendly by carefully segmenting the information into separate sections. For instance, begin with your career summary and your work experience. Then follow with research, education, credentials, honors and awards, publications, public-speaking engagements, professional affiliations, civic affiliations, technology skills, volunteer experience, foreign-language skills, and other relevant information you want to include. Put each into a separate category so that your resume is easy to peruse and your reader can quickly see the highlights. You'll read more about each of these sections in chapter 2.

Paper Color

Be conservative. White, ivory, and light gray are ideal. Other "flashier" colors are inappropriate for individuals in the education professions.

Graphics

An attractive, relevant graphic can really enhance your resume. When you look through the sample resumes in chapters 4 through 12, you'll see some excellent examples of the effective use of graphics to enhance the visual presentation of a resume. Just be sure not to get carried away…be tasteful and relatively conservative.

White Space

We'll say it again—readability is everything! If people have to struggle to read your resume, they simply won't make the effort. Therefore, be sure to leave plenty of white space. It really does make a difference.

ACCURACY AND PERFECTION

The very final step, and one of the most critical in resume writing, is the proofreading stage. It is essential that your resume be well written, visually pleasing, and free of any errors, typographical mistakes, misspellings, and the like. We recommend that you carefully proofread your resume a minimum of three times, and then have two or three other people also proofread it. Consider your resume an example of the quality of work you will produce on a company's behalf. Is your work product going to have errors and inconsistencies? If your resume does, it communicates to a prospective employer that you are careless, and this is the "kiss of death" in a job search.

Take the time to make sure that your resume is perfect in all the little details that do, in fact, make a big difference to those who read it.

CHAPTER 2

Writing Your Resume

For many education professionals, resume writing is *not* at the top of the list of fun and exciting activities! How can it compare to developing a new instructional methodology, designing and funding a new training center, increasing your school's enrollment numbers well beyond the projections, or working one-on-one to build a child's self-esteem? In your perception, we're sure that it cannot.

However, resume writing can be an enjoyable and rewarding task. Once your resume is complete, you can look at it proudly, reminding yourself of all that you have achieved. It is a snapshot of your career and your success. When it's complete, we guarantee you'll look back with tremendous self-satisfaction as you launch and successfully manage your job search.

The very first step in finding a new position or advancing your career, resume writing can be the most daunting of all tasks in your job search. If writing is not one of your primary job functions, it may have been years since you've actually sat down and written anything other than notes to yourself. Even for those of you who write on a regular basis, resume writing is unique. It has its own style and a number of peculiarities, as with any specialty document.

Therefore, to make the writing process easier, more finite, and more efficient, we've consolidated it into four discrete sections:

- **Career Summary.** Think of your Career Summary as the *master plan* of your resume. It summarizes all the components of your professional skills and experience that contribute to the success of a school, a classroom, or a corporate training and development center.

- **Professional Experience.** Professional Experience is analogous to the *courses and curricula* that you might teach. It is the specifics that make up the larger master plan. Your professional experience demonstrates how you put all of your capabilities to work.

- **Education, Credentials, and Certifications.** Think of this section as your *accreditation,* the third-party validation of your qualifications, knowledge, and expertise.

- **The "Extras"** (Publications, Public Speaking, Honors and Awards, Technology Qualifications, Professional Affiliations, Civic Affiliations, Foreign Languages, Personal Information, and so on). These make up the *extra-credit* section of your resume, the "extra stuff" that helps distinguish you from others with similar qualifications.

Step-by-Step: Writing the Perfect Resume

In the preceding section, we outlined the four core resume sections. Now, we'll detail the particulars of each section—what to include, where to include it, and how to include it.

CONTACT INFORMATION

Before we start, let's briefly address the very top section of your resume: your name and contact information.

Name

You'd think this would be the easiest part of writing your resume...writing your name! But there are several factors you may want to consider:

- Although most people choose to use their full, formal name at the top of a resume, it has become increasingly more acceptable to use the name by which you prefer to be called.

- Bear in mind that it's to your advantage to have readers feel comfortable calling you for an interview. Their comfort level may decrease if your name is gender-neutral, difficult to pronounce, or very unusual; they don't know who they're calling (a man or a woman) or how to ask for you. Here are a few ways you can make it easier for them:

> Lynn T. Cowles (Mr.)
>
> (Ms.) Michael Murray
>
> Tzirina (Irene) Kahn
>
> Ndege "Nick" Vernon

Address

You should always include your home address on your resume. If you use a post office box for mail, include both your mailing address and your physical residence address.

Telephone Number(s)

Your should include your home telephone number. If you're at work during the day, when you can expect to receive most calls, consider including a work phone number (if it's a direct line and you can receive calls discreetly). If others answer your work phone, you can't be assured of their discretion; so for professionals such as classroom teachers who are not readily available by phone during the day, we do not recommend including a work number. You might also include a mobile phone number (refer to it as "mobile" rather than "cellular," to keep up with current terminology) or a pager number (however, this is less desirable because you must call back to speak to the person who called you). You can include a private home fax number (if it can be accessed automatically), but do not include your work fax number. *Never* include your employer's or school's toll-free number, if it has one. This communicates the message that you are using your employer's resources and budget to support your own personal job search campaign. Not a wise idea!

E-Mail Address

Without question, if you have a private e-mail address, include it on your resume. E-mail is now often the preferred method of communication in job search, particularly in the early stages of each contact. Do not use your employer's e-mail address, even if you access e-mail through your work computer. Instead, obtain a free, accessible-anywhere address from a provider such as Yahoo!, Hotmail, or NetZero.

As you look through the samples in this book, you'll see how resume writers have arranged the many bits of contact information at the top of a resume. You can use these as models for presenting your own information. The point is to make it as easy as possible for employers to contact you!

Now, let's get into the nitty-gritty of the four core content sections of your resume.

CAREER SUMMARY

The Career Summary is the section at the top of your resume that summarizes and highlights your knowledge and expertise.

You may be thinking, "But shouldn't my resume start with an Objective?" Although many job seekers still use Objective statements, we believe that a Career Summary is a much more powerful introduction. The problem with Objectives is that they are either too specific (limiting you to a "Librarian position") or too vague (doesn't everyone want a challenging opportunity with a progressive organization offering the opportunity for growth and advancement?). In addition, they can be read as self-serving, since they describe what *you* want rather than suggesting what you have to offer an employer.

In contrast, an effective Career Summary allows you to position yourself as you wish to be perceived and immediately "paint a picture" of yourself in relation to your career goal. It is critical that this section focus on the specific skills, qualifications, and achievements of your career that are related to your current objectives. Your summary is *not* an historical overview of your career. Rather, it is a concise, well-written, and sharp presentation of information designed to *sell* you into your next position.

This section can have various titles, such as:

Career Summary	Management Profile
Career Achievements	Professional Qualifications
Career Highlights	Professional Summary
Career Synopsis	Profile
Executive Profile	Summary
Expertise	Summary of Achievements
Highlights of Experience	Summary of Qualifications

Or, as you will see in the first example format below (Headline Format), your summary does not have to have any title at all.

Here are five sample Career Summaries. Consider using one of these as the template for developing your Career Summary, or use them as a foundation to create your own presentation. You will also find some type of Career Summary in just about every resume included in this book.

Headline Format

HIGHER-EDUCATION EXECUTIVE / VICE PRESIDENT / DIRECTOR
Strategic Planning / Finance / Marketing / Facilities

MBA — Executive Leadership   MS — Educational Administration
MS — Instructional Systems & Technology

Paragraph Format

CAREER PROFILE

ASSISTANT PRINCIPAL / DEAN OF STUDENTS / COORDINATOR / EDUCATOR / TRAINER offering expertise in the development and teaching of educational programs designed to meet a broad cross-section of learner needs. Experience in teaching, project development, and behavioral management. Counseling and training abilities. Strong administrative, interpersonal, and communication skills as well as expertise in identifying instructional requirements and developing effective course curricula. Positive motivator skilled in educating both student and adult learners. Conversational Spanish.

Core Competencies Summary Format

QUALIFICATIONS SUMMARY

CORPORATE TRAINING & DEVELOPMENT PROFESSIONAL

Advanced Engineering & Technology Industries

- Organizational Needs Assessment
- Program Budgeting & Resource Management
- Trainer Training & Team Leadership
- Change Management & Revitalization
- Business & Process Optimization

- Curriculum Design & Development
- Multimedia Instructional Systems
- E-Learning & Distance Learning
- Training Materials Design
- Public Speaking & Executive Presentations

**Guest Speaker, 2000 "Technology Innovation in Education" Conference
Winner, 1999 Pioneer Electronics Award for Excellence**

Bullet List Format

PROFESSIONAL QUALIFICATIONS

- **Elementary School Educator** with 10 years of professional experience.
- Strengths in **literacy development** and **early language acquisition** for "English as a Second Language" learners.
- Extensive background working with **multi-cultural, special-needs, and at-risk** students and their families.
- **Award-winning** classroom management skills.
- Two years of experience as a **mentor teacher**.
- Outstanding communication, organizational, and project-management skills.

Category Format

PROFESSIONAL CAREER HIGHLIGHTS

Experience:	12 years as a Classroom Educator, Department Chairperson and School Services Administrator
Education:	**MS—Educational Administration**—University of Wisconsin **BS—Elementary Education**—Wisconsin State College
Publications:	"Integrating Technology into the Classroom," *Data Processing Management Association Annual Journal,* 1999 "Innovative Curricula to Accelerate Student Learning & Retention," *National Education Association,* 1998
Awards:	Teacher of the Year, Milwaukee Public Schools, 2000 Teacher of the Year, Detroit Public Schools, 1992

PROFESSIONAL EXPERIENCE

Your professional experience is the meat of your resume—the "courses and curricula," as we discussed before. It's what gives your resume substance, meaning, and depth. It is also the section that will take you the longest to write. If you've had the same position for 10 years, how can you consolidate all that you have done into one short section? If, on the opposite end of the spectrum, you have had your current position for only 11 months, how can you make it seem substantial and noteworthy? And, for all of you whose experience is in between, what do you include, how do you include it, and where do you include it?

These are not easy questions to answer. In fact, the most truthful response to each question is, "It depends." It depends on you, your experience, your achievements and successes, and your current career objectives.

Here are five samples of Professional Experience sections. Review how each individual's unique background is organized and emphasized, and consider your own background when using one of these as the template or foundation for developing your Professional Experience section.

Achievement Format

Emphasizes each position, your overall scope of responsibility, and the resulting achievements.

PROFESSIONAL EXPERIENCE

LEWISTON HIGH SCHOOL, Lewiston, Maine

MATHEMATICS TEACHER (1995 to Present)

Teach full spectrum of secondary school mathematics curricula (7th–12th grades) to a multicultural student body at this 1200-student public high school. Design/develop new curriculum, create instructional resources, lead two student associations, and serve as back-up for girls' basketball coach.

Achievements

- ❑ Initiated use of graphic calculators to facilitate introduction of technology-based learning tools, and transitioned students from manual to computerized calculations.

- ❑ Achieved an 8.2% increase in student test scores across all core mathematics disciplines, and a 6.8% increase in core science disciplines.

- ❑ Utilized math manipulatives (e.g., geoboards, tangrams) as well as varied assessment tools to supplement structured curriculum.

- ❑ Won a $25,000 grant from the Ford Motor Company to purchase scientific equipment and technology for chemistry and physics classes.

- ❑ Selected to train newly hired math and science teachers, precept student teachers, and participate on administrator selection panels.

- ❑ Coached two students to the finals in state-wide trigonometry competition.

Challenge, Action, and Results (CAR) Format

Emphasizes the challenge of each position, the action you took, and the results you delivered.

PROFESSIONAL EXPERIENCE

National Director of Corporate Training (1998 to Present)
National Training Implementation Manager (1994 to 1998)
VISA INTERNATIONAL, Atlanta, Georgia

Challenge: To lead the design, development, and nationwide launch of a comprehensive employee-training and leadership-development program impacting all 15,000 VISA employees worldwide.

Action: Built a 42-person training and support team, established a business infrastructure for the training unit, purchased over $1 million in technology training resources and instructional materials, and launched a nationwide marketing campaign to encourage employee interest.

Results:
- ☑ Orchestrated design, development, and roll-out of 25 new training programs offered in 12 locations throughout the U.S. and Europe. Trained more than 2000 employees in the first two years.
- ☑ Achieved/surpassed all corporate objectives for employee development and performance improvement.
- ☑ Conceived, launched, and won executive management support for the development and implementation of a complete Instructor Certification Program.
- ☑ Partnered with HP, IBM, and Dell to integrate their technologies into VISA's training curriculum. Received over $200,000 in technology resources at no charge to the company.
- ☑ Featured in the National Education Association's annual publication as one of 1999's *Leaders in Corporate Training*.

Functional Format

Emphasizes the functional areas of responsibility within the job and associated achievements.

EMPLOYMENT EXPERIENCE

Assistant Principal	WILLIAMS HIGH SCHOOL, Beaver Creek, Oregon	1996 to Present

Member of 6-person educational administration and management team of 800-student public high school in Southeastern rural Oregon. Scope of strategic planning, leadership, and decision-making responsibilities is extensive, with particular emphasis on:

Curriculum/Instruction:

❖ Supervise instructional planning, goals, and objectives; develop new course offerings in science, mathematics, English, foreign languages, and the creative arts.

❖ Direct staff, manage operational budgets, and coordinate all educational activities for GATE, ESL, SB 1882 Staff Development, Advanced Placement, Summer School, and SASI administrative computer system.

❖ Develop Master Schedule and direct the entire student scheduling process.

❖ Recruit, interview, hire, and direct the work performance of a 42-person teaching staff.

❖ Member of the Williams District Mentor Teachers Association.

Staff Development:

❖ Orchestrate professional-development opportunities for teaching staff across all curricula and grade levels.

❖ Use site-based management principles to support teachers' participation in school-wide decisions and to strengthen their ownership of school results.

❖ Conduct regularly scheduled performance reviews of teaching and support staff.

❖ Supervise and coordinate the work of chairpersons of staff-development committees at all 43 schools throughout the Williams District.

Outreach and Communications:

❖ Revitalized fledgling student newspaper, recruited a talented team of student writers and production personnel, and expanded distribution to include all parents.

❖ Write and publish press releases, fliers, and other promotional materials to encourage community participation in school-sponsored events.

❖ Lead public-speaking engagements at area middle schools to raise the level of enthusiasm of incoming freshmen.

Career-Track Format

Emphasizes fast-track promotion, overall scope of responsibility, and notable achievements.

—PROFESSIONAL EXPERIENCE & SELECTED EXAMPLES OF SUCCESS—

UNITED STATES AIR FORCE   May 1972–August 2000

More than 18 years in increasingly responsible positions as a commissioned Air Force Officer, including these recent assignments:

- *Promoted* to **Chief Learning Officer**, Air Force Doctrine Center (1995 to Present).
  The Center provides the basic corporate vision guiding the professional efforts of 371,000 employees worldwide.

  — Turned around a new organization that was swamped with urgent, unfocused tasks for two years. Guided a corporate-level needs analysis that integrated every level of proficiency in 12 major learning areas in our first master training plan.

  — *Payoffs:* Our **credibility — our stock in trade — rose fast**, as did our **productivity.**

- *Promoted* to **Director of Curriculum**, Air Force Extension Correspondence Institute (1993 to 1995).
  The Institute was recognized as the educational institution with the largest number of students in the world. With its $5.5 million budget, it serves learners in hundreds of disciplines at locations around the world.

  — Reignited an organization that had four CEOs in as many years, saw its staffing cut 36% in eight years, and suffered with stagnant budgets for four years.

  — *Payoffs:* Skilled, but "burned out," **employees revoked their retirement** papers. **Productivity rose** dramatically. **Conflicts** that had festered for years were **resolved**.

- *Promoted* to **Chief of Distance-Learning Policy**, Doctrine University (1990 to 1993).
  Our office served as the single point of contact for researching, employing, and delivering distance-learning technologies.

  — Went beyond the obvious fix to help our customers who had high-tech distance-learning technologies but not the training to use them. Found and removed potential roadblocks from every level.

  — *Payoffs:* Our combination users' handbook, **strategy** document, and "priority-setter" was in the field in just six months. **Customers very pleased**.

- *Promoted* to **Director of Training & Development**, North American Command Headquarters (1988 to 1990).
  Designed, developed, produced, delivered, evaluated, and validated "soft skills" training curricula servicing 1,700 people.

  — Overhauled a system that left new team members feeling left out of our organization for their first six months. Based new program on a detailed, organization-wide needs analysis.

  — *Payoffs:* **Spin-up time cut by a third**. Everybody won — from workers to managers.

Experience Summary Format

Briefly emphasizes specific highlights of each position. Best used in conjunction with a detailed Career Summary.

EXPERIENCE SUMMARY

Preschool Teacher, George Mason Child Development Center, Macon, GA – 2000 to Present
- Instructed 17 three- and four-year-old children in twice-weekly class.
- Assisted with school's reaccreditation process.
- Coordinated children's classroom literature, including thematic and individual reading.

Preschool Teacher, Green Day School, Valley Glen, GA – 1997 to 2000
- Instituted literature-based, early-childhood curriculum at NAEYC-accredited school. Supervised two assistant teachers.
- Presented "Learning Through Literature" workshop at Northern Georgia Regional Teachers' Conference.
- Transformed classrooms with creative decorations that tied in with weekly themes and classroom reading.

Secretary, Village Day Camp, Valley Glen, GA – 1994 to 1997
- Managed billing, registration, student scheduling, and site tours.
- Managed accounts payable for five affiliated summer camps.
- Administered employee time sheets, reporting, and payroll.

EDUCATION, CREDENTIALS, AND CERTIFICATIONS

Your Education section should include college, certifications, credentials, licenses, registrations, and continuing education. If any are particularly notable, be sure to highlight them prominently in your Education section or bring them to the top in your Career Summary (as demonstrated by the Headline format in the section on writing career summaries, earlier in this chapter).

Continuing professional education is vital in any industry or profession, and this is particularly true in education, where new teaching methodologies and educational concepts are introduced regularly. Professionals in other fields can briefly summarize their continuing-education courses at the end of their resumes. You, on the other hand, must be much more detailed and include most, if not all, of your courses, particularly those that are recent or demonstrate key qualifications and up-to-date knowledge of current educational trends. Try to consolidate as much as possible, but be thorough.

Here are five sample Education sections that illustrate a variety of ways to organize and format this information.

Academic Credentials Format

Ph.D., Education Administration, University of Oklahoma, 1998
M.Ed., Secondary School Education, University of Wisconsin, 1988
B.S., Secondary Education, University of Wisconsin, 1984

Highlights of Continuing Professional Education:
World-Management of the Classroom, Purdue University, 2001
Technology in Education, Purdue University, 2000
Executive Leadership Skills, Dale Carnegie, 1998
Conflict Resolution & Violence Management, Institute for Safety in Education, 1998

Certification:
Certified Secondary School Principal, State of Wisconsin, 1989
Certified Secondary School Teacher, State of Wisconsin, 1984

Executive Education Format

Executive Development Program	STANFORD UNIVERSITY
Executive Development Program	UNIVERSITY OF CALIFORNIA AT IRVINE
Master of Education Degree	UNIVERSITY OF CALIFORNIA AT LOS ANGELES
Bachelor of Education Degree	UNIVERSITY OF CALIFORNIA AT SAN DIEGO

Certifications Format

TEACHING CERTIFICATIONS & EDUCATION
- Certified Educational Diagnostician (K–12), State of Delaware, 1998
- Certified Generic Special Education Teacher (K–12), State of Delaware, 1994
- Certified Elementary Self-Contained Classroom Teacher (1–8), State of Delaware, 1992
- M.Ed. Candidate, University of Newark, expected 2002
- B.S., Elementary Education, University of Delaware, 1992

Professional Training Format

PROFESSIONAL TRAINING & DEVELOPMENT
- *Developing Creative Learners, National Education Association Annual Conference, 2001*
- *Appropriate Use of Behavior Management in the Classroom, Bedford County Public Schools In-Service Symposium, 2000*
- *Issues Impacting Children, Families & School Communities, Maryland State Teachers Association, 1999*
- *Observation & Assessment Methodologies, Maryland State Teachers Association, 1997*
- *Education Major, Catonsville Community College, Catonsville, Maryland, 1988–1990*

Non-Degree Format

TRAINING & EDUCATION:

UNIVERSITY OF ILLINOIS, Urbana, Illinois

BS Candidate—Nursing Education (senior class status)

UNIVERSITY OF MICHIGAN, Ann Arbor, Michigan

Dual Majors in Education & Nursing (2 years)

Graduate, 200+ hours of continuing professional education through the University of Illinois, University of Michigan and University of Wisconsin.

THE "EXTRAS"

The primary focus of your resume is on information (most likely, your professional experience and academic credentials) that is directly related to your career goals. However, you also should include things that will distinguish you from other candidates and clearly demonstrate your value to a prospective employer. And, not too surprisingly, it is often the "extras" that get the interviews.

Following is a list of the other categories you might or might not include on your resume, depending on your particular experience and your current career objectives. Review the information. If it's pertinent to you, use the samples for formatting your own data. Remember, however, that if something is truly impressive, you may want to include it in your Career Summary at the beginning of your resume in order to draw even more attention to it. If you include it there, it's not necessary to repeat the information at the end of your resume.

Honors and Awards

If you have won honors and awards, you can either include them in a separate section on your resume or integrate them into the Education or Professional Experience section, whichever is most appropriate. If you choose to include them in a separate section, consider this format:

- Winner, 1999 **"Recognition"** award from the National Library Association
- Winner, 1998 **"Innovation"** award for outstanding contributions to technology innovation from the National Library Association
- Named **"Librarian of the Year,"** Hofstra University, 1997
- **Summa Cum Laude Graduate**, Washington & Lee University, 1989

Publications

As an education professional, being published is a true mark of distinction. In fact, for those of you working at a university, foundation, or research institution, getting published is almost mandatory to further your professional career. Publications validate your knowledge, qualifications, and credibility. Only people in the medical fields have more pressure to publish than those in academia.

As such, if you are published, be sure to highlight your publications prominently on your resume. If you have a short list of publications, you might highlight them in your Career Summary. However, if your list is extensive, we recommend that you mention that you are a published author in your Career Summary and then list all of your publications after your Professional Experience and Education section.

Remember, publications can include books, articles, online Web site content, manuals, and other written documents. Here's an example:

> ❑ "Teachers' Attitudes Toward an Inclusive Classroom," *Journal of Teacher and Special Education*, Vol. 42, pp. 317–328, 2000.
>
> ❑ "Innovation in Educational Programming & Instruction," *School Psychology*, Vol. 22, pp. 123–135, 1999.
>
> ❑ "Graduate Curriculum in Learning Disabilities," approved by the Illinois State School District, 1999.
>
> ❑ Co-Author, "Teacher Technology Training Manual," Skokie Public School District, 1998.

Public Speaking

Experts are the ones who are invited to give public presentations at conferences, seminars, workshops, training programs, symposia, and other events. So if you have public-speaking experience, others must consider you an expert. Be sure to include this very complimentary information in your resume. Here's one way to present it:

> — **Keynote Speaker,** "Introducing Technology Innovation into the Classroom," 2000 National Education Association National Conference, Milwaukee.
>
> — **Presenter,** "Instructional Technology Finds Its Place in the Classroom," 1999.
>
> — **National Presenter,** "Management of Children with Behavior or Emotional Problems," Masterson County Department of Family and Children Services, 1994.

Teaching Experience

If you're a teacher, you'll include your teaching experience in the Professional Experience section of your resume. However, if you're a school administrator, school psychologist, or student services director, teaching is not your primary job function. Depending on your current career objectives, you can handle your teaching experience in one of two ways:

- If your objective is *not* teaching, then briefly mention your teaching experience within your job descriptions under Professional Experience.

- If your objective *is* teaching, we recommend that you include a separate Teaching Experience section on your resume. This way, you can visually attract your reader to an entire section devoted to teaching. Just as with everything else you do with your resume, you are constantly trying to push your reader in the direction in which you want to be perceived. If you want to be a teacher, show that you *are* a teacher!

Consider using the following format to present your teaching experience:

◈ **Adjunct Faculty**, Department of Education, Maryland State University, 1997 to Present Teach Learning Disabilities, Cultural Foundations in Education, Classroom Management, and Diagnostic and Prescriptive Education.

◈ **Adjunct Faculty**, Department of Education, Catonsville Community College, 1996 to Present. Teach Psychological Foundations of Education, Methods of Educational Evaluation, and School Administration.

◈ **In-Service Instructor**, Baltimore City Public School System, 1990 to Present. Taught high school core curriculum for behaviorally disordered students, the learning disabled, and those with severe behavioral and emotional problems.

Committees and Task Forces

Many education professionals serve on committees, task forces, and other special project teams either as part of, or in addition to, their full-time responsibilities. Again, this type of information further strengthens your credibility, qualifications, and perceived value to a prospective employer. Consider a format such as this:

• Member, 2000–01 Corporate Planning & Reorganization Task Force

• Member, 1999–00 Study Team on "Redesigning Corporate Training Systems to Maximize Employee Development"

• Chairperson, 1997–98 Committee on "Curriculum Planning for the New Millennium"

Professional Affiliations

If you are a member of any educational, professional, or leadership associations, be sure to include that information on your resume. It communicates a message of professionalism, a desire to stay current with the industry, and a strong professional network. What's more, if you have held leadership positions within these organizations, be sure to include them. Here's an example:

CALIFORNIA STATE TEACHERS ASSOCIATION
Professional Member (1988 to Present)
Resource Center Development Committee Member (1994 to 1996)
Recruitment Committee Member (1992 to 1993)

NATIONAL EDUCATION ASSOCIATION
Associate Member (1997 to Present)
Professional Member (1988 to 1997)
Curriculum Design Review Committee Member (1996 to 1998)
Instructional Software Development Committee Member (1996 to 1997)

Civic Affiliations

Civic affiliations are fine to include if they

• are with a notable organization,

• demonstrate leadership experience, or

• may be of interest to a prospective employer.

However, things such as treasurer of your local condo association and singer with your church choir are not generally of value in marketing your qualifications. Here's an example of what to include:

> ➤ Volunteer Chairperson, United Way of America—Detroit Chapter, 1998 to Present
> ➤ President, Lambert Valley Conservation District, 1997 to Present
> ➤ Treasurer, Habitat for Humanity—Detroit Chapter, 1996 to 1997

Technology Skills and Qualifications

Most education professionals will not need to add a separate section on their resumes for technology skills. Rather, you'll most likely incorporate relevant technology skills into your Career Summary with just a brief mention.

However, for those of you in technology-based education careers, this is a critical section. You need to list your experience with hardware, software, applications, operating systems, networks, multimedia graphics, and more.

You'll also have to consider placement of this section. Depending on your specific objectives, we would recommend you insert it immediately after your Career Summary (or as a part thereof) or immediately after your Professional Experience. This is extremely important information to a prospective employer, so be sure to display it prominently. Here's just one of many different formats you can use:

Technical Expertise

Operating Systems	Windows 3.0 — NT 4.0 — 95 — 98
Networks	LAN — WAN
Software	Microsoft Works — Word — Excel — PowerPoint — Publisher Lotus 1-2-3 — Notes Netscape Navigator — Internet Explorer

Personal Information

We do not recommend that you include such personal information as birth date, marital status, number of children, and related data. However, there may be instances when personal information is appropriate. If this information will give you a competitive advantage or answer unspoken questions about your background, then by all means include it. Here's an example:

- Born in Argentina. U.S. Permanent Residency Status since 1987.
- Fluent in English, Spanish, and Portuguese.
- Competitive Triathlete. Top-5 finish, 1987 Midwest Triathlon and 1992 Des Moines Triathlon.

Note in the above example that the job seeker is multilingual. This is a particularly critical selling point and, although it may be listed under Personal Information in this example, we think it is more appropriate to highlight it in your Career Summary.

Consolidating the Extras

Sometimes you have so many extra categories at the end of your resume, each with only a handful of lines, that spacing becomes a problem. You certainly don't want to have to make your resume a page longer to accommodate five lines, nor do you want the "extras" to overwhelm the primary sections of your resume. Yet you believe the information is important and should be included. Or perhaps you have a few small bits of information that you think are important but don't merit an entire section. In these situations, consider consolidating the information using one of the following formats. You'll save space, avoid over-emphasizing individual items, and present a professional, distinguished appearance.

PROFESSIONAL PROFILE

Affiliations	National Education Association
	Nevada State Teachers Association
	Las Vegas County Teachers Association
Public Speaking	Speaker, NEA Leadership Conference, Dallas, 2000
	Presenter, NEA National Conference, San Diego, 1998
	Panelist, NEA National Conference, Chicago, 1996
Languages	Fluent in English, Spanish, and German
Additional Information	• Founder and Program Chair, Detroit Education & Training Professionals Association.
	• Bilingual—Spanish/English.
	• Available for relocation.

Writing Tips, Techniques, and Important Lessons

At this point, you've done a lot of reading, probably taken some notes, highlighted samples that appeal to you, and are ready to plunge into writing your resume. To make this task as easy as possible, we've compiled some "insider" techniques that we've used in our professional resume-writing practices. We learned these techniques the hard way through years of experience! We know they work; they will make the writing process easier, faster, and more enjoyable for you.

GET IT DOWN—THEN POLISH AND PERFECT IT

Don't be too concerned with making your resume "perfect" the first time around. It's far better to move fairly swiftly through the process, getting the basic information organized and on paper (or onscreen), rather than agonizing about the perfect phrase or ideal formatting. Once you've completed a draft, we think you'll be surprised at how close to "final" it is, and you'll be able to edit, tighten, and improve formatting fairly quickly.

WRITE YOUR RESUME FROM THE BOTTOM UP

Here's the system:

- **Start with the easy things**—Education, Professional Affiliations, Public Speaking, Publications, and any other extras you want to include. These items require little thought and can be completed in just a few minutes.

- **Write short job descriptions for your older positions, the ones you held years ago.** Be very brief and focus on highlights such as rapid promotion, achievements, innovations, professional honors, or employment with a well-respected, well-known school system, university, or corporation.

Once you've completed this, look at how much you've written in a short period of time! Then move on to the next step.

- **Write the job descriptions for your most recent positions.** This will take a bit longer than the other sections you have written. Remember to focus on the overall scope of your responsibility, major projects and initiatives, and significant achievements. Tell your reader what you did and how well you did it. You can use any of the formats recommended earlier in this chapter, or you can create something that is unique to you and your career.

Now, see how far along you are? Your resume is 90 percent complete with only one small section left to do.

- **Write your career summary.** Before you start writing, remember your objective for this section. The summary should not simply rehash your previous experience. Rather, it is designed to highlight the skills and qualifications you have that are most closely related to your current career objective(s). The Summary is intended to capture the reader's attention and "sell" your expertise.

That's it. You're done. We guarantee that the process of writing your resume will be much, much easier if you follow the "bottom-up" strategy. Now, on to the next tip.

INCLUDE NOTABLE OR PROMINENT "EXTRA" STUFF IN YOUR CAREER SUMMARY

Remember the "extra-credit sections" that are normally at the bottom of your resume? If this information is particularly significant or prominent—you won a notable award, spoke at an international conference, developed a new teaching methodology, published a paper, or led a nationwide research study—you may want to include it at the top in your Career Summary. Remember, the Summary section is written to distinguish you from the crowd of other qualified candidates. As such, if you've accomplished anything that clearly demonstrates your knowledge, expertise, and credibility, consider moving it to your Career Summary for added attention. Refer to the sample career summaries earlier in this chapter for examples.

USE RESUME SAMPLES TO GET IDEAS FOR CONTENT, FORMAT, AND ORGANIZATION

This book is just one of many resources where you can review the resumes of other education professionals to help you in formulating your strategy, writing the text, and formatting your resume. What's more, these books are published precisely for that reason. You don't have to struggle alone. Rather, you should use all the available resources at your disposal.

Be forewarned, however, that it's unlikely you will find a resume that fits your life and career to a "T." It's more likely that you will use "some of this sample" and "some of that sample" to create a resume that is uniquely "you."

INCLUDE DATES OR NOT?

Unless you are over age 50, we recommend that you date your work experience and your education. Without dates, your resume becomes vague and difficult for the typical hiring manager or recruiter to interpret. What's more, it often communicates the message that you are trying to hide something. Maybe you haven't worked in two years, maybe you were fired from each of your last three positions, or maybe you never graduated from college. Being vague and creating a resume that is difficult to read will, inevitably, lead to uncertainty and a quick toss into the "not interested" pile of candidates. By including the dates of your education and your experience, you create a clean and concise picture that the reader can easily follow to track your career progression.

An Individual Decision

If you are over age 50, dating your early positions must be an individual decision. On the one hand, you do not want to "date" yourself out of consideration by including dates from the 1960s and early 1970s. On the other hand, it may be that those positions are worth including for any one of a number of reasons. Further, if you omit those early dates, you may feel as though you are misrepresenting yourself (or lying) to a prospective employer.

Here is a strategy to overcome these concerns while still including your early experience: Create a separate category titled "Previous Professional Experience" in which you summarize your earliest employment. You can tailor this statement to emphasize just what is most important about that experience.

If you want to focus on the reputation of your past employers, include a statement such as this:

- Previous experience includes tenured professorial positions with the Graduate Business Schools of **Harvard** and **Yale** Universities.

If you want to focus on the rapid progression of your career, consider this example:

- Promoted rapidly through a series of increasingly responsible teaching and teacher-training positions with the Massachusetts Public School System.

If you want to focus on your early career achievements, include a statement such as

- Member of the 6-person Curriculum Development Team that created the State of Virginia's "Standards of Learning" program, now a statewide institution and the guiding force of all public education initiatives.

By including any one of the above paragraphs, under the heading "Previous Professional Experience," you are clearly communicating to your reader that your employment history dates further back than the dates you have indicated on your resume. In turn, you are being 100 percent above-board and not misrepresenting yourself or your career. What's more, you're focusing on the success, achievement, and prominence of your earliest assignments.

Include Dates in the Education Section?

If you are over age 50, we generally do not recommend that you date your education or college degrees. Simply include the degree and the university with no date. Why exclude yourself from consideration by immediately presenting the fact that you earned your college degree in 1958, 1962, or 1966—probably about the time the hiring manager was born? Remember, the goal of your resume is to share the highlights of your career and open doors for interviews. It is *not* to give your entire life story. As such, it is not mandatory to date your college degree.

However, if you use this strategy, be aware that the reader is likely to assume that there is *some* gap between when your education ended and your work experience started. Therefore, if you choose to begin your chronological work history with your first job out of college, omitting your graduation date could actually backfire, because the reader may assume you have experience that predates your first job. In this case, it's best either to *include your graduation date* or *omit dates of earliest experience,* using the summary strategy discussed above.

ALWAYS SEND A COVER LETTER WHEN YOU FORWARD YOUR RESUME

It is expected, and it's appropriate job search etiquette. When you prepare a resume, you are writing a document that you can use for each and every position you apply for, assuming that the requirements for all of those positions will be similar. The cover letter, then, is the tool that allows you to customize your presentation to each company or recruiter, addressing their specific hiring requirements. It is also the appropriate place to include any specific information that has been requested such as salary history or salary requirements (see the following section).

NEVER INCLUDE SALARY HISTORY OR SALARY REQUIREMENTS ON YOUR RESUME

Your resume is *not* the correct forum for a salary discussion. First of all, you should never provide salary information unless a company has requested that information and you choose to comply. (Studies show that employers will look at your resume anyway, so you may choose not to respond to this request, thereby avoiding pricing yourself out of the job or locking yourself into a lower salary than the job is worth.)

When contacting recruiters, however, we recommend that you do provide salary information, but again, only in your cover letter. With recruiters you want to "put all of your cards on the table" and help them make an appropriate placement by providing information about your current salary and salary objectives. For example, "Be advised that my current compensation is $55,000 annually and that I am interested in a position starting at a minimum of $65,000 per year." Or, if you would prefer to be a little less specific, you might write, "My annual compensation over the past three years has averaged $50,000+."

ALWAYS REMEMBER THAT YOU ARE SELLING

As we have discussed over and over throughout this book, resume writing is sales. Understand and appreciate the value you bring to a prospective employer, and then communicate that value by focusing on your achievements. Companies don't want to hire just anyone; they want to hire "the" someone who will make a difference. Show them that you are that candidate.

CHAPTER 3

Printed, Scannable, Electronic, and Web Resumes

After you've worked so tirelessly to write a winning resume, your next challenge is design, layout, and presentation. It's not enough to read well; your resume must also have just the right look for the right audience. And, just as with everything else in a job search, there is no specific answer. You must make a few choices and decisions about what your final resume presentation will look like.

The Four Types of Resumes

In today's employment market, there are four types of resume presentations:

- Printed
- Scannable
- Electronic (e-mail attachments and ASCII text files)
- Web

The following sections give details on when you would need each type, as well as how to prepare it. Note that for virtually all education professionals, the printed resume is the most commonly used and widely accepted. However, month by month, this is changing as the latest and greatest in technology begins to establish itself firmly within the education industry. In fact, many school districts and other educational institutions around the country now prefer online applications in place of traditional mailed resumes, and your printed resume may come into play only during interviews. For those of you in corporate training and development positions, the scannable and electronic resumes are already well established. And, for those of you in technology-based educational services and professions, scannable, electronic, and Web resumes are already the norm.

THE PRINTED RESUME

The printed resume is what we know as the "traditional resume," the one that you mail to a recruiter, take to an interview, and forward by mail or fax in response to an advertisement. When preparing a printed resume, your objective is to create a sharp, professional, and visually attractive presentation. Remember, that piece of paper conveys the very first impression of you to a potential employer, and that first impression goes a long, long way. Never be fooled into thinking that just because you have the best educational qualifications in your industry, the visual presentation of your resume does not matter. It does, a great deal.

THE SCANNABLE RESUME

The scannable resume can be referred to as the "plain-Jane" or "plain-vanilla" resume. All of the things that you would normally do to make your printed resume look attractive—bold print, italic, multiple columns, sharp-looking type-style, and more—are stripped away in a scannable resume. You want to present a document that can be easily read and interpreted by scanning technology.

Although the technology continues to improve, and many scanning systems can in fact read a wide variety of type enhancements, it's sensible to appeal to the "lowest common denominator" when creating your scannable resume. Follow these formatting guidelines:

- Use a commonly used, easily read font such as Arial or Times New Roman.
- Don't use bold, italic, or underlined type.
- Use a minimum of 11-point type size.
- Position your name, and nothing else, on the top line of the resume.
- Keep text left-justified, with a "ragged" right margin.
- It's okay to use common abbreviations (for instance, scanning software will recognize "B.S." as a Bachelor of Science degree). But when in doubt, spell it out.
- Eliminate graphics, borders, and horizontal lines.
- Use plain round bullets or asterisks.
- Avoid columns and tables, although a simple two-column listing can be read without difficulty.
- Spell out symbols such as % and &.
- If you divide words with slashes, add a space before and after the slash to be certain the scanner doesn't misread the letters.
- Print using a laser printer on smooth white paper.
- If your resume is longer than one page, be sure to print on only one side of the paper, put your name and telephone number on the top of page 2, and don't staple the pages together.
- For the best possible results, mail your resume (don't fax it), and send it flat in a 9 × 12 envelope so that you won't have to fold it.

Of course, you can avoid scannability issues completely by sending your resume electronically, so that it will not have to pass through a scanner to enter the company's databank. The next section details electronic resume guidelines.

THE ELECTRONIC RESUME

Your electronic resume can take two forms: e-mail attachments and ASCII text files.

E-mail Attachments

When including your resume with an e-mail, simply attach the word-processing file of your printed resume. Because a vast majority of businesses use Microsoft Word, this is the most acceptable format and will present the fewest difficulties when attached.

However, given the tremendous variety in versions of software and operating systems, not to mention printer drivers, it's quite possible that your beautifully formatted resume will look quite different when viewed and printed at the other end. To minimize these glitches, use generous margins (at least .75 inch all around), don't use unusual typefaces, and minimize fancy formatting effects.

Test your resume by e-mailing it to several friends or colleagues, then having them view and print it on their systems. If you use WordPerfect, Microsoft Works, or another word-processing program, consider saving your resume in a more universally accepted format such as RTF or PDF. Again, try it out on friends before sending it to a potential employer.

ASCII Text Files

You'll find many uses for an ASCII text version of your resume:

- To avoid formatting problems, you can paste the text into the body of an e-mail message rather than send an attachment. Many employers actually prefer this method. Pasting text into an e-mail message lets you send your resume without the possibility of also sending a virus.

- You can readily copy and paste the text version into online job application and resume bank forms, with no worries that formatting glitches will cause confusion.

- Although it's unattractive, the text version is 100 percent scannable.

To create a text version of your resume, follow these simple steps:

1. Create a new version of your resume using the Save As feature of your word-processing program. Select "text only" or "ASCII" in the Save As option box.

2. Close the new file.

3. Reopen the file, and you'll find that your word processor has automatically reformatted your resume into Courier font, removed all formatting, and left-justified the text.

4. To promote maximum readability when sending your resume electronically, reset the margins to 2 inches left and right, so that you have a narrow column

of text rather than a full-page width. (This margin setting will not be retained when you close the file, but in the meantime you can adjust the text formatting for best screen appearance. For instance, if you choose to include a horizontal line of characters to separate sections of the resume, by working with the narrow margins you won't make the mistake of creating a line that extends past the normal screen width. You also won't add hard line breaks that create odd-length lines when seen at normal screen width.)

5. Review the resume and fix any "glitches" such as odd characters that may have been inserted to take the place of "curly" quotes, dashes, accents, or other nonstandard symbols.

6. If necessary, add extra blank lines to improve readability.

7. Consider adding horizontal dividers to break the resume into sections for improved skimmability. You can use any standard typewriter symbols such as *, -, (,), =, +, ^, or #.

To illustrate what you can expect when creating these versions of your resume, pages 43, 44, and 45 show one resume (top portion only) in three different formats: traditional printed format, scannable version, and electronic (text) format.

The Web Resume

This newest evolution in resumes combines the visually pleasing quality of the printed resume with the technological ease of the electronic resume. You host your Web resume on your own Web site (with your own URL), to which you refer prospective employers and recruiters. Now, instead of a "plain-Jane" version of your e-mailed resume, with just one click a viewer can access, download, and print your Web resume—an attractive, nicely formatted presentation of your qualifications.

What's more, because the Web resume is such an efficient and easy-to-manage tool, you can choose to include more information than you would in a printed, scannable, or electronic resume. Consider separate pages for achievements, publications, education and credentials, multimedia instructional projects, qualifications, management skills, and more if you believe they would improve your market position. Remember, you're working to sell yourself into your next job!

Educators in multimedia and related technology industries can even take it one step further and create a virtual multimedia presentation that not only tells someone how talented you are, but also visually and technologically demonstrates it. Web resumes are an outstanding tool for people seeking jobs in the technology-based education industry.

A simplified way to create a Web resume is to post your Microsoft Word resume on the Internet. Instead of attaching a file to your e-mail, you can include a link to the online version. This format is not as graphically dynamic as a full-fledged Web resume, but it can be a very useful tool for your job search. Using this method, you can offer the simplicity of text in your e-mail, and by including the link to your online site you can offer the instant availability of a word-processing document for the recruiter or hiring manager who is interested. For a demonstration of this format, go to www.e-resume-central.com and click on "See a Sample."

Laura Greystone

Lgreystone23@netscape.net

672 Oaklawn Drive
Cincinnati, Ohio 45242
(513) 555-0202

Expertise   **SENIOR-LEVEL UNIVERSITY ADMINISTRATION & LEADERSHIP**

Experience   **DEAN OF ADMISSIONS & FINANCIAL AID,** 1995–2001
ASSISTANT DEAN OF ADMISSIONS, 1993–1995

MORRISON COLLEGE, Cincinnati, OH

Planned and directed the reorganization and refinement of the Admissions and Financial Aid Departments. Redesigned core processes, streamlined operations, and accelerated program growth. Directed a staff of 14 and managed a $300,000 annual operating budget.

> **Recruitment:** Created and launched a multi-faceted recruitment program including high school visitations, open house visitations, targeted direct mail and e-mail, guidance counselor cultivation, and alumni admissions networking. Results included 185% increase in admissions inquiries, 53% increase in applications, and 10% increase in matriculants.

> **Strategic Planning:** Appointed to senior management team that developed and implemented the College's strategic planning processes for enrollment, facilities, curriculum, personnel, finances, and public relations.

> **Committee Memberships:** Served on the Middle States Accreditation Committee, Centennial Athletic Committee, College Retention Committee, Marketing Task Force, and Budget Advisory Committee.

The print version of the resume section.

Laura Greystone

672 Oaklawn Drive
Cincinnati, Ohio 45242
Lgreystone23@netscape.net
(513) 555-0202

EXPERTISE   Senior-Level University Administration and Leadership

EXPERIENCE   Dean Of Admissions And Financial Aid, 1995–2001
                      Assistant Dean Of Admissions, 1993–1995
                      Morrison College, Cincinnati, OH

Planned and directed the reorganization and refinement of the Admissions and Financial Aid Departments. Redesigned core process, streamlined operations, and accelerated program growth. Directed a staff of 14 and managed a $300,000 annual operating budget.

RECRUITMENT: Created and launched a multi-faceted recruitment program including high school visitations, open house visitations, targeted direct mail and e-mail, guidance counselor cultivation, and alumni admissions networking. Results included 185 percent increase in admissions inquiries, 53 percent increase in applications, and 10 percent increase in matriculants.

STRATEGIC PLANNING: Appointed to senior management team that developed and implemented the College's strategic planning processes for enrollment, facilities, curriculum, personnel, finances, and public relations.

COMMITTEE MEMBERSHIPS: Served on the Middle States Accreditation Committee, Centennial Athletic Committee, College Retention Committee, Marketing Task Force, and Budget Advisory Committee.

The scannable version of the resume section.

```
LAURA GREYSTONE
-----------------------------------------------------------
672 Oaklawn Drive
Cincinnati, Ohio 45242
Lgreystone23@netscape.net
(513) 555-0202
-----------------------------------------------------------

EXPERTISE
Senior-Level University Administration and Leadership
-----------------------------------------------------------
EXPERIENCE
Dean of Admissions and Financial Aid, 1995-2001
Assistant Dean of Admissions, 1993-1995

MORRISON COLLEGE, Cincinnati, OH

Planned and directed the reorganization and refinement
of the Admissions and Financial Aid Departments.
Redesigned core process, streamlined operations, and
accelerated program growth. Directed a staff of 14 and
managed a $300,000 annual operating budget.

--- RECRUITMENT: Created and launched a multi-faceted
recruitment program including high school visitations,
open house visitations, targeted direct mail and
e-mail, guidance counselor cultivation, and alumni
admissions networking. Results included 185 percent
increase in admissions inquiries, 53 percent increase
in applications, and 10 percent increase in
matriculants.

--- STRATEGIC PLANNING: Appointed to senior management
team that developed and implemented the College's
strategic planning processes for enrollment,
facilities, curriculum, personnel, finances, and
public relations.

--- COMMITTEE MEMBERSHIPS: Served on the Middle States
Accreditation Committee, Centennial Athletic
Committee, College Retention Committee, Marketing Task
Force, and Budget Advisory Committee.
```

The electronic/text version of the resume section.

The Four Resume Types Compared

This chart quickly compares the similarities and differences between the four types of resumes we've discussed in this chapter.

	PRINTED RESUMES	SCANNABLE RESUMES
TYPESTYLE/ FONT	Sharp, conservative, and distinctive (see our recommendations in chapter 1).	Clean, concise, and machine-readable: Times New Roman, Arial, Helvetica.
TYPESTYLE ENHANCEMENTS	**Bold,** *italics,* and underlining for emphasis.	CAPITALIZATION is the only type enhancement you can be certain will transmit.
TYPE SIZE	10-, 11-, or 12-point preferred... larger type sizes (14, 18, 20, 22, and even larger, depending on typestyle) will effectively enhance your name and section headers.	11, 12-point, or larger.
TEXT FORMAT	Use centering and indentations to optimize the visual presentation.	Type all information flush left.
PREFERRED LENGTH	1 to 2 pages; 3 if essential.	1 to 2 pages preferred, although length is not as much of a concern as with printed resumes.
PREFERRED PAPER COLOR	White, Ivory, Light Gray, Light Blue, or other conservative background.	White or very light with no prints, flecks, or other shading that might affect scannability.
WHITE SPACE	Use appropriately for best readability.	Use generously to maximize scannability.

ELECTRONIC RESUMES	WEB RESUMES
Courier.	Sharp, conservative, and distinctive... attractive onscreen and when printed from an online document.
CAPITALIZATION is the only enhancement available to you.	**Bold,** *italics,* and <u>underlining</u>, and color for emphasis.
12-point.	10-, 11-, or 12-point preferred... larger type sizes (14, 18, 20, 22, even larger, depending on typestyle) will effectively enhance your name and section headers.
Type all information flush left.	Use centering and indentations to optimize the visual presentation.
Length is immaterial; almost definitely, converting your resume to text will make it longer.	Length is immaterial; just be sure your site is well organized so viewers can quickly find the material of greatest interest to them.
N/A.	Paper is not used, but do select your background carefully to maximize readability.
Use white space to break up dense text sections.	Use appropriately for best readability both onscreen and when printed.

Are You Ready to Write Your Resume?

To be sure that you're ready to write your resume, go through the following checklist. Each item is a critical step that you must take in the process of writing and designing your own winning resume.

- ❏ Clearly define "who you are" and how you want to be perceived.

- ❏ Document your key skills, qualifications, and knowledge.

- ❏ Document your notable career achievements and successes.

- ❏ Identify one or more specific job targets or positions.

- ❏ Identify one or more industries that you are targeting.

- ❏ Research and compile key words for your profession, industry, and specific job targets.

- ❏ Determine which resume format is best for you and your career.

- ❏ Select an attractive font.

- ❏ Determine whether you need a print resume, an electronic resume, a Web resume, or all three.

- ❏ Secure a private e-mail address (not your employer's).

- ❏ Review resume samples for up-to-date ideas on resume styles, formats, organization, and language.

PART II

Sample Resumes for Teachers and Educators

CHAPTER 4

Resumes for Early-Childhood Educators

- Child Care Directors
- Preschool Teachers
- Kindergarten Teachers
- After-School Program Coordinators
- Preschool Enrichment Consultants
- Children's Librarians
- Head Start Teachers
- Nursery School Directors

PENNY CONWAY

973 Corbin Way • Modesto, California 95350 • (425) 881-3201

Director / Teacher / Early Childhood Education
~ Natural gift to relate to children ~

PROFILE

An enthusiastic, warm, and caring educator/administrator who wants all children to be successful learners and works to create an atmosphere that is stimulating, encouraging, and adaptive to their emotional needs. Follower of traditional teachings and values. Energetic and decisive leader able to effectively merge and develop effective communications between provider, parent, and child through unique triangular, team-centered concept.

PROFESSIONAL EXPERIENCE AND ACHIEVEMENTS

Director, APPLEBEE HOUSE CHILD CARE CENTER, Omaha, Nebraska   1987–1999

Management/Administration
Established start-up operating procedures for an eight-child in-home child care center that grew into a 45-child facility. Retained 92% of the children and continued to grow facility with an annual revenue of over $100,000. Ensured smooth-running operations concerning administrative, menu planning, scheduling, policies and procedures, and educational program elements. Recruited staff of 10 to 12 assistant directors and child care assistants for each shift. Consistently provided more staff than the "state-required ratio of children" in order to provide a quality child care center.

Communications/Training
Encouraged parent participation in creative craft-based activities (Jell-O, finger painting, blowing bubbles, baking, cooking, shaving cream, flour and water to create volcano foam, math, creative writing). Ensured all materials were biodegradable and non-toxic. Initiated and developed "triangular concept of communication," which strengthened communications and interaction among parent, child, and provider.

Trained and directed parents, assistant directors, and child care assistants to emphasize an active, positive learning environment. Worked with children to gain confidence and trust. Encouraged open communication and freedom of expression. Achieved measurable successes with all children, including at-risk and "problem" children. Increased parent involvement through regular communications and invitations to participate in classroom activities and field trips such as fishing, camping, and visiting the elderly.

Creativity/Imagination
Designed music programs using a variety of musical instruments including the harp, piano, and organ. Encouraged creative music style using pots, pans, and skillets to build hand dexterity skills. Developed build-up and tear-down exercises to stimulate their imaginations.

Dividing professional experience into functional paragraphs is a good way to keep the information manageable and easy to understand.

PENNY CONWAY

Page 2

LICENSES

In-home Child Care: 45 children, State of Nebraska
Foster Care: Ages 0–18, 1986–1999

PRESENTATIONS

Lectured on the "Triangular Concept of Communication" among parent, child, and provider for an audience of 3,000 at "Excellence in Early Childhood" conference.

SPECIALIZED TRAINING

UNIVERSITY OF OMAHA COOPERATIVE EXTENSION, Omaha, Nebraska

Certificates:

CPR/First Aid

Developing Creative Learners

Issues Affecting Children and Families

ADHD/ADD Workshop Early Intervention Team

Appropriate Use of Behavior Management

Good Stuff for Kids

Observation and Assessment in Early Childhood Programs

Encouraging Responsibility in Young Children through Choices/Consequences of Raising Children in a Socially Toxic Environment

COMPUTER SKILLS

PC computer literate: Windows 98, MS Office, and scanner

BEATRICE WRIGHT

648 Yale Drive
Alexandria, VA
22314
Home 703.579.6492
Cell 703.528.3164
BeaWright@aol.com

CAREER FOCUS

Creative and resourceful early childhood/elementary educator **dedicated to child and adult literacy**. Possess extensive **knowledge of children's literature** and **balanced literacy programs**. Experienced in multicultural classroom settings. Strong desire to work at grassroots level to educate inner-city children and adults on the importance of reading and literacy. Seeking admission to a graduate program specializing in **children's literature, language**, and **reading programs**. Expertise includes:

Balanced Literacy Programs ▪ Curriculum Development ▪ Course Design
Classroom Management ▪ Educational Administration ▪ Lifelong Learning
Accreditation ▪ Grant Administration ▪ Training & Development
Curriculum Mapping ▪ Parent/Teacher Conferences ▪ Student Retention

EDUCATION

B.A. George Mason University, Fairfax, VA, anticipated May 2001 with honors & distinction
Major: Honors English ▪ Minor: History

EXPERIENCE

Preschool Teacher, George Mason Child Development Center, Fairfax, VA, 2000
- Instructed 17 three- and four-year-old children in twice-weekly class.
- Assisted with school's reaccreditation process.
- Coordinated children's classroom literature, including thematic and individual reading.

Preschool Teacher, Village Green Day School, Great Falls, VA, 1994-96, 1998-99
- Instituted literature-based, early childhood curriculum at NAEYC-accredited school. Supervised two assistant teachers.
- Presented *Learning Through Literature* workshop at Northern Virginia Regional Teacher's Conference.
- Transformed classrooms with creative decorations that tied in with weekly themes and classroom reading.

Camp Director, American Camping Association, Great Falls, VA, Summers 1995-98
- Supervised activities for 200 children at nationally accredited children's camp. Chaired curriculum-development efforts.
- Recruited, trained, and managed staff of 40 counselors and 8 administrative assistants.
- Implemented First Aid, CPR, and Blood-Borne Pathogen certification for staff members.
- Camp earned first-ever 100% rating from evaluator with 17 years experience.

Manager, Children's Hour, New Orleans, LA, Summers 1996-97
- Directed non-profit literacy-awareness program for hospitals, schools, and pediatricians.
- Coordinated community book events and author visits.
- Promoted literacy awareness through seminars for teachers and administrators.

Summer Camp Director, U.S. Embassy, Community Service Association, Cairo, Egypt, 1993
- Orchestrated camp events and activities for 183 children from around the world.
- Created ethnically harmonious curriculum for diverse student group.
- Organized field trips to educational sites such as the Giza Pyramids.

AFFILIATIONS & COMMUNITY SERVICE

NAEYC Member ▪ Undergraduate English Society, George Mason University
Golden Key National Honor Society and English Honors Society
Virginia Association for Early Childhood Educators ▪ Read to Your Bunny Campaign
Northern Virginia Women's Shelter – Organized new children's library
Crescent House, New Orleans, LA – Raised $800 in book donations for women's shelter

"Once in a while a natural teacher is born and Beatrice is truly that person."

Linda A. Rodgers
Village Green Day
School Director
Great Falls, VA

"[Beatrice created] an innovative, totally integrated literature based curriculum... the children waited with anticipation to see where they would be visiting next...[Beatrice] presented an environment where children entered the world of a story..."

Patricia L. Dezelick
Parent & Teacher
Hemdon, VA

"...an incredible role model for the staff."

Lynne Simmons
President and Founder
Village Green Day School
Great Falls, VA

This resume uses a creative format, reserving the left column for contact information and testimonials. There is a strong key-word summary in the Career Focus section.

FREDERICK R. RICHARDS
134 Ridgefield Street
Framingham, Massachusetts 01701
508-877-8216
frichards@mediaone.net

EDUCATOR / INSTRUCTOR — EARLY CHILDHOOD

11+ years' hands-on experience in early childhood education... Nominated by parents of children in my care for Scholastic National Teacher of the Year... Outstanding communication skills... Readily establish rapport with wide range of people of various ages... Adapt presentation of material/coursework to ensure complete comprehension by students... Software proficiency includes Microsoft Word, PowerPoint, and QuickBooks.

Sought out by organizations to **present workshops** at statewide and regional conferences to early childhood educators on various topics, e.g., science for young children, professionalism for child care providers, development of handbooks and contracts.

PROFESSIONAL EXPERIENCE

Apple Tree Child Center – Sudbury, Massachusetts   1989 – Present
OWNER / DIRECTOR

- Oversee three staff members in care of 10 children aged infant – 11 in nationally accredited (NAFCC) child care program. Prepare and serve nutritional meals; teach good eating habits and personal hygiene.

- Help children explore interests, develop talents and independence, build self-esteem, and learn how to behave with others in child-centered, child-directed environment.

- Develop curriculum based on NAEYC standards for developmental appropriateness to stimulate children's physical, emotional, intellectual, and social growth. Nurture, motivate, and teach children.

- Assess children to evaluate their progress and discuss parents' involvement in their child's learning and developmental process.

Marlborough Hospital – Marlborough, Massachusetts   1994 – Present
CPR INSTRUCTOR / TRAINER, per diem
Teach pediatric safety and CPR to expectant parents, early childhood professionals, grandparents, and others.

PROFESSIONAL ORGANIZATIONS

National Association for the Education of
Young Children (NAEYC)

National Association for Family Child Care (NAFCC)

Mass. Alliance of Family Child Care Providers,
Treasurer, 1 term; President, 2 terms

Office of Child Care Services, Mentor

CERTIFICATION

Commonwealth of Massachusetts Teacher Certification, K–8

EDUCATION / CONTINUING EDUCATION

M.Ed., **Early Childhood Curriculum and Instruction**, 1998, Suffolk University – Boston, Massachusetts
B.S., **Special Education and Elementary Education**, 1977, Lowell State College – Lowell, Massachusetts

With a colorful graphic and creative headline font, this resume for an early-childhood educator stands out from the ordinary.

Joanne Cavanagh

60 Orchard Terrace, Bronxville, NY 10708
(914) 961-9823 Home ✳ (610) 896-8969 College
joanne.cavanagh@haverford.edu

Objective

Kindergarten Teacher. Qualified by academic training as an educator, extensive experience working with young children, and leadership roles.

Education

Bachelor of Science, English Education (expected May 2001)
Haverford College, Haverford, PA
✳ Major: Education – Minor: English – GPA in Major: 3.4
✳ Admitted to the National Honor Society in high school

Ongoing training/certification:
✳ CPR for the Professional Rescuer (2000)
✳ Lifeguard Training and Community First Aid & Safety (1998)

Relevant Experience

Co-Facilitator (2000–2001)
Haverford College, Haverford, PA
✳ Selected to lead weekly group meetings with 20 freshmen to discuss issues related to adjusting to college life.

Swim Instructor (Summers 1999–2000)
Lake Isle Country Club, Eastchester, NY
✳ Taught young children to swim one-on-one and in small-group lessons.
✳ Utilized self-taught techniques acquired through 12 years of competitive swimming experience and book research.
✳ Entrusted with simultaneously managing head lifeguard duties.

Head Lifeguard/Lifeguard (Summers 1995–2000)
Lake Isle Country Club, Eastchester, NY
✳ Promoted to Head Lifeguard in 1999 based on demonstrated work ethic.
✳ Ensured a safe environment by scheduling coverage, supervising lifeguards, and testing pool water regularly.
✳ Organized special holiday games for children.

Junior Achievement Kindergarten Teacher (Spring 2000)
St. Mary's Elementary School, Broomall, PA
✳ Conducted educational activities that followed the curriculum.
✳ Selected books to read based on coursework in children's literature.

Community Service

Special Olympics Volunteer, Haverford, PA (1997–1999)
✳ Supported an assigned group throughout all games and meals.
✳ Participated as "Team Hugger" for two years, hugging participants at the conclusion of their events.

Catholic Worker, West Philadelphia, PA (1997–1998)
✳ Mentored group in an after-school program, providing structured play and individual homework help.

This resume shows quite a bit of experience for a newly graduated kindergarten teacher and clearly relates this youthful experience to her new role.

Chloe Kelley

7 Oak Lane, Waldwick, NJ 07463   201-555-1212

Child Care Professional

Excellent ability to establish and maintain rapport with both children and parents based on superb interpersonal and communication skills. Provide facilitated learning environment with well-planned and organized curriculum. Able to assess each child to determine their personalities and relate to them as individuals. Intuitive ability to control children while providing a relaxed and fun atmosphere for them. Solve problems quickly and well with total focus on the welfare of the child.

Professional Employment

AFTER-SCHOOL PROGRAM COORDINATOR
YWCA of Old Hills, Old Hills, NJ   1995 – present
Design and deliver after-school programs for 35–40 children from K–7th grade.
- Develop age-appropriate curriculum linked to monthly themes.
- Cultivate respect of children through consistent deployment of policies while creating an atmosphere where children can relax and have fun.
- Establish and maintain good working relationships with parents through constant communication regarding vacations, policies, and upcoming events.
- Develop and maintain solid relationships with principals, school nurses, and secretaries.
- Recruit, develop, train, and supervise four to five staff members.
- Ensure compliance with state regulations for child care, administration of medications, staff-to-children ratio, attendance books, and fire drills.
- Implement parental requests regarding supervision of homework and participation in sports and recreational activities.

SECRETARY – NURSERY SCHOOL and CAMP
- Coordinate billing, registration, site tours, and word processing.
- Order all supplies and snacks.
- Manage accounts payable for five separate nursery school sites.
- Administer employee time sheets.
- Schedule day classes and trips for camp.
- Manage all details for special parties, including booking, billing, scheduling, and staffing.

TEACHER
Happy Times School, Inc., Oakland, NJ   1993 – 1995
Supervised the activities of 12–13 children ranging from two to three years old at this privately owned pre-school.
- Developed and delivered thematic monthly curriculum appropriately geared to age ranges with reinforcement through all bulletin boards and banners throughout the school.
- Taught colors, shapes, numbers, weather, and science.
- Conducted walking trips and organized fund raisers.

ASSISTANT DIRECTOR
- Conducted tuition billing for 60 families.
- Created and administered staff schedules.
- Performed diverse administrative duties: word processing, filing, and answering telephones.
- Conducted site tours.

A strong introduction focusing on educational philosophy is a notable feature of this well-organized resume.

Chloe Kelley 201-555-1212

page two

Professional Employment, cont.

ASSISTANT TO DIRECTOR

The Exceptional Child Pre-School, Rye, NJ   Summer 1993

- Designed bulletin boards and classrooms around monthly themes.
- Served as half-day floating teacher in afternoons for classes with infants through kindergarten.
- Conducted daily projects and various lesson plans.

ART TEACHER

Ridge Hills Recreation Commission, Ridge Hills, NJ   Summer 1993

- Instructed art for 20 three-year-olds at this morning summer recreation program.

ASSISTANT TO PROGRAM COORDINATOR

YMCA of Middletown, Middletown, NY   1989–1993

- Assisted in the after-school latchkey program for 20–25 children in 1st through 5th grades.
- Supervised homework, indoor/outdoor games, special classes, and craft projects.
- Served as summer camp counselor.
- Supervised vacation programs.
- Acted as birthday party hostess for weekend programs.

Education

Associate Degree — Early Childhood Education

Ramapo Community College, Oak Ridge, NJ   1993

Student Teaching:

— Supervised all room centers and activities and conducted various lesson plans for a class composed of 20 three- and four-year-olds.

Relevant coursework:

— *Early Childhood Education I and II, Child and Educational Psychology, Sociology of Family, Human Service, Parenting Young Children, Curriculum Materials & Methods, Developing and Implementing Curriculum, Supervised Field Work Experience I and II, Field Work Seminar I and II; Infants and Toddlers.*

Languages

Spanish: some knowledge

Computer Skills

Windows 95, Microsoft Word, Excel: some knowledge

Certifications

First Aid, Level 1 and CPR Adult, Child and Infant, National Safety Council

Professional Affiliations

NJ Association for the Education of Young Children (NJAEYC)

Joyce A. Morrison

133 Bertram Island Road
Hopatcong, New Jersey 07843
973-398-1832

PRESCHOOL ENRICHMENT CONSULTANT / CHILDREN'S LIBRARIAN

Dynamic professional career promoting literacy and language development through programs encouraging parent/child interaction... Knowledge of wide variety of information sources to assist patrons in locating information for use in their personal and professional lives... Communicate effectively with people of all ages... Recognize opportunities for outreach; develop and implement programs... Excellent research and organizational skills.

Toddler Presentations - Hopatcong, New Jersey   1996 – Present
PROGRAM LEADER / CONSULTANT

- Design specific single-day or multi-session programs for children ages 2 and up. Present home workshops for children ages 6 and up during school vacations. Promote interaction between parent(s) and child(ren). Programs include a story and craft focusing on a specific theme:

    Storytime with Simple Science   Holiday Sampler for Young Children
    Red is Best (Valentine's Day)   You're So Silly (April Fool's)
    Mother's Day Coffee/Story Hour   Tea Party

- Develop and present customized party activity related to party theme, child's age and interests. Offer complete party planning services. Make quality-time happen.

Sussex County Public Library - Hopatcong, New Jersey   1990 – Present
CHILDREN'S LIBRARIAN

- Manage children's department; supervise circulation; train children's department staff. Contributed to development of training manual and library policy.
- Manage budget of $10K–$15K; preview and purchase print and non-print materials. Follow trends and consider patron's requests to effectively oversee selection and organization of library materials.
- Design and present all programs for ages 2 through 10 and family, focusing on stimulating children's emotional, intellectual, and social growth. Write all press releases for children's programs.
- Interface with school and community to develop informational programs and systems to meet needs of patrons. Complete reference inquiry interview through information retrieval. Assist users with searching techniques, including use of Internet.
- Assisted in grant writing to obtain Community Partnerships Grant through the New Jersey Department of Education. Developed and implemented outreach program to promote literacy for children in a day-care setting while concurrently providing support for caregivers.

Randolph Public Library - Randolph, New Jersey   1986 – 1990
ASSISTANT DIRECTOR / CHILDREN'S SERVICES

- Supervised children's department and encouraged teamwork to ensure quality service to the public. Assisted Director in administrative duties.

MEMBERSHIPS / VOLUNTEER ACTIVITIES

Lenape Valley Early Childhood Advisory Council   Netcong Arts Council, Chairperson
Hopatcong Parks Department, Volunteer Coordinator   Executive Board of HCC, Past Treasurer

EDUCATION

M. S., 1989, Early Childhood and Child Development, Montclair University - Montclair, New Jersey
B. A., 1978, English Major, Drew University - Madison, New Jersey

An owl reading a book is the perfect graphic to enhance this resume for a children's librarian.

Tanisha Jones

Home: 724.555.8735

14000 Sixth Avenue

Work: 724.555.8004

Sun City, PA 16000

E-Mail: Teacup@searchforth.net

Objective: To continue my track record for dedication, responsibility, and leadership in education as an Early Childhood Education Teacher with County Head Start.

Education & Certification

Pennsylvania State University
University Park, PA
- Bachelor of Science Degree in Elementary / Kindergarten Education
- Pennsylvania Instructional 1 Teaching Certificate
- Pennsylvania Private Academic School Certificate (Early Childhood Elementary)

Scholastic Highlights
- Dean's List: 5 semesters.
- Chaired / sat on relevant committees.
- Attended education seminars: Penn State Cooperative Extension-Middle County.
- Maintained continuous employment to fund education.

Relevant Employment

Community Child Care Center (Present)
Hudson, PA
- Center Supervisor
- Preschool Teacher

Pierre Indian Learning Center
Pierre, SD
- Teacher

Ferguson Township Elementary School
Pine Valley, PA
- Teaching Internship

Townsend Primary School
Townsend, PA
- Teaching Internship

Teaching Qualifications

Class Instruction
- Capable of providing expert instruction for students ranging from learning-disabled to gifted.
- Responsibly lead daily learning activities based on development of monthly themes.
- Ably contribute to building new curriculum framework / units.
- Successfully initiate classroom management plans promoting individual responsibility / positive reinforcement.
- Provide tactful, stern classroom mediation whenever necessary.
- Innovate and test stimulating educational games.
- Build excellent, productive relationships via daily contact with parents and guardians.
- Create clear monthly calendars to aid students and parents in coordinating school activities.

Administrative Strengths
- Possess superior time-management skills.
- Perform above and beyond daily requirements to achieve project success.
- Professionally versatile working in a team effort or independently.
- Active participant in staff meetings, in-services; serve on and chair committees.
- Easily adapt to new assignments / willing to take extra time to learn skills.
- Expertly assemble staff schedules and calendars to increase efficiency.
- Lead others and take initiative.
- Coordinate peer-tutor programs.

Committee Involvement

- College Women's Association: President 2000-01
- Young Authors Conference: Chair, 1997
- Year-Round Schooling: Research Committee Member
- School Scheduling: Committee Member
- Peer Tutoring Program: Coordinator

Computer Proficiency

Windows, Works, Word, WordPerfect, Internet navigation, Graphics versatility

Personal Highlights

Mature and Stable / Thorough / Innovative / Pleasant / Professional / Conscientious

A multicolumn format makes the most of the available space. Note the interesting addition of a Personal Highlights section at the very bottom.

Jennifer R. Haglund

1861 Pascal Avenue
Roseville, MN 55113
651-555-3892
jrhaglund.uminn.edu

Profile

✦ Enthusiastic, committed educator with innate ability to understand and motivate children.
✦ Keen interest in and hands-on experience working with students who have special needs.
✦ Strive to build student self-esteem and encourage understanding of cultural diversity, gender differences, and physical limitations.
✦ Create a cooperative community in the classroom; model for students the importance of mutual respect and cooperation among all community members.
✦ Skilled in adapting to students' diverse learning styles.

Education

Macalaster College • St. Paul, MN
Pursuing **Master's Degree — Special Education**
  • Anticipated completion: Fall 2002
  • Working toward Emotionally Impaired specialty

University of Minnesota • Minneapolis, MN
Bachelor of Science in Education (1995)
  • Language Arts major; Math and Early Childhood Education minors
  • Earned *Class Honors* and named *Gopher Scholar*

Certification

Minnesota Provisional Elementary with Early Childhood Specialty (K–8)

Relevant Experience

Preschool Teacher — Ready, Set Succeed! Program/Perry Community Schools • Perry, MN (1995–Present)
  • Oversee all aspects of state-funded program for at-risk four-year-olds modeled after Head Start.
  • Plan and implement age-appropriate curriculum to academically prepare students for kindergarten and provide opportunity for development of socialization skills.
  • Utilize wide range of instructional techniques (centers, cooperative groups, individual work) with emphasis on providing a language-rich environment.
  • Interview parents; determine eligibility for program based on income and other guidelines.
  • Make home visits; build rapport with families as well as students.
  • Administer four-year-old Brigance screening to assess students' developmental levels.
  • Developed duties for and direct program assistant.
  • Trained in and taught Minnesota Literacy Progress Profile to five-year-olds (Summer 1999).

Substitute Preschool Teacher — College Child Development Center • Minneapolis, MN (1994–1995)
  • Interacted with infants and children up to kindergarten age.

Student Teacher — King Elementary/Roseville Community Schools • Roseville, MN (1995)
  • Taught all subjects to 17-member first-grade classroom.
  • Organized and facilitated reading group.

Student Intern — United Way First Call for Help & Volunteer Center • St. Paul, MN (1995)
  • Referred callers in need to community service agencies and directed volunteers to assignments.

Tutor Aide — Columbia Middle School/Columbia Community Schools • Columbia, MN (1994)
  • Assisted 6th-grade Language Arts teacher with lesson plan preparation and instruction.
  • Tutored students individually and in small groups.

Tutor — Self-employed (1992–1994)
  • Privately tutored high school student in all subjects.

Volunteer Tutor — Brooklyn Middle School/Brooklyn Community Schools • Brooklyn, MN (1990–1994)
  • Completed Lit Start program and tutored middle school students.

References available on request

Note how professional, student, and volunteer experiences are blended to present a substantial Relevant Experience section.

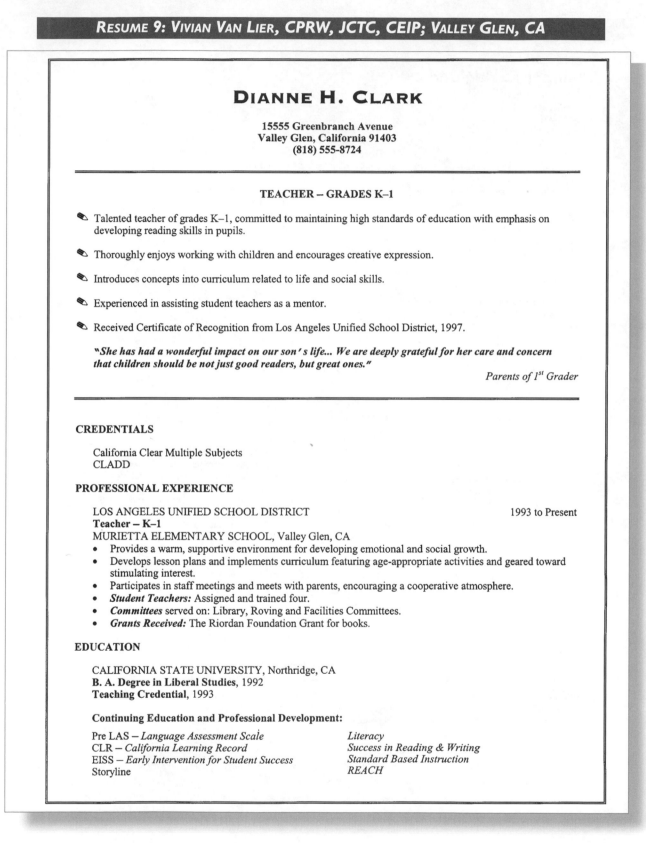

DIANNE H. CLARK

15555 Greenbranch Avenue
Valley Glen, California 91403
(818) 555-8724

TEACHER – GRADES K–1

- Talented teacher of grades K–1, committed to maintaining high standards of education with emphasis on developing reading skills in pupils.

- Thoroughly enjoys working with children and encourages creative expression.

- Introduces concepts into curriculum related to life and social skills.

- Experienced in assisting student teachers as a mentor.

- Received Certificate of Recognition from Los Angeles Unified School District, 1997.

"She has had a wonderful impact on our son's life... We are deeply grateful for her care and concern that children should be not just good readers, but great ones."

Parents of 1st Grader

CREDENTIALS

California Clear Multiple Subjects
CLADD

PROFESSIONAL EXPERIENCE

LOS ANGELES UNIFIED SCHOOL DISTRICT   1993 to Present
Teacher – K–1
MURIETTA ELEMENTARY SCHOOL, Valley Glen, CA
- Provides a warm, supportive environment for developing emotional and social growth.
- Develops lesson plans and implements curriculum featuring age-appropriate activities and geared toward stimulating interest.
- Participates in staff meetings and meets with parents, encouraging a cooperative atmosphere.
- *Student Teachers:* Assigned and trained four.
- *Committees* served on: Library, Roving and Facilities Committees.
- *Grants Received:* The Riordan Foundation Grant for books.

EDUCATION

CALIFORNIA STATE UNIVERSITY, Northridge, CA
B. A. Degree in Liberal Studies, 1992
Teaching Credential, 1993

Continuing Education and Professional Development:

Pre LAS – *Language Assessment Scale*	*Literacy*
CLR – *California Learning Record*	*Success in Reading & Writing*
EISS – *Early Intervention for Student Success*	*Standard Based Instruction*
Storyline	*REACH*

The summary section is enhanced by the addition of an effective testimonial. The experience summary is brief yet comprehensive.

MARY BARTEN, MA

1422 Manor Avenue • Somerset, NJ 08873 • (609) 567-6359

EARLY CHILDHOOD EDUCATOR

Innovative professional offers an extensive background in early childhood education with broad pedagogical base, covering Piaget through Harold Gardner.... Experienced in developing curriculum as well as conducting teacher training and parenting programs.... Accustomed to working in a multicultural environment that emphasizes inclusion.

—— *Selected Accomplishments* ——

- ◆ Recipient of New Jersey Governor's Award for excellence in education.
- ◆ Nominated ten times and recipient of locally sponsored award for excellence in teaching.
- ◆ Nominated by school PTA for national award, Phoebe Apperson Hearst Outstanding Educator Award.
- ◆ Speaker at national conferences on varied topics such as Montessori education and portfolio assessment.
- ◆ Designated a Clinical Faculty Member at Rutgers University.

"Mary Barten effectively demonstrates leadership capabilities and follow-through. She contributes to and exerts a positive influence on the total school community."... Principal's comment on evaluation, 1999.

CAREER EXPERIENCE:

SOMERSET BOARD OF EDUCATION, Somerset, New Jersey   1987–2000

Teacher/Subject Matter Leader

Spearheaded the development of **Montessori Magnet School** for Pre-K/kindergarten students. Starting as pilot program, school expanded to fifth grade by popular demand, servicing over 350 children.

- Served in both administrative and teaching capacities (Pre-K & kindergarten). Supervised teachers in developing stages of program. Collaborated with principal in hiring staff.

- Key member of School Review Committee, working with principal, teachers, and parents to resolve educational issues and adjust curriculum to students' needs. Committee played a leadership role in expansion of school through fifth grade.

- Selected to serve as on-site Educational Mentor for student teachers from Rutgers University. Facilitated improvement in instruction and overall performance through regular observations and evaluations. Coordinated all visitations and teaching assignments directly with University.

- Developed and conducted in-depth training program for teaching assistants that included educational philosophy, methodology, and constructive discipline. Prepared staff for more active participation in classroom instruction.

- Created and delivered parent education programs, dealing with a wide range of topics such as homework, discipline, and Montessori principles. Offered in the evening, these popular programs greatly enhanced parent-school relations.

- Actively advanced staff-development programs in district. Developed and delivered in-service workshops dealing with portfolio assessment along with all aspects of early childhood education. Coordinated training for implementation of performing arts program with Lincoln Center.

Continued....

This resume for an experienced teacher appropriately focuses on her accomplishments, both in the summary and in the position descriptions.

MARY BARTEN   Page 2
(609) 567-6359

CAREER EXPERIENCE: (continued)
PRE-SCHOOL FOR ALL CHILDREN, Somerset, NJ   1981–1987
Director/Montessori Division
Started as Head Teacher and advanced to School Director for this Nursery/Kindergarten
program, serving up to 75 students.

- Supervised and trained six teachers in Montessori methods, focusing on language and
  math skills integrated with social development. Gained excellent results in student
  reading levels by end of program.

- Liaison with parents regarding school issues as well as behavioral and educational
  concerns.

- Developed and delivered parenting programs that enhanced application of Montessori
  methods within the home.

PREVIOUS EXPERIENCE includes teaching positions in New York City and Baltimore,
Maryland, School Systems. Credited with developing curriculum for first experimental
kindergarten in Baltimore. Basic program and theory are still in use.

EDUCATION/CERTIFICATION:
Rutgers University, Piscataway, NJ — **Master of Education/Specialty in Parenting** —
Pi Lambda Theta (International Honor and Professional Association in the field of education)
Oneonta State Teachers College, NY — **Bachelor of Science Degree**

Specialized Training
American Montessori Society — Certified Montessori Teacher
Fairleigh Dickinson University, Madison, NJ — Montessori Certificate

State Certification
New Jersey Early Childhood & Elementary School Certifications

SELECTED SEMINARS/WORKSHOPS:

Inner City Family	Creating a World-Management of the Classroom
Young Children and Computers	Teaching for Critical Thinking
Preparing to be an Educational Mentor	Mentoring/Coaching Strategies
Conflict Resolution—Way to a Peaceable School	Technology in Early Childhood Classroom
Implementing Jean Piaget's Theories	Big Books and Whole Language
Encouraging Emerging Readers	Literature and Science Together

SELECTED CONFERENCES ATTENDED:

Diversity in Public Schools	Administrator's Workshop on New Innovations
State Principal's Forum on Early Childhood	Inclusion Conference
Montessori National Conferences	World-Wide Montessori Congress

SELECTED COMMITTEE PARTICIPATION:

Primary Unit Task Force	Parent Workshop Involvement
Kindergarten Language Arts	Creating New Kindergarten Report Card
Creating Rubrics for Assessment	Creating Standards Handbook for Kindergarten
Staff Development Day	Pre-Kindergarten Evaluation
Homework Assessment	Montclair Pride in Education
Book Report/Performance Assessment	Summer Camp Programs/Montessori Camp

Helen F. Shalk

2 Rigel Road, Kingston, ON K1C 0B2 (613) 777-9999
Chillin@hotmail.com

PROFILE

A self-directed, action-oriented professional with over 10 years' experience in education and community service. Proven abilities in problem solving, people management, and motivation. A self-starter with high energy enabling maximum and efficient work under pressure.

"This individual gives her all to everything she does. Her participation in a project is like having your own King Midas!" — *quote from her performance appraisal as Nursery School Director (1997).*

SUMMARY OF QUALIFICATIONS

Organizational Skills

As a leader, organized, coached, and lead people of all ages in a variety of activities and events.

- Coordinated the National Capital Marathon route control by planning for the protection of the participants, **recruiting resources from the community**, and assigning roles and responsibilities at various geographic locations throughout the National Capital Region (secured route of 21 kilometres).
- Recruited, trained, and supervised a volunteer staff of 20 responsible for registering over 1500 children in Gloucester Recreational soccer league.
- Managed family needs in the context of an absent spouse, which involved **facilitating the development and education of special-needs children**, managing the family finances, coordinating special-needs child care, and orchestrating all related logistics.
- Established the T-Ball league at Rockcliffe that involved scheduling games and acquiring equipment and uniforms. For 2 years, guided the coaches and ensured all participants, including coaches, received acknowledgement and trophies. **Set budgetary goals** to maintain previous years' expenses. The program resulted in happy kids and satisfied parents in the community.

Administrative Functions

- Performed Nursery School Director duties at Rockcliffe Army Base for over 2 years and Trenton Army Base for over 4 years, planning activities, teaching children, and **maintaining a daily log on each child.**
- Volunteered with St John Ambulance as a brigade member, attending weekly meetings to review skills, drills, and equipment usage following strict protocols with the purpose of **providing quality patient care.**
- Managed medical records, answered inquires, directed people to appropriate locations, managed file system, handled mail, performed word processing (self-taught), and coordinated other **administrative tasks** associated with the gymnasium.
- Pooled resources to transport people and children to events and activities in the community and **coordinated child care for families** within the community.

A functional style worked well for this individual, whose primary professional experience had taken place on military bases. A quote from the job seeker herself is a nice touch at the end of the resume.

Helen F. Shalk

Community Service

Over 10 years of active service within the community in a variety of capacities.

- Participated in the needs assessment and **facility planning** for the community centre at Rockcliffe Army Base.
- Recruited and coordinated volunteers for the community centre.
- Performed councillor duties, enforcing community bylaws and supporting the mayor in **policy development** and implementation.

"The professional attitude that Helen portrays is evident in the way she approaches everyone she comes in contact with." – Mayor of Rockcliffe Army Base

---

WORK AND VOLUNTEER EXPERIENCE

Nursery School Director   1997–current
Rockcliffe Base, Ottawa Ontario

Registrar   1998
Gloucester Recreational soccer, Gloucester, Ontario

Volunteer Coordinator   1997
National Capital Marathon, Ottawa, Ontario

Mayfair Coordinator   1996
Manor Park Elementary School, Ottawa, Ontario

Community Councillor   1995–1998
Rockcliffe Base, Ottawa, Ontario

Gymnasium Clerk and Secretary   1991–1995
National Defence, Trenton, Ontario

PROFESSIONAL DEVELOPMENT AND EDUCATION

Early Childcare Certificate   1998–1999
Algonquin College, Ottawa, ON

Business Management   1999
Ottawa Carleton Night School, Ottawa, ON

French Language Training   1996
Berlitz School of Language

Bachelor of Arts, Psychology   1987
University of Manitoba

REFERENCES AVAILABLE UPON REQUEST

"Children help supply the energy that warms our hearts; without them, the world would be a mighty cold place." – Quote from Helen Shalk

---

CHAPTER 5

Resumes for Elementary Educators

- Elementary Teachers
- Bilingual Educators

RESUME 12: PATRICIA S. CASH, CPRW; PRESCOTT, AZ

COMMITTED TO THE CARE AND EDUCATION OF YOUNG CHILDREN

LINDSAY M. SHULL

lindsayteaches@primenet.com

5963 Oakview Circle
Oklahoma City, Oklahoma 59109

405.134.8163

This four-page resume with a distinctive cover can be printed on single sheets of paper or in a "booklet" style. Inside, good organization makes the pages highly readable.

PROFILE

Professional Educator with diverse experience and strong track record fostering child-centered curriculum and student creativity. A warm and caring teacher who wants all children to be successful learners and works to create a classroom atmosphere that is stimulating, encouraging, and adaptive to the varied needs of students. Committed to professional ethics, standards of practice, and the care and education of young children.

Certifications	*Oklahoma Department of Education, 1998*	*Elementary K through 12*
	Endorsement: TESL — in progress	*(Teaching English as Second Language)*
	Texas Department of Education, 1996	*Elementary K through 8*
	Spalding Method — a reading program	

ACHIEVEMENTS

- **CERTIFICATE** — Developmentally Appropriate Music Experiences for Young Children.
- Originated and developed **CHILDREN'S ACTIVITY GROUP CENTER**:
  - Provided children from the age of 4 to 12 with educational activities.
  - Designed and implemented programs for crafts and science experiments.
  - Planned and directed field trips encompassing "*How The World Works*" venues.

SUMMARY OF QUALIFICATIONS

- Successfully develop and instruct child-centered, integrated, thematic unit curriculum, utilizing multiple intelligences, to create an atmosphere of learning and fun.
- Demonstrate ability to consistently individualize instruction, based on students interests and needs, at the most appropriate level.
- Positive coaching and motivational proficiencies.
- Key member in designing and developing operating procedures for the opening of a new school.
- Implement strategies to create innovative units enabling students to master academic skills.
- Utilize solid organizational, work, and time management skills.
- Strong interpersonal relations, effective oral and written communication skills with students, colleagues, principal, parents, and individuals on all levels.
- Perform effectively both as an autonomous, self-motivated individual and as an active, contributing team member.
- Demonstrate decision-making skills with problem-solving abilities.

Computer Skills: Mac, PCs, DOS, Windows 98, word processing, Internet search and e-mail procedures.

EDUCATION

UNIVERSITY OF OKLAHOMA	Norman, Oklahoma
MASTER'S PROGRAM — in progress	
UNIVERSITY OF TEXAS	Dallas, Texas
BACHELOR OF SCIENCE DEGREE — 1996	
Major: Elementary Education	
UNIVERSITY OF TEXAS — 1992 to 1994	Austin, Texas
Major: Elementary Education; *Minor:* History	

TEACHING EXPERIENCE

JACKSON ELEMENTARY SCHOOL, 1999 to current   Oklahoma City, Oklahoma
TEACHER — FIRST GRADE
- Year-round school with *Back to Basics* academic curriculum.
- Effectively instruct "at-risk" students.
- Implemented Accelerated Reading Program (ARP), encompassing assessing students for tier placement and performing ongoing testing, evaluating comprehension improvement.
- Integrate multiple subjects and provide students with hands-on projects, creating an atmosphere of learning and fun.
- Maintain a structured, monitored environment, including adhering to mandated mps (minutes per subject) requirements, and setting and achieving daily student goals.
- Provide weekly progress reports assessing student comprehension on subjects taught.
- Work effectively in team-teaching situations.

DUNCAN LIBERTY SCHOOL   Stillwater, Oklahoma
TEACHER — K THROUGH EIGHTH GRADE, August 1997 to June 1999
- Head teacher, reported directly to school board, supervised three employees.
- In addition to teaching duties, created lesson plans for eight grade levels adhering to Oklahoma Academic Standards; performed office manager functions; allocated time to teach P.E., Music, Art, Social Skills; responsible for application and evaluation in all subject areas.
- Coordinated services for special needs children, i.e., OT, PT, Speech Therapist, Special Education teacher, with community agencies.
- Performed administrative responsibilities including reporting to Oklahoma Department of Education on various compliance issues for the school district.

CAHLAN CHARTER SCHOOL, August 1996 to June 1997   Irving, Texas
TEACHER — PRIMARY (K-3), MIDDLE (4-8), SECONDARY (9-12)
- Prepared and administered lesson plans in all levels. Developed and implemented multiple intelligence and learning modalities in lesson planning.
- As *Career Development Advisor* for upper grades, provided guidance/counseling to address students' academic and emotional needs.
- Accountable for Learning Center activities and programs.

VALLEY SCHOOL DISTRICT, August 1994 to June 1996   Ft. Worth, Texas
STUDENT TEACHER — KINDERGARTEN
- Resourceful at working with special needs children; behavioral problems, ADD, and at-risk.
- Collaborate with community resource and child support personnel.

HARRIS COUNTY SCHOOL DISTRICT, 1993 to 1994   Austin, Texas
TEACHER AIDE — ADD, BEHAVIORAL DISORDERS, AND AT-RISK CHILDREN
- Performed evaluations and assessments for referral and mainstreaming.
- Designed and implemented programs to involve children in creative expressions of art and music.

TEXAS COUNCIL OF GOVERNMENTS, 1992   Austin, Texas
INSTRUCTOR
- Assisted preschool students from three years through five years old.
- Developed, designed, and implemented indoor and outdoor children's activities and teaching lessons.
- Extensive knowledge of community resources, support systems and social services.

PROFESSIONAL AFFILIATIONS National Science Teachers Association
                Big Brothers – Big Sisters Organization

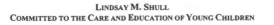

LINDSAY M. SHULL
COMMITTED TO THE CARE AND EDUCATION OF YOUNG CHILDREN   PAGE 2

CONTINUING EDUCATION AND PERSONAL DEVELOPMENT

SEMINARS, WORKSHOPS AND SPECIAL TRAINING

March 2000	Classroom Management Seminar	Norman, OK

- Methods and new strategies to motivate children toward positive learning behavior
- Teaching students consistency and structure

February 2000	Super Teaching Workshop	Norman, OK

- Teaching students how to learn
- Teaching test-taking strategies

January 2000	Reader's Theater	Norman, OK

Strategies and techniques for educators
- Methods and strategies for enabling students to become independent readers
- Educational styles that enforce "Round Robin" instruction

July 1999	Language Acquisition Workshop	Tulsa, OK

- Methods for teaching English to second-language learners

June 1999	G.E.M.S. Society — Math and Science Workshop	Oklahoma City, OK

OKLAHOMA STATE UNIVERSITY
- Using Math and Science to solve "real world" problems
- Environmental Issues and Our Children

August 1998	Project Wild — Creating Environmental Activities	Stillwater, OK

- People, Culture and Wildlife
- Responsible Human Actions

April 1997	Texas Mathematics & Science Consortium	Dallas, TX

- Problem Solving in Math and Science

February 1996	Early Childhood Education Conference	Irving, TX

- Early Learning Difficulties
- Assessment in Early Childhood Education
- Creative Thinking for Early Learners

August 1995	Accepting Individual Differences and Change	Dallas, TX

- Insights into Listening and Communication
- Developing Appropriate Activities For Special Needs Children
- Family Changes in Changing Times

April 1994	Linguistic Bias	Austin, TX

- Language Reflecting Culture Values
- Gender Bias Relating to Interaction With Children
- Traditional and Historical Usage of Language

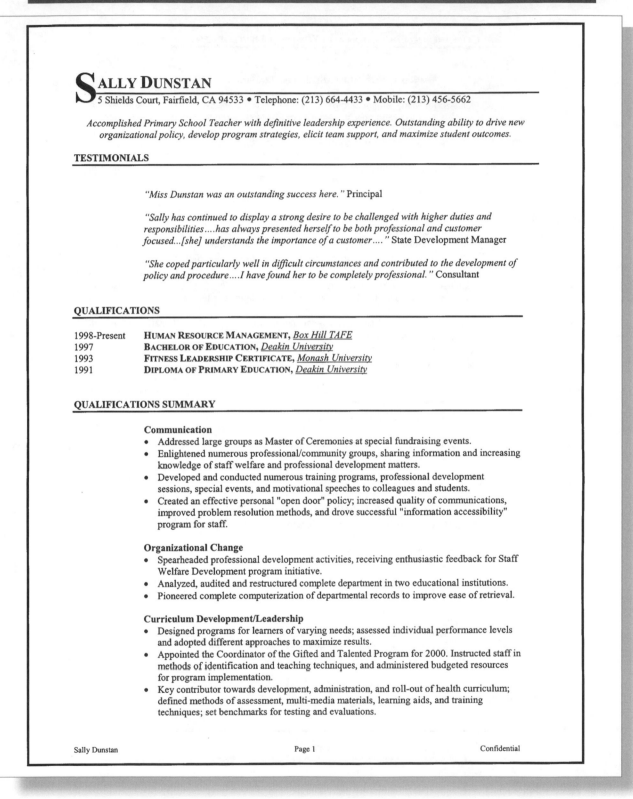

SALLY DUNSTAN

5 Shields Court, Fairfield, CA 94533 • Telephone: (213) 664-4433 • Mobile: (213) 456-5662

Accomplished Primary School Teacher with definitive leadership experience. Outstanding ability to drive new organizational policy, develop program strategies, elicit team support, and maximize student outcomes.

TESTIMONIALS

"Miss Dunstan was an outstanding success here." Principal

"Sally has continued to display a strong desire to be challenged with higher duties and responsibilities....has always presented herself to be both professional and customer focused...[she] understands the importance of a customer...." State Development Manager

"She coped particularly well in difficult circumstances and contributed to the development of policy and procedure....I have found her to be completely professional." Consultant

QUALIFICATIONS

1998-Present	HUMAN RESOURCE MANAGEMENT, *Box Hill TAFE*
1997	BACHELOR OF EDUCATION, *Deakin University*
1993	FITNESS LEADERSHIP CERTIFICATE, *Monash University*
1991	DIPLOMA OF PRIMARY EDUCATION, *Deakin University*

QUALIFICATIONS SUMMARY

Communication
- Addressed large groups as Master of Ceremonies at special fundraising events.
- Enlightened numerous professional/community groups, sharing information and increasing knowledge of staff welfare and professional development matters.
- Developed and conducted numerous training programs, professional development sessions, special events, and motivational speeches to colleagues and students.
- Created an effective personal "open door" policy; increased quality of communications, improved problem resolution methods, and drove successful "information accessibility" program for staff.

Organizational Change
- Spearheaded professional development activities, receiving enthusiastic feedback for Staff Welfare Development program initiative.
- Analyzed, audited and restructured complete department in two educational institutions.
- Pioneered complete computerization of departmental records to improve ease of retrieval.

Curriculum Development/Leadership
- Designed programs for learners of varying needs; assessed individual performance levels and adopted different approaches to maximize results.
- Appointed the Coordinator of the Gifted and Talented Program for 2000. Instructed staff in methods of identification and teaching techniques, and administered budgeted resources for program implementation.
- Key contributor towards development, administration, and roll-out of health curriculum; defined methods of assessment, multi-media materials, learning aids, and training techniques; set benchmarks for testing and evaluations.

Sally Dunstan   Page 1   Confidential

Leading off with strong testimonials, this resume uses a functional format to emphasize qualifications before displaying chronological work history.

EMPLOYMENT CHRONICLE

1992-Present   **EDUCATION**
Classroom Teacher/Librarian, Department of Education
Current assignment: Mt. Evelyn Primary School
Eight years' teaching Grades Prep to 6 across all curriculum areas. Key contributor in curriculum, procedure, and policy planning/development. Share information with colleagues and conduct well-received workshops in employee welfare and special programs. Includes experience in London and USA.

- Developed and implemented social skills program for Grades 5/6 (1998, 2000).
- Instruct children in Grades 5/6 to use Internet/CD-ROMs and word processing.
- Key contributor in coordinating three Grade 5/6 camps.
- Pioneered school Chess Club. Encouraged student participation and nurtured competitive spirit, coordinating successful interschool championships.
- Jointly implemented a health curriculum; defined a holistic approach with proactive student participation. Program reinforced all learning modalities and ensured retention.
- Appointed to leadership roles; allocated and used budget resources to coordinate and present sessions for gifted/talented children, selected as Environmental Coordinator.

1991-Present   **FITNESS INDUSTRY**
Nine years' hands-on fitness sector experience as a swimming instructor and aerobics/gym instructor. Encourage achievement of personal goals, assess client's physical fitness levels and design age/level appropriate programs. Academic achievements include Fitness Leadership Certificate (Monash University) and Aerobic Instructor's Certificate (ACE).

1985-1997   **CUSTOMER SERVICE**
Vast experience servicing client needs and troubleshooting problems across commercial, retail and hospitality sectors. Includes employment with First National Bank, Clayton Fitness Centre, Rembrandts, and Hungry Jacks.

PROFESSIONAL DEVELOPMENT

Energetically embrace opportunities for further education. Have attended numerous training courses, workshops, and conferences including CAPC (Computing Across the Primary Curriculum), Behavior Management, IT Workshops, Senior First Aid, Time Management, Staff Welfare, Social Skills, and Resume Writing/Interviews.

PERSONAL

Leisure interests include gym work, motivational seminars, self-improvement books, reading, and traveling.

REFERENCES

Available upon request.

Susan Cowalski

3456 Orange Avenue   Mason, OH 45040

513.555.0073

Career Objective: An elementary teaching position

Education

YOUNGSTOWN STATE UNIVERSITY
Youngstown, OH

Special Education Certification Courses
(1996-Present)
Studies in Exceptional Children / Learning
Disabilities / Communication & Consultation

Bachelor of Science Degree in Education 1992
Elementary Education
Social Science

Student Teaching / Field Experience
(Ten-week rotations in each grouping)

4th Grade	West Elementary	(Youngstown, OH)
Kindergarten	Curtis Elementary	(Brookville, OH)
Kindergarten-6th Grade	Musser Elementary	(Shantey, PA)

Relevant Employment & Qualifications

CREATIVE PRE-SCHOOL AND DAYCARE   *Assistant Director / Teacher / Group Supervisor* (1992-2001)
Shantey, PA

MGC SERVICES, INCORPORATED   *Therapeutic Staff Support, Wraparound Program*   (1996-98)
Shantey, PA
Recognized by parents, co-workers, and supervisors for high-quality teaching and therapeutic support.
- Modify curriculum for children with special needs to make classroom experience positive for all participants.
- Understand adaptations needed to skillfully instruct children aged 9 months to 13 years.
- Independently increase daily teaching responsibilities.
- Frequently institute dialogue with community resources and nurture professional relationships with parents.
- Work closely with children to increase self-esteem, anger management, decision-making, and coping skills.
- Assist child, parents and teachers with behavior management strategies.
- Fluent in Sign Language.

Other Leadership Employment Experience

PIZZA WORKS, INCORPORATED   *Shift Leader*   (1986-95)
Youngstown, OH
- Responsible for entire operation of establishment during shift.
- Consistently maintained restaurant in a state of cleanliness and productivity.
- Supervised and trained employees to work as efficient team in all disciplines.
- Accurately filed daily activity reports and financial transactions.

Community Involvement
March of Dimes
St. Jude's Children's Hospital, Event Organizer

This resume makes good use of available space on the page to present education, teaching positions, and other relevant experience.

RHONDA L. LeCOMPTE

202 Arborway
Jamaica Plain, MA 02130

Telephone: (617) 555-3571   E-mail: RLecompte@aol.com

CREDENTIALS:

- Certified to Teach Bilingual Education (K-8)
- Certified to Teach Special Education
- Certified to Teach Elementary Education (K-8)

EDUCATION:

M.A. Applied Linguistics (Bilingual, ESL Education)   **Summa Cum Laude, 1999**
— University of Massachusetts, Boston, Massachusetts

B.S. Special Education   **Magna Cum Laude, 1990**
Dual Major: *Special Education, Mental Retardation & Elementary Education*
Concentration: *Psychology*
- University of Maine at Farmington   1986-1990
- Université du Maine, LeMans, France   Spring Semester 1987
- University of Maine, Orono   1985-1986

Academic Awards / Achievements:
- Certificates of Award for Highest GPA in MR Major (1988, Spring)   UMF
  & Outstanding Academic Achievement (1988, Spring)
- Alpha Lambda Delta / National Scholastic Honor Society for Freshmen   UMO
- Selected (1 of 3 Students at the University) to participate in a
  Special Education Delegation to the People's Republic of China   UMF

QUALIFICATIONS:

- Bilingual (English & Spanish).
- Experience in one-on-one tutoring and group instruction of ESL.
- Experienced in client assistance working with the mentally retarded - teaching living skills to adolescents and adults.
- Designed and implemented a new program for teaching life skills which is currently successfully being used in a high school setting.
- Experienced in conceptualization, consultation, and presentation of varied-level educational workshops/conferences.
- Serve as a teaching consultant to other teachers involved in the process of integrating students into other programs and classes.
- Published in *Racenicity: The Whitewashing of Ethnicity* by Pepi Leistyna (Chapter 6) / Publisher: Roman & Littlefield (forthcoming)

(Continued on Page Two)

This resume for a bilingual/special/elementary teacher was very effective in generating interviews for positions in highly competitive school districts.

Rhonda L. LeCompte   Curriculum Vitae (Page Two)

TEACHING EXPERIENCE:

Bi-Lingual (Spanish) Special Education Teacher   **Fall 1999-Present**
Cambridge High School (Cambridge, Massachusetts)
 — Designed, implemented, and administer new Life Skills Program
 — Mentor to several high school students

Spanish Instructor   **Summer 1998**
UMASS, Boston, Massachusetts / Veteran's Upward Bound Program

Substitute Teacher   **1996-1999**
Boston School System (Boston, Massachusetts)

ESL Instructor   **1996-1998**
Cambridge Center for Adult Education (Cambridge, Massachusetts)

Bilingual Special Education Teacher   **1995-1996**
Thomas Jefferson Elementary School (Boston, Massachusetts)
 — K-3 Self-contained language room

Peace Corps Volunteer (Cuenca, Ecuador)   **1993-1995**
Special Education Teacher Consultant
Instituto Psicopedagogico Agustin Cueva Tamariz (Cuenca, Ecuador)
 — Total program conducted in the Spanish language, grades K-6.
 — Consulted with multiple teachers, classrooms, and students.
 — Implemented/presented individual and classroom consultation programs
  for teachers.
 — Demonstrated planning/presentation of lessons through model teaching.

Special Education Teacher (Behaviorally Impaired)   **1990-1993**
Montello Jr. High School (Lewiston, Maine)
 — Self-contained classroom for 7th and 8th grade students.
 — Supervised 1-2 Education Techs.
 — Outstanding Teacher Award (1992-1993), Lewiston Teacher's Association.

ANNE C. ELLIS

210 Candlewood Court, Lacey, Washington 98509
ellisedu@earthlink.com   378-245-1256

OBJECTIVE

A position as an Elementary School Teacher that will utilize strong teaching abilities to create a nurturing, motivational, and stimulating learning environment to help children achieve their potential.

PROFILE

- Highly motivated, enthusiastic, and dedicated educator who wants all children to be successful learners.
- "Believe in the impossible"; continually research educational programs and procedures to benefit students.
- Committed to creating a classroom atmosphere that is stimulating and encouraging to students.
- Demonstrated ability to consistently individualize instruction, based on student's needs and interests.
- Exceptional ability to establish cooperative, professional relationships with parents, staff, and administration.

EDUCATION

B.S. in Elementary Education, Troy State University, Troy, Alabama   2000
- Summa Cum Laude — President's Honor List — Kappa Delta Phi
- National Collegiate Education Award Winner
- Who's Who Among Students in American Universities and Colleges
- Participated in the Test for Teaching Knowledge field project, 2000

A.A. in Arts and Sciences, Pierce College, Tacoma, Washington   1995

CREDENTIALS

Elementary Education: 1-6:   Alabama License (Pending) — Washington License (Pending)

STUDENT TEACHING

Student Teacher, Harrand Creek Elementary School, Dothan, Alabama   Fall 2000
- Completed 200 hours hands-on teaching; resulting in a total of 488 hours experience in a first grade classroom. Utilized children's literature to teach and reinforce reading, writing, grammar, and phonics. Coordinated and taught math lessons and activities. Collaborated with teacher in planning, preparing, and organizing thematic units. Observed the use of teaching techniques to meet the needs of visual, kinesthetic, and auditory learners for all subject areas. Assisted in the quarterly grading.

Classroom Intern, Harrand Creek Elementary School, Dothan, Alabama (60 hours)
2nd Grade, Reading, Clover Park Elementary School, Dothan, Alabama
4th Grade, Reading, Science, Social Studies, Headland Elementary School, Dothan, Alabama
4th Grade, Math, EastGate Elementary School, Dothan, Alabama
5th Grade, Art & Social Studies, EastGate Middle School, Ozark, Alabama
1st Grade, Reading Tutor for student at-risk program, Troy State University, Alabama

RELATED EXPERIENCE

Director, Kinder-Care Learning Center, Lacey, Washington   1993 to 1995
Oversaw day-to-day operations of child care center for 65 children. Ensured all local, state, and federal rules and regulations were adhered to.

AFFILIATIONS

Member, National Council for Exceptional Children
Leader, Girl Scouts of America

This resume for a newly qualified teacher makes a strong visual impression through the use of unusual fonts and a striking graphic.

The *ABCs* for Hiring TYLER TORRES

23 Gold Street
Peoria, AZ

(623) 555-7654
tyler@net.com

Qualified for a position as a **Substitute Elementary School Teacher.** Certified to teach children from kindergarten to eighth grade. Hold a Bachelor of Science in Elementary Education and a Master of Arts in Education.

Highlights of Qualifications A – L

Attitude is geared towards empowering children to learn to their fullest potential.

Believe every child has the ability to learn if placed in a nurturing environment.

Create and implement lesson plans for students with special needs; adapt teaching style to accommodate different levels of learning.

Demonstrate ability to engage students in the educational process and facilitate learning.

Employment history – **Teacher, Pine Park Elementary (2 yrs), Twin Pines Elementary (18 yrs).**

Foster an encouraging educational setting to meet the objectives of each student.

Girl Scout Leader for 5 years.

Hands-on teaching style; take an active interest in the progression of each student.

Interact with parents, teachers, and administrators, establishing open oral and written communication.

Judged Spelling Bees.

Keen ability to pique students' interest by providing a creative and supportive environment.

Led successful parental workshops that focused on how to improve homework habits and nurture a love for reading.

continued...

With a unique format that makes the connection between teaching and the "ABCs," this resume is a real attention-getter. Note how essential information is in boldface to ensure that the reader absorbs it in a quick skim of the resume.

TYLER TORRES page 2

Highlights of Qualifications <u>M - Z</u>

Maintain a stimulating and nurturing classroom setting. Promote free thinking and expression of ideas.

Natural talent for engaging students.

Open-minded and culturally sensitive.

Prepare lesson plans to meet the needs of the individual student and the curriculum set forth by the state.

Qualified educator with an impressive teaching ability.

Respected teacher with over **20 years experience.**

Served on the PTA to help bridge the gap between parents and teachers.

Team-taught various subjects including **Math, English, Science, and History.**

Undeniably powerful, compassionate, and dedicated.

View teaching as an opportunity to enrich the lives of children.

Wear many hats; one of teacher, motivator, and role model.

Xtremely conscientious when developing classroom material.

Yawns are nonexistent in the classroom.

Zest for educating!!

LINDA QUI

1502 Lin Grove Blvd. #615 — Houston, TX 77087 — (713) 555-5555

OBJECTIVE: A full-time elementary school teaching position

HIGHLIGHTS OF QUALIFICATIONS:

- More than 8 years of successful work experience in an academic environment
- Bachelor of Fine Arts degree and currently working toward Master's degree in Education
- Experience working with preschool and elementary-age children
- Exceptionally creative with proven organizational, planning, and leadership skills

RELEVANT EXPERIENCE:

Teaching

KILLEEN INDEPENDENT SCHOOL DISTRICT - Killeen, IA
Student Teacher's Assistant for summer art program *(Kindergarten through first grade)*

FIRST BAPTIST CHURCH - Southtown, TX
Vacation Bible School and Sunday School Teacher *(Preschool through first grade)*

UNIVERSITY OF RICHMOND, THE HONORS COLLEGE - Richmond, TX
Academic Advisor, Orientation Advisor, and Retreat Counselor for students of the Honors College

Planning and Organization

UNIVERSITY OF RICHMOND, THE HONORS COLLEGE - Richmond, TX
Coordinator – "Little Wrangler Day" in cooperation with the Richmond Independent School District. During this successful event, over 3000 elementary school students observed cultural exhibits.

Chairman - University of Richmond Annual Fiesta Association
(A student-run festival event benefiting community scholarship programs)

- Advised and oversaw all event committees.
- Created and produced the Annual Fiesta Policy Manual and the Annual Fiesta Gazette.
- Created recruitment programs and served as Scholarship Coordinator and Director of Community Relations.
- Held overall responsibility for event's $126,000 budget.

EMPLOYMENT HISTORY:

UNIVERSITY OF RICHMOND, THE HONORS COLLEGE - Richmond, TX	
Administrative Assistant	1996 to Present
Chairman - Annual Fiesta Association	1995 to 1996
Assistant to the Scholarship Coordinator	1992 to 1994
UNIVERSITY OF KILLEEN - Killeen, IA	
Residential Clerk	1992
THE PHOTOGRAPHERS - Stafford, TX	
Office Assistant	1988 to 1992

Without a teaching certificate, this individual used a functional style to show her experience with young children and was successful in landing a position with the school district's Alternative Certification Program.

Linda Qui — Page 2

EDUCATION:

UNIVERSITY OF RICHMOND - Richmond, TX
Bachelor of Fine Arts (1997)
GPA 3.4 / Graduated with membership in The Honors College
*Currently enrolled in coursework toward **M.Ed. in Educational Psychology***

Awards:

- Outstanding Senior Service Award
- Ambud of the Year
- Ambassador of the Year
- Areté Award

MEMBERSHIPS & CERTIFICATIONS:

- University of Richmond Alumni Association, *Young Alumni Board of Directors*
- Annual Fiesta Association, *Chairman*
- Honors College Student Governing Board
- Honors College Advisory Board
- Honors Advocates, *Coordinator*
- Richmond Livestock Show and Rodeo Committee
- Certified Alcohol Intervention Trainer

Excellent references and letters of recommendation available

Shayla Miller

3211 Pine Grove Lane • Richmond, Virginia 23219
804-555-9278 • smiller02@richmond.com

OBJECTIVE

To obtain a teaching position in Elementary Education, K-6

SUMMARY OF QUALIFICATIONS

- Initiate programs to foster inclusivity and respect among students.
- Collaborate with other educators to create new learning experiences for students.
- Use creativity and the arts to promote enjoyment of learning.
- Gear teaching style to include students with various abilities and functional levels.

PROFESSIONAL EXPERIENCE

9/2000 – present
Pine Grove Elementary School, Richmond School District, Richmond, Virginia
Teacher, Grade 3, Leave Replacement Position

- Plan and implement Virginia Standards in all subject areas.
- Encourage extra reading by developing extensive classroom library.
- Utilize manipulatives in mathematics and science for hands-on understanding.
- Participate in district's math curriculum writing team.
- Direct third grade Drama Club.
- Team-teach with fourth grade teacher for combined-group reading lessons.
- Participate in PTA.
- Initiated and continue weekly inclusion of students from Boces special education class.

12/1999 – 6/2000
Madison Central School District, Madison, Virginia
Substitute Teacher, Grades K-6

- Managed classroom as appropriate to each grade level.
- Implemented lesson plans and added personal expertise to classroom activities.

STUDENT TEACHING EXPERIENCE

9/1999 – 12/1999
Centerton Elementary School, Madison, Virginia
Student Teacher, Grade 3 and Kindergarten

- Enacted strategic planning procedures to facilitate students' meaningful engagement with curriculum.
- Developed personal teaching approach centered on active engagement and cooperative learning.
- Created instructional materials and strategies consistent with students' learning and behavioral needs.
- Evaluated and analyzed students with special needs; attended instructional support meetings.

This highly readable resume concentrates on teaching experience on page 1, then includes other work experience and qualifications on page 2. The pencil border strikes just the right note.

Shayla Miller   **Resume – page 2**

ADDITIONAL WORK EXPERIENCE

6/1994 – 2/1998
Lazarus, Columbus, Ohio
Sales Manager

- Responsible for all aspects of daily operation: recruitment, training of personnel, store presentation, inventory control, scheduling, and customer relations.
- Assumed New Store Coordinator position with additional responsibilities of organizing and opening of all new stores in Tri-State area including recruitment, staffing, employee development, receiving, and store setup.

ARTISTIC BACKGROUND

- Classically trained in voice and piano.
- Various recitals in Chicago area; performed with Chicago Opera Company and various regional and national opera companies.
- Fifteen years of theatrical training: directing, acting, cabaret, and improvisation.

COMPUTER SKILLS

- Microsoft Word
- Microsoft Excel
- Internet browser and e-mail applications

EDUCATION AND CERTIFICATION

Richmond University, Richmond, Virginia
- *Master of Science in Elementary Education*, 12/1999
  GPA: 3.8/4.0
- *Certification Program of Reading*, in process

Ashland University, Ashland, Ohio
- *Bachelor of Fine Arts*, 5/1998
  Major in Opera Performance

Virginia State Provisional Certification, Grades K-6, 5/2000

Virginia State Provisional Certification, Grades K-12, Music, 5/2000

Family Math Training Workshop, 10/99

Identification and Reporting of Child Abuse and Maltreatment, 3/1999

AUGUST JAGGER

10 Front Street, Santa Monica, CA 90403 ◆ (310) 934-6673

OBJECTIVE	To secure a position in elementary education teaching grades K-6
CERTIFICATION	California State Provisional Certification, N-6
EDUCATION	State University of California at Santa Monica, Santa Monica, CA **Bachelor of Science, Elementary Education, May 2000** —with a concentration in Psychology; Dean's List - Fall 1998/1999 and Spring 2000

TEACHING EXPERIENCE

1/00 - 5/00 — **STUDENT TEACHER, FIRST GRADE**
MASON ELEMENTARY SCHOOL, Deer Ridge, CA

- Demonstrated excellent classroom management skills and a passion for teaching.
- Employed an integrated approach towards teaching by incorporating multiple teaching methods that included: cooperative learning, story mapping, compare and contrast, math manipulatives, sequencing, charting, prediction, discussion, music, and arts and crafts.
- Conceptualized an integrated unit on Earth Day that provided students with an understanding and appreciation for their global environment through hands-on experiments and project-oriented exercises in all subject areas.
- Taught time and money concepts, and created a math learning center to develop students' higher-level thinking skills at an appropriate pace.
- Utilized computers and visual aids as educational tools to further students' understanding of course material, and to develop/reinforce computer and keyboarding skills.

9/99 - 12/99 — **STUDENT TEACHER, FOURTH GRADE**
JUNIPER INTERMEDIATE SCHOOL, Deer Ridge, CA

- Assisted in preparing students for upcoming English Language Arts test.
- Developed and implemented lessons in all subject areas, and accessed students' prior knowledge through a combination of KWL charts and semantic mapping.
- Directed reading groups with full responsibility for the selection of all materials.
- Successfully used enrichment activities and behavior modification techniques as a motivator for completing homework and projects, and for improving overall class conduct.
- Attended various conferences, meetings, and reading workshops.

3/98 - 6/98 — **VOLUNTEER TEACHER'S ASSISTANT, SECOND GRADE**
1/98 - 3/98 — **TEACHER OBSERVER, SECOND GRADE**
SOUTHERN WAY ELEMENTARY SCHOOL, Deer Ridge, CA

- Assisted in all aspects of classroom management and chaperoned students on class trips.
- Observed teaching methods with a focus on lesson content and teacher-student interaction.

9/95 - present — **PRIVATE MATH & READING TUTOR**

- Provide one-on-one tutoring to third, fourth, and sixth grade students to achieve and sustain target levels in areas of reading, writing, division, and multiplication.

WORK HISTORY — Customer Service Representative, Partners, Deer Ridge, CA, 1994 - present

SPECIAL INTERESTS

- Avid collector of new and classic children's books for personal and professional use.
- Enjoy sharing books with students and bringing in "Student Selections of the Week."

COMPUTER SKILLS — Windows 95, Word Perfect, MS Word, MS Works, Internet Research
Jump Start, Little Bear, Freddie Fish, Thinking Adventures, School House Rock, Madeline

This concise resume is enlivened with an appropriate graphic and diamond-shaped bullets.

Mary Elizabeth Hardy

1937 McKenzie Drive • Lapeer, MI 48446 • 810-555-8211

Profile

- ✓ Reputation for motivating students and making learning fun.
- ✓ Finely honed communication skills; equally effective with students, parents, colleagues, and administrators.
- ✓ An advocate for children from educational, as well as personal, perspectives.
- ✓ Highly organized yet flexible.
- ✓ Energetic and optimistic personality.

"Your patience and kindness has truly paid off. Mark's self-esteem and confidence in himself has really improved, thanks to you!"
—Joan Dailey

"It's nice to see someone who truly cares about the kids and contributes so much to their learning experience."
—John Edwards

Career Highlights

- ✓ Tutored at-risk students during non-instruction hours and after school.
- ✓ Successfully integrated special education and inclusion students into classroom; prepared individual lesson plans for autistic student. Participated in IEP sessions.
- ✓ Collaborated with students and support staff to set short- and long-term student goals.
- ✓ Consulted with administrators on MEAP preparations targeting at-risk students.
- ✓ Piloted reading series and prepared reaction report contributing to district's decision to adopt program.
- ✓ Coordinated school-wide fund-raiser for Seeing Eye Dogs program in conjunction with multi-disciplinary unit on Helen Keller.
- ✓ Served on School Improvement Team and Social Science Curriculum Committee.
- ✓ Co-organized biannual career exploration program "Student Career Day."
- ✓ Supervised classroom aide and student teacher.
- ✓ Earned State of Michigan Professional Teaching Certificate.

Professional Experience

Lapeer Community Schools • Lapeer, Michigan
Elementary Teacher (Johnson Elementary - 2nd & 3rd grades)   1990-Present
Student Teacher

Additional experience as a Private Tutor.

Education

Oakland University • Rochester, Michigan
Master of Art - Teaching & Curriculum   1996
9+ additional postgraduate hours in Conflict Management

Eastern Michigan University • Ypsilanti, Michigan
Bachelor of Science - Elementary Education   1990
    Major: Social Science   Minor: Natural Science

Delta College • University Center, Michigan
Associate of Arts with Honors   1986

Ongoing continuing education through Lapeer Intermediate School District on relevant topics including Conflict Management and Cooperative Learning.

The testimonials to the right of the Profile show a very effective way to let others do the "selling" for the job seeker.

MIDORI TAKASAKI

31 Masters Road
Augusta, Ontario A2B 3C4

Phone: (905) 333-4455
Email: mtakasaki@sprint.ca

QUALIFICATIONS AND PERSONAL STRENGTHS

"Midori has very high expectations for her students and she teaches them study skills and organizational skills that will make them independent learners."

Extremely organized, resourceful, and dedicated teacher with over 21 years classroom experience. Consistently recognized for ability to create exciting and enriching classroom environments in which students are motivated to achieve and develop into independent learners.

- Extremely resourceful and self-sufficient – independently created exhaustive in-class student resources to complement curriculum and facilitate research and learning.
- Consistently able to engage students, meet their collective and individual learning needs, and assist them in reaching or exceeding their learning goals.
- Exceptional sensitivity working with special needs children, including Gifted, Remedial, ADD, and other unique and/or identified students.
- Participated as a Marker in the scoring of Grade 3 Assessment (Mathematics).

PROFESSIONAL DEVELOPMENT

"Midori sets clear rules and expectations for her class and communicates frequently with parents to share the good news as well as the problems."

In-Service Training
Technology & Learning with Computers (TLC)	Augusta Board of Education	1999
First Steps Training	Cedar Bay Public School	1997

Certification
Certified Kumon Instructor – Reading and Mathematics	1999

Qualifications
Primary (Summer 2000), Junior, Intermediate, and Senior

Graduate / Post-Graduate Education
Bachelor of Education (French Language, Literature)	University of Augusta	1979
Master of Arts Program (French Language, Literature)	University of Pinehurst	1978
Bachelor of Arts (Honours French)	University of Augusta	1977

ACCOMPLISHMENTS

"Midori is extremely well organized and her long-range plans and weekly plans are meticulously prepared. She is always on the lookout to find new ideas, new strategies, new rewards to make her class more interesting and to motivate her students."

- Compiled, prepared, and submitted comprehensive proposal for Hilroy Fellowship Program entitled *Please Teach Me How To Read and Write.* Designed to increase oral/written communication and reading comprehension for Grade 4 French Immersion students, the proposal recommended a unique teaching methodology based upon the compilation and integration of most successful personal teaching strategies and resources.

- Independently opened Augusta Kumon Centre in 1995 and received full instructor certification. Current enrollment exceeds 50 part-time students instructed by a staff of 7 student instructors. Responsible for teaching and overseeing all aspects of business, including hiring, supervision, training, and administration.

- Successfully self-taught on recorder and developed extremely effective teaching approach based upon three accepted methodologies: *Je m'amusique, Musicabec,* and the *Ed Sueta Baroque Recorder Method.* Grade 4 and 5 students able to write their own pieces and perform in school functions, including Augusta Citizenship Celebration.

This classic-style resume is enhanced through the addition of testimonials in the left column.

Midori Takasaki (905) 333-4455 2

PROFESSIONAL EXPERIENCE

Professional teaching career dedicated to designing and implementing highly structured and effective programs in accordance with Provincial curricula guidelines. Lessons are highly structured yet specifically designed to permit the flexibility required to meet the particular needs of students. Methodologies employed include cooperative learning strategies, modeling, and outcome-based approaches designed to encourage self-learning and independence.

CEDAR BAY PUBLIC SCHOOL, Augusta, Ontario   1995 - Present
Positions/Responsibilities:
Teacher – Grade 4 French Immersion, Grade 4 English
French Remedial Teacher – Grades 1-6
Junior Arts & Crafts Club

* Created comprehensive in-class Sciences research library on index cards – students encouraged to use, administer, and maintain all materials.
* Successfully implemented in-class use of *Math Concepts & Skills* computer-based learning program. Currently instructing school staff on use and benefits.
* Presented a variety of French Immersion information sessions to parents and incoming students, discussing all aspects of the program and fielding all inquiries.

SOUTHWOOD PUBLIC SCHOOL, Pinehurst, Ontario   1988 - 1995
Positions/Responsibilities:
Teacher – Grades 4/5, 5, 5/6 French Immersion, Grade 4 English
French Immersion Teacher/Librarian
French Immersion Art Teacher – Grades 1-5
French Immersion Academic Resource Assistant – Grades 2-6
School Display Coordinator
Junior Arts & Crafts Club
Concours Oratoire
Fetons la Parole

* Independently developed "Mille Mots Merveilleux", a comprehensive 70-page vocabulary development handbook designed to enhance student writing proficiency.
* Contributed to development of Durham Board's French Language Curriculum.

FRENCHMAN'S BAY ACADEMY, Warwick, Bermuda   1979 – 1987
Positions/Responsibilities:
Teacher – Grades 9-12 French, Grade 9 English

* Created and implemented dynamic lessons to prepare students for the University of London General Certificate of Education Ordinary level examination.

LANGUAGE SKILLS

* Fluent in French
* Knowledge of German, Italian, and Spanish.

References and supplemental information available upon request.

"Midori aims at perfection, and the materials that she prepares for her class, her classroom decorations, [and] her art projects...are always perfectly polished."

"Mme Takasaki's greatest strength lies in her planning and organization skills. She is always in complete control of the class and is the epitome of a poised and confident teacher."

"Her classroom management skills are refined...no difficulty, at any time, getting the students' attention."

CHAPTER 6

Resumes for Secondary-School Educators

- Middle School Teachers
- High School Teachers
- Coaches

TIMOTHY SMITH

1234 Main Street   tsmith@email.com
Millville, CA 96062   (530) 654-3210

SUMMARY OF QUALIFICATIONS

STUDENT-FOCUSED EDUCATOR offering 20 years of diverse teaching and educational programming and administration experience. Uncompromising advocate of the view that all students can learn; facilitate learning through a positive environment that encourages student exploration and promotes self-confidence. Strengths include:

❑ Personable, dependable, visionary leader, active in the community and recognized in the field for rigorous instruction, outstanding staff supervision, and innovative curriculum development.

❑ Effective project leader able to facilitate cooperation among administrators, faculty, students, and the community.

❑ Special knowledge in administering and evaluating assessments, researching best teaching practices, and interpreting standards and directives.

PROFESSIONAL EXPERIENCE

MILLVILLE MIDDLE SCHOOL, Millville, CA   1986 – Present
<u>English and History Teacher</u>

- Teach 5 periods of English Composition, Creative Writing, and Literature to 7th and 8th grade students.
- Teach 5 periods of 18th Century American History, World History, and Current Events to 7th and 8th grade students.
- Voted by faculty Teacher of the Year in 1995.
- Appointed to Chair of English Department (1995 – 1998).
- Served as Student Activities Advisor with full responsibility for projects, field trips, and assemblies (1988 – 1992).
- Selected as Blue Team Leader of the CSLA Leadership Team in 1995.

MILLVILLE CHRISTIAN SCHOOLS, Millville, CA   1982 – 1986
<u>History Teacher</u>

- Taught 6 periods of 18th Century American History, World History, and Current Events to 9th –12th grade students
- Served as Sophomore Class Advisor to 120 students, providing counseling and academic advisement.

MONTVIEW COLLEGE, Keene, CA   1972 – 1980
<u>Building and Grounds Supervisor</u>

- Oversaw maintenance and security of a five-acre campus.
- Supervised three-member maintenance salaried staff and 15 part-time student workers.
- Represented staff on school council.
- Earned designation as Worker of the Year in 1976.

This traditional resume is enhanced by an appropriate graphic and attractive layout. Note the Civic Leadership section toward the end that highlights community activities relevant to teaching.

Timothy Smith
Page 2

EDUCATION

WEST ED, Fairfield, CA
- Certificate in Reading Strategies (to be conferred June 2001)

SONOMA STATE UNIVERSITY, Rohnert Park, CA
- "Computers for Educators" course (2000)

FAIRFIELD UNIFIED SCHOOL DISTRICT (SB 395), Fairfield, CA
- CLAD Credential (2000)

CALIFORNIA STATE LEADERSHIP ASSOCIATION, Fairfield, CA
- Certificate in Staff Management (1996)

SAN FRANCISCO STATE UNIVERSITY, San Francisco, CA
- Master of Arts in Secondary Education: Arts Emphasis (1986)
- Clear Credential: English and Social Studies (1985)

SIMPSON COLLEGE, Redding, CA
- Bachelor of Arts in Communications and English (1982)

CIVIC LEADERSHIP

CENTRAL BAPTIST CHURCH, Millville, CA   1995 – Present
Teacher – Teach theology courses to 30 students.
Choir Director – Lead 30-member choir. Select music, coordinate practice sessions, and conduct performances.
Deacon – Provide pastoral care and facility oversight.

PROFESSIONAL MEMBERSHIPS
- SOLANO COUNTY READING ASSOCIATION (SCRA) – **School Representative**
- SIMPSON COLLEGE ALUMNI ASSOCIATION – **Bay Area Chapter Officer**

COMPUTER SKILLS
- IBM PC
- Macintosh
- Windows 95 & 98
- Microsoft Word & Microsoft PowerPoint
- JavaScript
- E-mail

Rhoda Peterson

502 Madison Avenue ◆ Leonia, NJ 07605 ◆ (201) 522-6442 ◆ rhoda9@aol.com

◆ ◆ ◆ ◆ ◆

SECONDARY SCHOOL EDUCATOR

—— *Key Qualifications* ——

✓ Proactive teacher with diverse background from educational, corporate, and military sectors.

✓ Experienced in training student teachers and orienting new staff members.

✓ An effective presenter, who conducts monthly chapter meetings for teaching staff.

✓ Demonstrated leadership potential, advancing to rank of staff non-commissioned officer in military.

——————————

"Your demeanor and patience lend themselves in creating a positive learning environment....You take the profession of teaching seriously on a daily basis." (Principal's Evaluation, 2000)

EDUCATION/CERTIFICATIONS:

William Paterson College, Wayne, NJ — **MS Degree/Multicultural Education**

State University at Oswego, NY — Courses in Education, Math, and Student Teaching

University of California, Los Angeles — **BS Degree/Computer Science**
- Graduated Magna Cum Laude

- New York State — Secondary School Mathematics, 1999
- New York City — Mathematics in Day High Schools/Junior High Schools, 1999
- New York State — Provisional Teaching Certification in Secondary School Mathematics, 1995

CAREER EXPERIENCE:

G.W. CARVER HIGH SCHOOL, New York, NY   1995-Present

Mathematics Teacher

Teach full spectrum of secondary school math curriculum (7th–12th grades) to a multicultural student body at this comprehensive high school, focusing on math and science. Scope of position covers pre-algebra through pre-calculus courses, including instruction to ESL students.

- Initiated use of graphing calculators as a way to incorporate technology into program. Demonstrated transition from manual to computerized calculations.

- Utilized math manipulatives such as geoboards and tangrams as well as varied assessment tools to supplement structured curriculum.

- Participated in Saturday and after-school tutoring programs, gaining a high student attendance rate. Produced above average scores on Regents Exams, with 97% passing Trigonometry exam.

- Selected to train student teachers and help new math teachers acclimate to program.

VARIOUS HIGH SCHOOLS AND JUNIOR HIGH SCHOOLS, New York, NY   1993-1995

Student Teacher

Covered Jr. and Sr. High School curriculums, including consumer math and investing.

COMPUTER SYSTEMS CO., New York, NY   1989-1993

Systems Analyst

Part of team for confidential project involving design, development, and testing code for mainframe operating system (MVS).

- Made regular presentations at team meetings on technical topics.

Continued....

This resume rounds out a strong Key Qualifications section with a testimonial taken from a recent performance evaluation.

Rhoda Peterson

Page 2

(201) 522-6442

CAREER EXPERIENCE (Continued):

US NAVY

1983-1987

Corporal

Advanced through ranks, attaining level of non-commissioned officer during four years of active duty. Served abroad as well as in US.

- Participated in many leadership programs. Gained valuable experience supervising personnel and making presentations.

Sergeant

1987-Present

- Continue in Reserves, leading logistics team.

Awards/Medals

- Letters of Achievement   - National Defense Medal   - Good Conduct Medal

LEADERSHIP EXPERIENCE:

- **Chapter Leader/United Federation of Teachers (UFT)** – Elected to this position, acting as liaison with UFT headquarters, maintaining communications with staff, and orienting new staff members.

- **School Supporter** – One of the most avid staff participants at Urban High School, taking a highly visible role in all school community events such as field trips, PTA functions, and athletic competitions.

PROFESSIONAL DEVELOPMENT:

Seminars & Inservice Programs

- The Dale Carnegie Course in Effective Speaking and Human Relations
- Thinking Math: Secondary School Summer Institute
- Demystifying Technology in Education
- Using Manipulatives in High School Classrooms
- Significant Math Topics for Grades 7-10
- Writing in Math

Affiliations

- National Council of Teachers of Mathematics – Attended educational conferences.
- Association of Mathematics Teacher of New York State – Attended educational conferences.

References available on request.

RICHARD OLSON
3605 North 86th Street
Superior, Wisconsin 54880
(715) 555-1692 or olson@cc.com

OBJECTIVE:

Elementary or Middle School Social Studies Teacher

HIGHLIGHTS OF QUALIFICATIONS:

- ❑ Numerous practica experiences in local schools.
- ❑ Total commitment to students, district, school, and community.
- ❑ Highly effective communicator.
- ❑ Compassionate and sensitive to needs and emotions of children.
- ❑ 11 years' experience coaching boys' baseball. Expertise in both on-field coaching and off-field administration of game.
- ❑ Committed to personal lifelong learning as well as offering quality education to children.

LICENSE:

Wisconsin teaching license. Certified to teach elementary education and Social Studies Grades 7 – 9.

EDUCATION:

University of Wisconsin – Superior (UWS)
BS, Elementary Education with **Social Studies** minor, May 2000.
GPA: 3.79. Involved in Future Teachers Association.

AWARDS:

UWS, Dean's List of Academic Achievement, 1998 – 1999; Fairbrother Academic Scholarship, 1999 – 2000; Lakehead Pipeline Company, Incorporated, Academic Scholarship, Spring 1999; Maurice Brown Academic Scholarship, 1998 – 1999; and UWS Foundation Academic Scholarship, 1997 – 1998.

PRACTICA:

Social Studies Methods, Lester Park Middle School, Duluth, MN, Spring 1999
Language Arts Methods, St. James Elementary School, Superior, WI, Fall 1998
Reading Methods, St. James Elementary School, Superior, WI, Fall 1998
Physical Education Methods, Cooer Elementary School, Superior, WI, Spring 1998

COACHING:

Baseball, Boys Legion (ages 16-18), Great Falls, MI, Youth Baseball Association, 1987 – 1994
Baseball, Boys Senior Little League (ages 13-15), Great Falls, MI, Youth Baseball Association, 1984 – 1986
- ❑ American Legion Baseball Program experienced phenomenal growth during tenure. Player enrollment increased to such an extent as to necessitate need for Junior Varsity Club. Promoted Legion baseball in community, raising awareness of it to higher level.
- ❑ Assisted several players to continue playing in college through on-site coaching and personal contacts with college coaches.
- ❑ Effectively assisted American Legion Club members in securing funds for program allowing for expenditures to be used in more beneficial manner.
- ❑ Work, tireless commitment, and knowledge of game earned me position with Atlanta Braves as Associate Scout.

There is a lot of information packed into this resume for a newly qualified teacher. It was important to include coaching and employment activities that gave him lots of experience working with children.

Richard Olson   Page 2

EMPLOYMENT:

School District of Superior, WI
Intern, January – June 2000
Interning in 6th grade classroom at Great Falls Elementary School. Assume responsibilities of regular classroom teacher: recording attendance, teaching all subjects, administering and correcting tests, and exercising needed discipline. Already employed as substitute teacher where I have interacted with other teachers and school employees in various capacities.
- Coordinated 6th grade fundraiser that raised over $2,000.
- Co-director of district-wide spelling bee that involved communications with district principals and teachers.
- Participated in after-school "Math Olympiad" program, a supplemental math activity for students seeking additional challenges.
- Assisted in school's participation in nationwide oration and writing contests.

University of Wisconsin–Superior
Game Management, 1997 – Present
Administer smooth, effective execution of all sports programs. Welcome visiting teams and provide necessary assistance. Secure and supervise workers for events.
- Key player in significantly improving UWS's hospitality image through hard work, effective planning, and personable communication.
- Successfully assisted in staffing 2000 NCAA Division III Men's Hockey National Finals Tournament.

VISTA (Volunteers in Service to America), Superior, WI
Summer Associate, May – August 1999
Strived to improve literacy of at-risk students. Created and learned about several literacy assessment tools used to select appropriate literacy experiences and assessed impact of total summer school experience on students. Served as resource person for paraprofessionals and helped prepare resource materials for other tutors.
- Effectively tutored 4 primary grade students in reading and writing daily.
- Developed evaluation tools including rubrics, surveys, and other assessments that were used as before-and-after measures for program.
- In conjunction with other summer associates, developed recruitment and training plan.

City of Great Falls Parks Department, Great Falls, MI
Park Maintenance Worker, Summers 1994 – 1997
Resurrected and maintained beauty of 22-acre city baseball complex.

Sheridan Lanes, Great Falls, MI
Assistant Manager, 1986 – 1997
Successfully ensured customer satisfaction for business by establishing rapport and communication.
Managed leagues and maintained facility.
- Reestablished youth bowling leagues.
- Successfully managed/hosted annual tournaments.
- Remained loyal during several ownership changes.

JILLIAN SMITH
3498 Oak Grove, Miami, Florida 32890
(305) 872-6545 · jillian_smith@internet.com

PROFESSIONAL PROFILE

Award-Winning Educator ... Applied Learning Advocate ... Student Mentor ... Published Author

Accomplished cooperative education coordinator and business relationship manager with an impressive track record of creating solid, synergistic alliances with socially conscious corporate entities. Substantial contributions in functioning as a liaison for the Dade County Public School System; building links between profit-driven business organizations, retail management executives, and entry-level talent pools; and driving development and implementation of specialized curriculum in Retail Mall Marketing. MBA candidate. Notable accomplishments include:

Greater Miami Chamber of Commerce Teacher of the Year — 1996

Competition Coaching: Empowered students to achieve advancement to the DECA State Marketing Competition (5 of 5 years) and the DECA National Marketing Competition (4 of 5 years).

Marketing Consultant: Co-authored *Securing Our Students' Future in a High-Tech Global Economy,* written for FCPS administration to spearhead marketing campaign on critical need for information technology curriculum development.

Executive Recruitment: Secured commitments from major corporate executives (Ford Motor, Citibank, MCI, Cirque Du Sole, Chick Fil-A, etc.) to present workshops at the annual *Dade Association of Marketing Educators* state conferences (1995-2000). Negotiated engagement from Bill Newcombe, 10-year veteran of the Miami Dolphins, to be the featured speaker at the DECA State Breakfast (2000).

Co-Author: *Putting Retail Skill Standards to Work,* published by National DECA for National Retail Federation.

Featured Author: Developed concept and wrote *Ethics in Advertising,* teaching unit highlighted in the *Washington Post.*

Extensive, Regular, and Highly Visible Community Involvement: Energetic in tackling challenging extracurricular, volunteer, and community assignments; very successful in managing fundraising programs generating up to $500,000. Involvement includes Fashion Group International, Junior League of Dade County, and the Miami Beach Rotary Club.

CAREER SYNOPSIS

DADE COUNTY PUBLIC SCHOOLS, Miami, Florida   **1990 to Present**

Execute diverse scope of responsibilities: marketing education curriculum development; applied education teaching; public relations; comprehensive program management. Coordinate unique activities, presentations, and seminars to facilitate community involvement in supplementing classroom instruction. Held Marketing Teacher-Coordinator positions at Miami South, Dade Central, and Oceanside High Schools. Featured roles include:

Marketing Education Teacher and Program Coordinator (1990 to Present)

Chair — Technology Department, Miami South (1994-1997)
Chair — Ethics Seminar, Miami South (1995-1997) · Chair — Career Day, Miami South (1996-1997)
Member — Marketing Advisory Board, Classroom-on-the-Mall (1997-2000)

- Surmount all challenges in bringing excellence to an off-site *Classroom-on-the-Mall* program designed to offer specialized Retail Mall Marketing. Brought real retail experience by coordinating student interaction with designers, public relations specialists, general managers, and human relations executives.

- Leverage retail merchandising expertise and industry experience with upper-level retail management executives to form strategic alliances, detail potential economic benefits of participation in a cooperative learning program, and engender socially responsible perspectives. Secured free use of storefront (normally generating in excess of $100,000 in monthly rent), creating an opportunity for students to benefit from laboratory and/or applied learning experiences.

- Conceive innovative "outside the box" educational experiences incorporating a series of applied learning activities. Moved program to mall and secured support of a cadre of owners and store managers fully committed to participating in workforce development. Negotiated for student management of Holiday Gift Wrap Center that continues to provide students with a real-world understanding of market-driven marketing, management and profitability fundamentals. Proceeds from fund-raiser used for students' annual field trip behind the scenes of New York's garment district.

Numerous notable achievements are included in an expansive Professional Profile. Note references to "Teacher of the Year," publications, and media coverage...things that make this individual stand out.

JILLIAN SMITH
Page Two

SENIOR RETAIL MERCHANDISING MANAGEMENT EXPERIENCE

PALM RIVER DEPARTMENT STORES, Miami, Florida   **1986 to 1989**
General Merchandise Manager · Area Customer Service Manager

Excelled in developing and implementing customer service training program to earn promotion to senior executive position directly responsible for $35 million in sales volume and placement of all merchandise in a 120,000-square-foot store.

- Coached, mentored, supervised, and evaluated 5 Area Managers and a support staff of up to 50.

- Delivered sales volume increase of 13% in 1 year, outperforming 26 regional stores.

EDUCATION

Advanced Academic Development:

MIAMI STATE UNIVERSITY
MBA Candidate – April 2001

Professional Licensure:

MIAMI CITY COLLEGE
Teaching Certification – 1972

Undergraduate Preparation:

UNIVERSITY OF FLORIDA
BS – Business Administration – 1970

SPECIAL EVENTS, ACTIVITIES, PRESENTATIONS, AND SEMINARS

General Manager, **The Limited** · Director of Public Safety, **The Limited**
Manager, **Johnson Fine Clothing** · **Chloe Morgan,** Designer · Owner, **The Samantha Store**
Dade Performing Arts Society, Silent Auction · **Gimbels** Fall Fashion Show
General Manager, **Dillard's** · Visual Display Artist, **The Limited**
WTKS FM104.1 Spring Fashion Show · **Burdines** Fall Fashion Show · **Men's Wearhouse** Suit Seminar
Famous Designer Trunk Show, **Dillard's** · Spring Trend Seminar, **Gimbel's**
Hudson Belk Super Saturday · **Belk Lindsey** Private Event

THOMAS B. KLEIN

89 Kensington Road • Manahawkin, NJ 08050 • 609-612-8985

— High-School English Teacher for Your Most Challenging Students —
— Football Coach —

SUMMARY

Spirited, optimistic education professional with an excellent reputation for spurring dramatic improvements in the classroom performance, behavior, and attitude of lower-track high-school students deemed "unteachable." Able to gain the trust and respect of youngsters and convey confidence in their abilities. Successful in using innovative, unconventional approaches to engage students' interest, strengthen reading and writing skills, develop an appreciation for literature, and achieve high passing rates on standardized proficiency tests. Initiator and manager of a unique, highly effective in-school suspension program. Extensive coaching background.

SKILLS AND ACCOMPLISHMENTS

Classroom Teaching

- Consistently sought the challenge of teaching and inspiring lower-track high-school students.
- Achieved outstanding success in strengthening their reading and writing abilities, building life skills, and motivating them to consider job / career goals; 25% of students pursued higher education.
- Encouraged students to become active classroom participants and join in the decision-making process.
- Attained an HSPT passing percentage in the upper 80% range among students who had previously failed.
- Effectively used comic books and other unconventional resources to build grammar and punctuation skills.
- Organized spirited debates on controversial topics.
- Sparked students' interest in literature through role playing and lively discussions.
- Arranged for monthly guest speakers to address career topics.

Behavior Management / Counseling

- Achieved one of the lowest rates of discipline problems in the school.
- Created a fun, free-spirited environment in which students adhered to stated rules of conduct.
- Worked closely with parents to reinforce behavior management.
- Developed trusting relationships with students and frequently served as a sounding board for problems.
- Helped them develop a better outlook and a solution-oriented approach to dealing with challenges.

Program Development and Management

- Initiated the introduction of a learning-based in-school suspension program to deal with a high rate of daily suspensions; later instituted the program at a middle school based on outstanding results.
- Coordinated each student's assignments with classroom teacher and provided one-on-one instruction in all subject areas. For the first time in the school's history, required suspended students to perform schoolwork.

Coaching

- Coached several undefeated football teams, including one that went on to win the state championship.
- Helped sharpen the skills of many players who later played college football.
- Oversaw the entire football program for 6 Pop Warner teams; interacted with local school coaches to integrate their philosophies into the program, so players are well-prepared for high school football.

PROFESSIONAL EXPERIENCE

Pomeranz High School, Newark, NJ:
Director of In-School Suspension Program / Teacher (1996 – Present)
English Teacher, Grades 9 - 12 (1971 – 1995)
Assistant Football Coach (1982 – 1990) / Head Football Coach (1975 – 1978) / Head Baseball Coach (1974)
Assistant Coach, Football / Baseball / Wrestling (1971 – 1974)

COMMUNITY SERVICE / AWARDS

Football Commissioner, Angels Athletic Association / Pop Warner Football, Manahawkin, NJ (1994 – Present)
Football Coach, Pop Warner Football, Manahawkin / Newark, NJ (1976 – 1994)
Community Service Award, Kaitland County Chamber of Commerce (1999)

CERTIFICATION / EDUCATION

Certification as Teacher of High School English, State of New Jersey
B.A., English / Communications, 1971 • Rutgers University, New Brunswick, NJ
Graduate Credits in Curriculum and Administration • Monmouth University, W. Long Branch, NJ

This high school teacher wants to take on a school's "most challenging students," and the functional Skills and Accomplishments list effectively highlights his ability to do so.

David Dumas
555 Overland Drive
Union City, NJ 07087
(201) 583-5555
dd322@hotmail.com

GOAL
High School Teacher
and / or Coach

PROFILE
➢ Over three years' experience in teaching, coaching, and motivating.

➢ Demonstrated gift for inspiring individuals and teams toward higher achievements.

➢ Poised and competent; able to maintain a sense of humor under pressure.

➢ Reputation for excellence; enthusiastic, high-energy, and creative professional.

EDUCATION

1997 BA, History
Southern University
South Grove, SC

COMPUTER SKILLS

Windows 98 and 95
Microsoft Office 97
Microsoft Word 6.0
Microsoft Excel
Microsoft Access
Microsoft Outlook
Internet Explorer

EXPERIENCE
1998 - Present   **Teacher / Coach / Moderator**
Union City High School, Union City, NJ

Teacher – World History, Government, and Contemporary Issues
- Teach 3 classes of 9th – 12th graders, engaging their curiosity and analytical problem-solving abilities in structured classroom activities.
- Plan and create innovative lesson plans and learning environment emphasizing relevancy and group task cooperation.
- Participate in staff meetings, addressing problems including family relations, staff cooperation, community support, and problem issues with individual children.
- Selected to serve on the Discipline Board (three years); actively involved as judge and as student advocate.
- Conduct interviews for incoming freshmen in person and by telephone, screening applicants for high school admittance.

Coach – Football, Winter & Spring Track
- Successfully built cooperative athletic teams and promoted winning attitudes in teams, including co-ed teams and varsity sports, by:
  - treating athletes with respect and maintaining a sense of humor;
  - welcoming constructive criticism and input on improvements;
  - encouraging athletic, social, and team skill development.
- Produced impressive record of winning teams in the last three years:
  - girls' track team achieved state championship every year;
  - boys' track team were champions in two of the last three years;
  - varsity football team made state playoffs twice.
- Provided coaching and oversight for the annual summer football camp of 6th and 7th graders.

Moderator – African-American Student Union
- Oversee all facets of this extracurricular program including:
  - arranging for college prep and career days with speakers;
  - planning, organizing, and conducting two field trips per semester;
  - designing and implementing successful fundraising activities.
- Revitalized and increased student and parent involvement in the African-American Student Union, building it into a high-profile program on the campus and within the community.
- Acted as liaison between the African-American Student Union, parents, community groups, and the school administrative hierarchy.
- Initiated the establishment of a Parents' Association for support, communication, and networking.

This resume highlights the three important roles (teacher, coach, and student union moderator) filled by this educator in his current position. The narrow left column makes good use of space on the page to present his credentials.

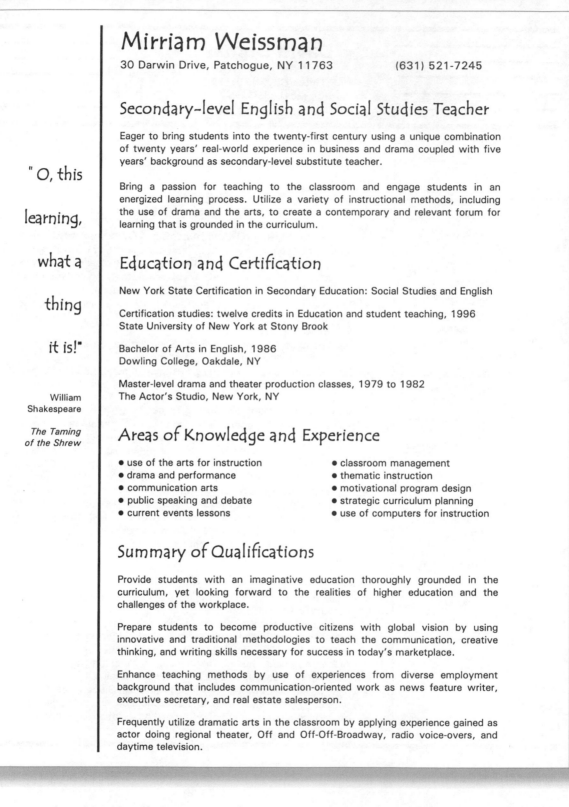

" O, this

learning,

what a

thing

it is!"

William
Shakespeare

*The Taming
of the Shrew*

Mirriam Weissman

30 Darwin Drive, Patchogue, NY 11763   (631) 521-7245

Secondary-level English and Social Studies Teacher

Eager to bring students into the twenty-first century using a unique combination of twenty years' real-world experience in business and drama coupled with five years' background as secondary-level substitute teacher.

Bring a passion for teaching to the classroom and engage students in an energized learning process. Utilize a variety of instructional methods, including the use of drama and the arts, to create a contemporary and relevant forum for learning that is grounded in the curriculum.

Education and Certification

New York State Certification in Secondary Education: Social Studies and English

Certification studies: twelve credits in Education and student teaching, 1996
State University of New York at Stony Brook

Bachelor of Arts in English, 1986
Dowling College, Oakdale, NY

Master-level drama and theater production classes, 1979 to 1982
The Actor's Studio, New York, NY

Areas of Knowledge and Experience

- use of the arts for instruction
- drama and performance
- communication arts
- public speaking and debate
- current events lessons

- classroom management
- thematic instruction
- motivational program design
- strategic curriculum planning
- use of computers for instruction

Summary of Qualifications

Provide students with an imaginative education thoroughly grounded in the curriculum, yet looking forward to the realities of higher education and the challenges of the workplace.

Prepare students to become productive citizens with global vision by using innovative and traditional methodologies to teach the communication, creative thinking, and writing skills necessary for success in today's marketplace.

Enhance teaching methods by use of experiences from diverse employment background that includes communication-oriented work as news feature writer, executive secretary, and real estate salesperson.

Frequently utilize dramatic arts in the classroom by applying experience gained as actor doing regional theater, Off and Off-Off-Broadway, radio voice-overs, and daytime television.

This is an unusual and highly effective resume for someone whose only teaching experience is as a substitute teacher—but you'd never know that by reading her first-page presentation of qualifications. Original formatting adds to the appeal.

Mirriam Weissman   page 2

Representative Methodologies and Lessons

As a substitute teacher, immediately try to develop a rapport with students and engage in discussion of current events. Facilitate the discussion to steer towards daily lesson plan. Discussion and debate keeps topic relevant, and keeps students centered, entertained, and open to learning.

Construct creative lessons to maintain interest, yet thoroughly cover curriculum. As a student teacher, planned vocabulary lessons that removed the "boredom" factor and utilized creative writing to enhance learning of vocabulary. Students used vocabulary words in contextual sentences to create exciting weekly class stories. Lessons were a great success.

Observed a student lunch-time incident and used it to develop a discussion on respect and compassion. Discussion became a two-day theme culminating in a better understanding of the phrase "walking in another person's shoes." Lesson was so effective that compassion theme was carried throughout quarter.

Always maintain students' curiosity about "what will happen next." Keep a keen focus on the tempo of the class to maintain control and flow of work. Deal with disruptive students immediately and firmly; will not tolerate inconsiderate behavior. Built excellent relationships and still have contact with some students from earliest teaching days.

Experience in Education

Substitute Teacher, grades 7 through 12   1996 to present
Patchogue-Medford School District
Sachem School District

Additional Experience

Licensed Real Estate Salesperson   1994 to present
Caldwell-Banker, Inc., Patchogue, NY

Feature Writer   1988 to 1989
The Advance Newspapers, Coram, NY
(Clippings available upon request)

Storyteller   1983 to 1987
Patchogue-Medford Library, Patchogue, NY

Dream Pursuer (Actor and Drama Student)   1979 to 1982
New York, NY

Executive Secretary to the Vice President of Operations   1976 to 1980
Saks Fifth Avenue, New York, NY

Assistant to the Vice President of Advertising   1975 to 1976
Banker's Trust Company, New York, NY

TONY C. RICHARDSON

328 Shattauck Avenue
Palm Bay, FL 32907
(321) 725-5135

PURSUING A POSITION IN TEACHING

Certifications and Endorsements: K-12 Physical Education, Health, and Science 6-12

SUMMARY OF QUALIFICATIONS

Professional committed to achieving favorable results in education through a positive impact on the children of today and the future. Recognized leader for professional, academic, and community contributions. Experience and academic training include:

• Teaching Practices	• Curriculum Inquiry	• Measurement & Evaluation
• Management Info. Systems	• Violence in Schools	• Educational Systems
• Personnel Evaluations	• Time Management	• Classroom Dynamics
• Future Planning	• Leadership	• Curriculum Evaluation
• Classroom Evaluation	• Athletic Coaching	• Community Relations

EDUCATION

M.S. in Educational Leadership, Florida State University — 12/99; GPA: 3.88
B.S. in Human Performance Dynamics; Concentration in Teaching K-12, University of South Florida — 12/96; GPA: 3.68

RELEVANT EXPERIENCE & SKILLS

Curriculum Development / Inquiry
- Developed curriculum for student teaching projects for health and social sciences.
- Researched the effectiveness of utilizing different styles of tests as assessments of learning.
- Wrote paper on preparing teachers for dealing with issues on mainstreaming, classroom behavior, perceived ability to teach special needs, classroom management, and academic development of the special needs child.

Educational Measurement
- Examined various assessment methods, tools, techniques, processes, and procedures in evaluating student performance for Measurement and Evaluation in Education.
- Completed a project on student learning styles to ascertain the prevalence of oral and visual learners and their related study habits.

Teaching / Presentation
- Developed strong presentation and teaching style by utilizing a variety of educational tools including games, team-building exercises, use of videos, lectures, and alternative activities.
- Skilled speaker, comfortable in presenting to groups as a manager and community volunteer.

VOLUNTEER / EMPLOYMENT EXPERIENCE

Volunteer
- Student Teacher, University High School, Orlando, FL — 1999 to 2000
- Coach, Volunteer, Youth Football League of Sanford, FL — 1996 to Present
- Den Leader, Boy Scouts of America, Orlando, FL — 1995 to Present
- Coach, Volunteer, Youth of America, Orlando, FL — 1994 to 1997
- Park Supervisor, Seminole County Recreation Department, Orlando, FL — 1990 to 1993

Employment
- Operations Manager, B.J.'s Wholesale Warehouse, Merritt Island, FL — 1997 to Present
- Department Supervisor, B.J.'s Wholesale Warehouse, Merritt Island, FL — 1994 to 1997
- Sales Associate, B.J.'s Wholesale Warehouse, Merritt Island, FL — 1993 to 1994

With no teaching experience but lots of pertinent volunteer and coaching activities, this individual highlighted "Relevant Experience & Skills" to add weight to his qualifications.

Cecilia M. Diaz

55 Magnolia Lane, Oakland, NJ 07436
201-405-5555 ▪ cmdiaz@net.com

Career Target

Middle School Science Teacher in a child-centered school district.

Summary

☑ Highly motivated, energetic educator with 15 years of middle school teaching experience.
☑ Strong track record of fostering student curiosity, creativity, and enhanced learning.
☑ Enthusiastic, warm, and caring professional, sensitive to students' specialized and changing needs.
☑ Demonstrated ability to deliver individualized instruction, appropriate to each student's abilities.
☑ Ability to act as liaison, harmoniously and effectively, between parents, school, and community.

Key Skill Areas

Instructional Strategies
- Designed and developed integrated, thematic physical science curriculum for middle school students, aligned to meet core content and state standards.
- Use cross-curriculum, cooperative learning, motivational environment, team planning, and "real-world" examples to stimulate learning and learner retention.

Learning Styles
- Achieve educational goals by incorporating learning modality principles into all instruction. First special-service teacher incorporated into an inclusion class.
- Emphasize an active learning environment, high student expectations, and individualized instruction in a student-centered, heterogeneous classroom.

Educational Technology
- Championed innovative physical science programs and activities utilizing instructional media to enhance the scope and quality of education.
- Accomplished in the use of hands-on materials, manipulatives, and technology (electron microscopes, research on the Internet, video cameras, software).

Leadership
- Pioneered "Scientists in the Classroom" Program, partnering with local companies to provide scientific demonstrations and Q&A sessions.
- Selected as judge for state-run program, "21st Century Science" – 3 years.

Student / Parent Relations
- Fostered parent involvement through regular communication (telephone calls or notes daily) and invitations to participate in classroom activities and events.
- Natural gift for getting young students excited about learning.

Certifications and Education

New Jersey Permanent Certification K-8 Elementary
New Jersey Permanent Certification K-12 English

1991 M. Ed., Stockton State College, Stockton, NJ
1979 B.S., Elementary Education & English, Clemson University, Clemson, SC

Continuing Education:
1997 Meteorology Course, Union College, School of Meteorology
1994 Certificate, Computer Educator, Passaic County College, Passaic, NJ
1992 Materials Science Conference, sponsored by Rutgers University
1988 Cooperative Learning, Conference on Scientific Curriculum

Computer Skills

Macintosh PCs	MS Word 97	MS Works	Netscape Navigator
Claris Works	MacGrade	Internet	E-mail

This two-page resume devotes as much attention to activities leadership as it does to teaching descriptions. It also uses a broad Key Skill Areas section to emphasize relevant achievements.

Cecilia M. Diaz
201-405-5555 ▪ Page 2

Experience

1985 – present **Morris County Middle School,** Morristown, NJ
Science Teacher – 8th Grade
- Teach Chemistry, Physics, Geology and Meteorology as well as enrichment classes for 3 classes daily, with up to 30 students per class, utilizing curriculum compacting and tiered instruction with 5 tiered teams in a block-scheduling system.
- Designed self-learning and small-group cooperative learning activities as well as hands-on science activities such as the Cliffton House archeological excavation.

1999 **Central State Middle School,** Harrison, NJ
Substitute Teacher – Physical Science

1984 – 1985 **Oakland Township School District,** Oakland, NJ
Substitute Teacher – K-12, primarily 6th Grade

1980 – 1984 **Tiny Tots Pre-school,** Rahwah, NJ
Kindergarten Teacher / Director
- Full administrative, staffing, and budgeting responsibility for this mini-school within the district, with 13 teachers, aides, cook, and school bus driver, in addition to duties as kindergarten teacher.

Activities

1985 – 1997 **Advisor, MCMS Newspaper: The Tiger Ledger**
- Provided proactive leadership for this student-run newspaper. Introduced students to assignments as cartoonists, reporters, photographers, proofreaders, and editors.
- Collaborated with Morristown News to meet quarterly production deadlines. Upgraded original cut and paste layout to computer layout. Forged parent partnerships for fundraising activities.

1985 – 1996 **Advisor, MCMS Video Imaging Program Production**
- Led creative team of student volunteers in the design, editing, and production of an annual 8th grade video production, a reprise of their 8th grade year, which was shown to parents, faculty, administration, and students at the end of the school year.
- Spearheaded successful fundraising campaign that raised $10K within one year for multimedia equipment. Spun-off to become the MCMS TV Studio, a fully functioning studio with a network of TV monitors installed in every classroom.

1985 – 1991 **Advisor, MCMS Yearbook: The Tiger**
- Oversaw this student-run production by 7th and 8th graders, culminating in a hardcover yearbook. Students learned photography, layout, cropping, editing, and the entire production process. Raised funds to support this annual activity.

Committees & Awards

Discipline Committee – established demerit system
Mission Statement Committee – Morristown Township "Millennium Mission"
Who's Who in American Education
Board of Education Honoree – for contributions to MCMS newspaper

Professional Associations

National Education Association (NEA)
New Jersey Education Association (NJEA)
New Jersey Science Teachers Association (NJSTA)

DONALD GUNDERSEN

500 Bird Court ■ Canoga Park, CA 95555 ■ Tel: 818-551-7830 ■ FAX: 818-551-7831

CAREER OBJECTIVE — Science Teacher — High School Level

SUMMARY OF QUALIFICATIONS

Seasoned entrepreneur with a Bachelor of Science Degree and more than 15 years' experience in:

Agricultural Sciences	**Operations Management**	**Business Development**
Market Identification & Penetration	**Financial Management**	**Inventory Management**

ADDITIONAL QUALIFICATIONS

- Adept at managing multiple tasks, problem isolation and resolution — Achieved an efficient balance of organizational requirements and employee needs, whether managing corporate operations or agricultural workers.
- Multilingual communication skills (English/Spanish). — Sensitivity in dealing with multicultural and diverse socio-economic topics and situations. — Hired and directed work forces of up to 50 farm workers as well as professional and support services staff without experiencing attrition problems.
- Strong analytical and writing abilities. — Developed business plans, loan proposals, bids, and market surveys for own business and for other agricultural brokerages.
- Computer proficiency in business and accounting software including Word, Excel, Internet Explorer, and Peachtree.

EDUCATION

Bachelor of Science in Agriculture
California Polytechnic State University, Pomona, California
Additional coursework in Biology, Chemistry, Animal Sciences, Zoology, and Microbiology

CAREER HISTORY

- **PRESIDENT/OWNER: CalAsia Trading Company** — Los Angeles, California (1992 - Present)
  Founded a produce brokerage that grosses $4 - $5 million in annual sales. Oversee financial/inventory planning, acquisition, and management. Design and implement product-marketing campaigns. Recruit and train 6 sales staff.

- **BROKERAGE DIVISION HEAD: Finest Produce Company** — Los Angeles, California (1991-1992)
  Created a national brokerage division. Planned and directed distribution of California and Arizona produce to terminal markets nationwide.

- **PRODUCE BROKER: Venice Distributing Company** — Los Angeles, California (1986 - 1991)
  Located commodity markets. Bought produce from primary sources. Negotiated sales between the sources and the markets. Performed sales analysis and reporting. Revised marketing strategies according to sales performance.

- **SALESMAN: Acme Fresh Vegetables** — San Jose, California (1983 - 1986)
  Developed and maintained accounts with wholesale markets, terminal market, and chain stores for Dole vegetable products. Provided customer support and account troubleshooting. Completed public speaking training.

- **OWNER: Gundersen Farms** — San Jose, California (1971 - 1983)
  Operated a 500-acre farm, growing vegetable crops. Initiated capital and inventory procurement. Planned annual budgets and secured operating funds from lenders. Interviewed, evaluated, scheduled, trained, and supervised 50 seasonal workers and 6 full-time employees.

—References furnished upon request—

This resume was written for a seasoned business professional transitioning to a career in teaching.

Ann Thomas

10 Henry Street, Wycoff, New Jersey 07401
H: (201) 886-1125 — E-mail: Athomas@Yahoo.com

OBJECTIVE

A position as a Middle School Mathematics Teacher where I can create an energized learning environment that focuses on individual understanding and expression.

PROFILE

Dedicated, talented, resourceful teacher skilled in building rapport and respect with students. Possess the ability to establish a creative and stimulating classroom environment. Experienced in using innovative computer software to enhance learning process. Background includes: tutoring in high school, student teaching in high school and middle school, and serving as a mathematics teaching assistant at the college level.

SUMMARY OF QUALIFICATIONS

- Over 8 years' experience as a mathematics teacher and tutor.
- Introduced "Studio Calculus" at Dover Institute of Technology (DIT) as a new teaching tool utilizing Maple Software.
- Received award for "Outstanding Teaching Assistant" from DIT student body.
- Tutored students in high school and college in mathematical principles.
- Able to make subject material "come alive" for students through enthusiasm and creativity.

EDUCATION
1996-Present
1993-96

DOVER INSTITUTE OF TECHNOLOGY, Jersey City, NJ
Ph.D. work in Mathematics. Stanley Fellowship recipient.
Master of Science in Applied Mathematics (GPA 4.0)

WILLIAM PATTERSON UNIVERSITY, Wayne, NJ
1990-93
Bachelor of Arts in Secondary Education (GPA 4.0), magna cum laude

EXPERIENCE
1994-Present

DOVER INSTITUTE OF TECHNOLOGY, Jersey City, New Jersey
Teaching Assistant/Lecturer
Prepared curriculum and materials for Freshmen Precalculus and Calculus courses. Served as recitation instructor for Mathematical Analysis up to senior level. Recitation instructor for Logic and Discrete Mathematics. Explained solutions, administered tests and quizzes, and fielded questions about material.
- Recipient of "Outstanding Teaching Assistant Award" from student body for both 1994-95 and 1995-96.
- Utilized Maple Computer Software to implement "Studio Calculus."
- Presented statistics paper on "Time Series Analysis" to faculty and guests.

1993-94

SHARPE CAPITAL, New York, New York
Researcher
Responsible for encapsulating financial news in fact sheets for client use.

1991-93

WILLIAM PATTERSON UNIVERSITY, Wayne, New Jersey
Mathematics Tutor
Tutored in university's "drop-in" math-help center.

CERTIFICATIONS

New Jersey Teaching Certificate in secondary education.

AFFILIATIONS

American Mathematical Society (AMA)
Mathematics Association of America (MAA)
American Statistical Association (ASA)

COMPUTER SKILLS

Proficient in Microsoft Word 7.0, Microsoft Excel 5.0, PowerPoint 4.0, Maple Software (mathematical software package), C++, and FORTRAN

This is an efficient one-page format for an experienced teacher. Note the effective Profile and Summary of Qualifications.

SHARON WELLS

4344 East Franklin Street, Apt. 5
New Haven, Connecticut 06525
(203) 336-8041   Email: germanteach@home.com

GOAL:

High School German teacher, In-service Instructor, or Computer Technician.

EDUCATION:

Southern Connecticut State University
B.A. Education – Anticipated 2001
Major: **German**
Minor: **Educational Computing & Technology Certificate** – May 1998
GPA: 3.31

Coursework for the Educational Computing & Technology Certificate included: The Computer in Education, Teaching with Technology, Utilizing Technology for the Administrative Tasks of Teaching, Current Issues in Computers and Educational Technology, and Advanced Educational Media Production.

COMPUTER SKILLS:

Hardware
Public access terminals, Apple Macintosh microcomputers with Ethernet LAN connections, Sun workstations running UNIX operating system, X-terminals, laser and color printers, scanners, video phones, video conferencing, and digital cameras.

Software
WordPerfect, Claris Works, Claris Home Page, Hyper Studio, Avid Videoshop, Fetch, PageMill, Top Class, PageMaker, QuarkXpress, PhotoShop, Swivel 3D, Director, Illustrator, MiniCad, Excel, FileMaker Pro, Telnet, Netscape, Fetch, and TurboGopher.

LANGUAGES:

German. Intermediate to advanced proficiency. Able to read, write, speak, and understand.

VOLUNTEER:

Taught English as a Second Language at the New Haven Adult Learning Center, Fall 1997. Worked in small groups with adults with various languages and 2 Bosnian students.

EXPERIENCE:

1996 – Present: **DELI CLERK**
Gala Jubilee, Hamden, CT

Merchandise products, order food, and work events. Relate well to a wide variety of people.

1994 – 1996: **WAITRESS/CASHIER**
Bonanza, West Haven, CT
Sold more side orders than anyone previously at restaurant. West Haven Bonanza rated top in nation. Performed other tasks as needed.

1993 – 1995: **VISUAL SPECIALIST MERCHANDISER**
J.C. Penney, West Hartford, CT
Promoted from Hamden store because of excellent merchandising skills.

Ordered merchandise via computer. Maintained a monthly budget that varied seasonally.

Worked cooperatively with other merchandisers in store as well as district managers.

Continually planned for future events/seasons.

Utilized self-management skills. Managed 2 employees.

1993 – 1995: **SALES ASSOCIATE**
J.C. Penney, Hamden, CT
Sold in various departments. Merchandised store products.

An unusual format makes this attractive, well-organized resume stand out. For a soon-to-be-qualified teacher, education and volunteer activities are as important as work experience.

CHAPTER 7

Resumes for Specialty Teaching Positions

- Adjunct Faculty
- Cooperative/Adult Education Teachers
- Art Teachers
- Computer Instructors
- Dance Teachers
- Distance-Learning Professionals
- E-Learning Specialists
- English as a Second Language (ESL) Teachers
- Community Health Educators
- Outdoor Skills Teachers
- Music Teachers
- Physical Education Teachers
- Special Education Teachers
- Educational Assistants
- Tutors

Melanie E. Powers, CFM

5 Redleaf Lane
Birmingham, Alabama 35222
(205) 591-9807
E-mail: mpowerscfm@msn.com

Objective: An adjunct faculty position teaching business-related topics to traditional and continuing education students.

Summary: *Top-performing business executive with extensive experience training, recruiting, and mentoring employees. Exceptional track record of outstanding sales and marketing performance, based on excellent ability to develop and maintain long-term client relationships and strategic business alliances.*

Education: **Master of Arts, Sociology**
University of Alabama; Birmingham, AL

Bachelor of Arts, Sociology
University of Alabama; Birmingham, AL

Associate of Arts, Social Science
Smith County Community College; Midville, AL

Professional Development:

Certified Financial Manager
Certified Financial Planner (In-Process)

NASD Series 7 & 8; Series 3, 63, 65 & 68

Professional Experience:

HOWELL AND LOVELL
1987 - Present   **Financial Consultant / Certified Financial Manager**
Provide financial services to over 600 individual and small business clients, managing assets in excess of $70 million.
- Build client base through diligent prospecting and follow-up.
- Develop new business through seminars, referrals, and networking.
- Perennial incentive trip winner and Chairman's Club member.

1995 – 1999   **Resident Manager; Birmingham, AL**
In addition to servicing a substantial account base, fulfilled managerial and administrative responsibilities for branch office operations.
- Supervised financial consultants and office staff.
- Reviewed performance and motivated sales force.
- Coordinated professional development activities for team members.

1992 - 1995   **Manager - Professional Development; Birmingham, AL**
Administered two-year professional training program for newly hired representatives. Maintained client base and regular sales duties while fulfilling the responsibilities of this position.
- Conducted seminars in prospecting and client development at National Training Center in Baltimore, MD.
- Implemented training programs for up to twenty interns.
- Delivered weekly two-hour training sessions for interns on topics including maintaining relationships and servicing clients, making sales presentations, and prospecting/client development.
- Mentored interns, offering advice on setting goals and developing marketing plans.

This successful businessperson wanted to pursue part-time teaching positions at local community colleges, focusing on areas that capitalized on her business career.

Melanie E. Powers, CFM
Résumé – Page Two

Additional Experience:

TRI-STATE STRUCTURES; Tuscaloosa, AL
1981 - 1987   **Vice President, Sales & Marketing**
Developed / implemented marketing plan and managed sales force for firm manufacturing and erecting wood and metal buildings in Alabama, Georgia, and Mississippi.
- **Increased sales volume by 330% over three-year period.**
- Designed and executed print and electronic advertising campaigns.
- Developed direct-mail marketing campaign and collateral materials.
- Established strategic relationships with lending institutions to assist customers in obtaining financing.
- Prospected for individual and small business accounts through diligent cold calling.
- Hired, trained, and supervised staff of twelve sales representatives in three branch offices.

Computer Literacy:

Windows 98, Microsoft Office (Word, Excel, PowerPoint),
Internet, IP Telephony, Electronic Books, DVD, audio/visual applications.

Community Involvement:

Birmingham Area Foundation
St. Mary's School of the Holy Childhood
Birmingham Rotary
United Way

References Available Upon Request

BETTE DENISE BLAKE

4457 South End Land
Virginia Beach, Virginia 23454
757-853-7658

JOB OBJECTIVE:

Full-Time Faculty or Staff position in a growing, innovative Cooperative Education Department.

EDUCATION:

Silver Gate University, San Francisco, California. Honors Graduate.
M.S. in Human Relations Management. 1984

Peterson State University, Peterson, Kansas.
B.S. Business Education. Minor in Music. 1981

EXPERIENCE:

Faculty Member, Job Development Specialist, Assistant Director, Cooperative Education and Job Placement. Tides Community College, 1984–2001

Musicologist with Church Choral Groups. 1981–1984

Counseling: Developed, organized, promoted, coordinated, and served as an Administrator and Instructor for an experiential learning program in Portfolio Development, a 3-credit course designed as an alternative, nontraditional method of Prior Learning.

Informational interviewing for budget counseling and crisis intervention for Navy Relief Society.

Interviewer: Primary instructor for workshops including creative job-seeking skills, résumé writing, and interviewing.

Instructor: Taught Business Communications, Word Processing, General Business Procedures, and Executive Stress Management.

Recruiting: Instrumental in recruiting and training faculty members for evaluation process. Active in public relations and outreach to the community, business, industry leaders, and greater area employers.

Supervision: Administration and supervision of a Cooperative Education program in the business and commerce center of a large city. Acted as a liaison between the college and employers with direct contact to students, members of the administration, teaching faculty, and student services.

Telecourse Instructor: Coordinator-Instructor for telecourse in Job Seeking Skills to be a credit course and marketed nationally. Instrumental in developing additional courses for credit in Preparation for Employment with seminars and workshops in résumé writing, interview skills, and job search strategies.

PROFESSIONAL ORGANIZATIONS and COMMUNITY INVOLVEMENT:

American Business Communicators Association
National Association for Professional Saleswomen
National Business Education Association
National Cooperative Education Association
Returning Women's Network
Tides Community College Secretarial Science Advisory Committee
Transportation Management Advisory Committee
Virginia College Placement Association
Virginia Community College Association

Key job qualifications from various job experiences are highlighted in brief paragraphs with bold functional headings. This avoids redundancy in restating job duties from similar jobs and puts the emphasis squarely on relevant skills.

Lisa D. Messina

23 Beverly Drive, Greenlawn, NY 11740
Home (631) 757-3221 • Cell (516) 321-6795

Profile

Enthusiastic, self-motivated **ART EDUCATION TEACHER** who uses creativity and innovation to motivate, impart knowledge and facilitate learning. Effectively incorporate the love of literature and art history into all lessons, creating an enriched learning environment. Possess outstanding interpersonal, presentation, and classroom management skills. Continually encourage diversity among children to accomplish a common goal — "a Love of Art." These qualities have earned the respect of faculty, peers, and students.

"One hundred years from now it will not matter what my bank account was, the sort of house I lived in, or the kind of car I drove. But the world may be different because I was important in the life of a child."
— Anonymous

Certifications

New York State Art Certification K-12 (pending)
Certification in Interior Design, Parsons School of Design, 1988

Education

Long Island University, C.W. Post, Brookville, NY
☛ **Bachelor of Arts in Art Education**   December 2000
G.P.A. - 3.87 • Dean's List

Student Teaching

MURPHY JUNIOR HIGH SCHOOL • Stony Brook, NY   11/00 to 12/00
☛ **Student Teacher, Seventh through Ninth Grade**
— Taught studio art, drawing and painting, sculpture, and multi-media.
— Designed and implemented well-received lessons utilizing various techniques, and developed cooperative learning strategies and interdisciplinary learning.
— Established learning environments which met the intellectual, social, and creative needs of students.
— Developed murals, displays, and presentations of artwork.
— Utilized slide presentations and audio/visual equipment.
— Created multicultural diverse lesson plans.
— Incorporated technology into the classroom.
— Exercised a positive and assertive approach to discipline for modeling behaviors.

NASSAKEAG ELEMENTARY SCHOOL • Setauket, NY   9/00 to 11/00
☛ **Student Teacher, Kindergarten through Sixth Grade**
— Utilized a literature-based approach, facilitated learning consistent with the diverse needs and interests of all students, while following the curriculum according to New York State and District Art Standards.
— Taught clay, sculpture, drawing, painting, and graphic design classes.
— Incorporated art history, art appreciation, and art criticism in all lesson plans.
— Created interdisciplinary lessons, i.e., incorporated language arts (poetry) and color theory (palettes) integrating the expressive quality of color.
— Maintained an active, disciplined classroom while activities occurred simultaneously.

A variety of elements are brought together to form a cohesive resume for an art teacher: a decorative font, text box, relevant educational quote, and pencil-point bullets.

Lisa D. Messina

Related Art Experience	DEBORAH VASSAR INTERIORS • Nissequogue, NY 1/88 to 6/89 ☛ **Residential Department Manager** — Developed design layouts and blueprints for residential projects.

Employment History

ZORBA THE GREEK RESTAURANT • Oakdale, NY   2/82 to 6/97
(Two Full-service Greek Restaurants • 70 Seats)

☛ **Owner / General Manager**
Co-directed the daily operations of this restaurant chain with two locations. Pioneered and launched innovative advertising campaigns; created logo design. Directed all aspects of interior design needs, new construction, and renovations. Diverse responsibilities were expansive and included: ordering food/beverages, handling all aspects of menu design, booking/catering parties, promotions, P&L, inventory control, labor controls, profit margins, and forecasting. Oversaw payroll procedures and developed/monitored budgets. Interviewed, hired, fired, trained, and scheduled 15-20 employees, i.e., managers, cooks, server staff, and hostesses.

Community Service

  — Setauket PTA
  — Girls Scouts - Brownie Leader
  — Unitarian Universalist Fellowship at Stony Brook
  — Three Village Character Counts Coalition - Character Development
  — Senior Seminar - Community High School Group

Professional Development

  — P.R.A.I.S.E. - Parents Raising Adolescents, Increasing Self-Esteem
  — Character Development Classes
  — Facilitated Parenting Skills Classes

Interests

  — Museums
  — Literature
  — Traveling
  — Salsa Dancing
  — Physical Fitness
  — Tennis

TRAVIS A. JONES

1908 Irish Avenue
Atlanta, GA 30067
(770) 494-1005
jazzman@cc.rr.com

COMPUTER (MCSE) INSTRUCTOR ~ MCT
Microsoft Certified Systems Engineer & MCP + Internet / Certified Network Engineer

---

SUMMARY OF QUALIFICATIONS

Computer Technology Instructor with extensive experience in Network Administration, Project Management and Quality Management. Consistently recognized and awarded for performance. Key areas of expertise include:

Instruction:
- Technical Instruction
- Curriculum Development
- MS Curriculum
- Lecture Techniques
- Student Assessment
- Lesson Plans

Computers:
- Microsoft Operating System
- Network Administration
- Windows 95
- Peripheral Equipment
- Novell Operating System
- Hardware Configuration
- Windows NT
- Proxy Server
- Internet Technology
- Software Configuration
- TCP / IP
- MS Office Professional

PROFESSIONAL EXPERIENCE

- **MCSE Instructor & MCT**, Computer Information Technology, Atlanta, GA, 1999-Present
- **Computer Instructor**, Adult Ed. Program, Marietta Community School, Marietta, GA, 1998
- **Software Instructor**, Hillsborough Community College, Tampa, FL, 1990-1997
- **Teacher**, Garden District High School, Tampa, FL, 1982-1989

Technical Instructor / Trainer
- Developed curricula, assembled training materials, prepared goals and objectives, created lesson plans, and taught college level computer classes in computer applications, data processing, operating systems, and Microsoft Network Engineering.
  - Demonstrated ability to prepare goals and teach a diverse adult student body.
  - Provided innovative lecture techniques and teaching strategies for students.

Network Administration
- Provided complete knowledge of Novell and Microsoft network administration as a MCSE / CNE / A+ Certification and as instructor of the MCSE Program at CIT.
  - Performed course instruction in: Networking Essentials ... NT 4.0 Core ... NT 4.0 Administration ... NT 4.0 Enterprise.
- Skilled in troubleshooting to the board level; excellent ability to facilitate, diagnose and troubleshoot networking and configuration problems of both hardware and software.

EDUCATION & TRAINING

- **B.S. in Education**, Marietta State College, Marietta, GA – GPA: 3.8
- **Computer Science Teaching Certification**, State of Georgia Education Program
- **MCSE, CNE and A+**, Valley Technical Institute, Atlanta, GA

For this technology instructor, the list of computer knowledge is as important as instructional expertise and work experience. The headline, centered between a double-line border, makes the job seeker's objective and expertise crystal clear.

CLAIRE JEAN MONET

DANCE TEAM DIRECTOR
Jazz (including Character, Lyrical, Modern) • *Hip-Hop* • *Ballet* • *Tap*

CREATIVE Team Leader and Dancer experienced in all phases of dance from **choreography and instruction** to successfully creating and directing **star quality performances.**

PROFESSIONAL DANCE PROFILE

- **Professional Dancer and Instructor with over 20 years' experience** in all facets of dance.
- **Danced 3 years for NBA Salt Lake City Dixie Twister's dance team.**
- **Choreographed NBA Denver Power Dancers jazz routine,** Denver, CO (1996-1998).
- **Studied Modern and Jazz Dance** at Utah State University (1986-1990).
- **Excellent teaching skills** encompassing all styles, levels, and students ages 5 to 40.

CHOREOGRAPHY BACKGROUND

- *The Wizard of Oz*, Children's Jazz Productions, Salt Lake City, UT (1997-1998)
- *A Lyrical Jazz Solo*, Salt Lake City, UT (1997)
- *Avita,* Procter's Theatre, Salt Lake City, UT (1996)
- *USA NBA Jazz Dance Camps*, all styles, one-minute routines, various cities in US (1995-1998)
- *Betty Morris Dance Company*, Lyrical Jazz piece, Salt Lake City, UT (1988)

PROFESSIONAL PERFORMANCES

- Solo artist (Lyrical Jazz), *The Looking Glass Theater*, Salt Lake City, UT (1997)
- *Martin Shore Dance Art* (Modern Jazz, Lyrical Jazz, Character Jazz, Jazz, Tap, Hip-Hop), Sacramento, California (1994)
- *NBA Salt Lake City Dixie Twister's Dance Team* (Jazz, Lyrical Jazz, Hip-Hop, Character Jazz), Salt Lake City, UT (1990-1993)
- *Martin Shore Dance Art* (Modern Jazz), Salt Lake City, UT (1988-1990)
- *Betty Morris Dance Company* (Jazz, Modern Jazz, Lyrical Jazz, Character Jazz), Utah State University, Salt Lake City, UT (1987-1989)

PROFESSIONAL EXPERIENCE

The Blue Moon Dance Studio, Salt Lake City, UT   1989-2001
DANCE INSTRUCTOR/DIRECTOR-OWNER

United Spirit Association (Road tour of several US cities)   1987-1989
JAZZ DANCE INSTRUCTOR

1613 East Glenn Terrace, Salt Lake City, UT 84109
Phone: (801) 276-6299 E-mail: cmonet@us.net

This concise, well-organized resume for a dance teacher and director is enhanced by an appropriate graphic.

Curriculum Vitæ

Fred Fiero

1449 Jackson Court		[334] 891-7325 (Office)
Montgomery, Alabama 36116	ffiero@coolspring.com	[334] 864-0074 (Home)

WHAT I CAN BRING TO **BMS** AS A **DISTANCE LEARNING PROFESSIONAL** _____

❑ The **vision and experience** to guide strategic E-learning programs from concept to tangible results that serve your customers quickly,

❑ The **leadership** to transform groups of diverse employees into impassioned stakeholders, and

❑ The **skill** to manage risk well enough to help build your productivity faster than your competition.

RELEVANT WORK HISTORY WITH SELECTED EXAMPLES OF SUCCESS _____

More than 18 years in increasingly responsible positions as commissioned Air Force officer, including these recent assignments:

❑ *Promoted to* **Chief Learning Officer**, Air Force Doctrine Center, Cranston Air Force Base, Alabama, August 1995 — Present
The Center provides the basic corporate vision guiding the professional efforts of 371,000 employees worldwide.

> Turned around a new organization that was swamped with urgent, unfocused tasks for two years. Guided a corporate-level needs analysis that integrated every level of proficiency in twelve major learning areas into our first master training plan. *Payoffs:* Our credibility — **our stock in trade** — **rose fast**, as did our **productivity**.

❑ *Promoted to* **Director of Curriculum**, Air Force Extension Correspondence Institute, Cranston Air Force Base, Marboro Annex, Alabama, November 1993 — August 1995
The Institute was recognized as the educational institution with the most number of students in the world. With its $5.5 million budget, it serves learners in hundreds of disciplines at locations around the world.

> Served as direct reporting official for senior- and mid-level managers; indirectly supervised 35 curriculum editors and writers.

> Reignited an organization that had four CEOs in as many years, saw its staffing cut 36% in eight years, and suffered with stagnant budgets for four years. *Payoffs:* Skilled, but "**burned out**," **employees revoked** their **retirement** papers. **Productivity rose** dramatically. **Conflicts** that had festered for years were **resolved**.

> Did what others had tried, and failed, to do for years: convinced senior corporate levels of our true **value to our customers**. Guided our team to make a powerful presentation in just eight weeks. *Payoffs:* **Management increased our budget** by **$1 million at once**. Previously discouraged employees became convinced there was **no problem they couldn't tackle**.

More indicators of performance ➤

This resume for the up-and-coming field of distance learning is an excellent example of how to transition military experience to the private sector.

Fred Fiero   **Distance Learning Professional**   [334] 891-7325 (Office)

Enlisted my team to teach me every aspect of their jobs. Then led these top-notch professionals to change from an outdated — but highly praised — development system to much more responsive methods. *Payoffs:* Typical course **development time dropped** from 22 days to 10 days. **Quality** remained **high**.

Restored responsiveness to thousands of customers when demand threatened to outstrip our resources and cause our customers' missions to fail. *Payoffs:* **My proposal documented savings of $1 million** by delivering formerly mailed material electronically.

❑ *Promoted to* **Chief of Distance Learning Policy**, Headquarters, Doctrine University, Cranston Air Force Base, Alabama, April 1990 — November 1993
Our office served as the single point of contact for researching, employing, and delivering distance learning technologies.

Went beyond the obvious fix to help our customers who had high-tech distance learning technologies, but not the training to use them. Found and removed potential roadblocks from every level. *Payoffs:* Our combination users' handbook, strategy document, and "priority-setter" was in the field in just six months. **Customers very pleased**.

❑ *Promoted to* **Director of Training and Development**, Headquarters, North American Command, Marly Air Force Base, Wyoming, June 1988 — April 1990
Designed, developed, produced, delivered, evaluated, and validated "soft skills" training curricula serving some 1,700 people.

Overhauled a system that left new team members feeling left out of our organization for their first six months. Based my new program on a detailed needs analysis. *Payoffs:* **Spin-up time cut by a third**. Everybody won — from workers to managers.

Built a training program that helped our staff serve senior decision makers better and faster than ever. *Payoffs:* After we trained 600 professionals, production **error rate fell from 84% to 15%**.

❑ *Promoted to* **Training Instructor Developer**, Headquarters, Air Force Near Earth Command, Grizzly Air Force Base, Colorado, June 1985 — June 1988
Managed traditional and distance learning programs covering 120 contact hours of highly technical skills training to customers across the United States.

Selected by a senior executive vice president **over hundreds of eligibles** for this position.

Salvaged a mission-critical program that had cost $2 million, but wasn't doing the job. Enlisted our experts to help streamline our methods. *Payoffs:* **Cut workload by a factor of 17**. The new system's quality was so high a foreign government asked to copy the methods.

❑ *Promoted to* **Training Branch Chief**; *promoted to* **Training Division Chief**, 91st Missile Wing, Frank Air Force Base, North Dakota, October 1982 — August 1985
Guided highly technical programs that delivered training to 400 skilled professionals each month.

Page 2 of 3

Fred Fiero — **Distance Learning Professional** — [334] 891-7325 (Office)

COMPUTER SKILLS_____

- Expert in **Web page design, evaluation of distance learning software**, Internet search protocols, **PowerPoint**, Word, proprietary event reporting software

- Proficient in Excel, Outlook, Quicken

- Working knowledge of Access

EDUCATION AND PROFESSIONAL DEVELOPMENT _____

- Pursuing **Evaluator** Certificate Program, **Distance Education and Training Council**

- Pursuing **Certified Distance Educator Credential**, University of Wisconsin at Madison

- MA, **Organizational Communication**, University of Northern Colorado at Greeley, 1985
  Earned this degree while working 45 hours a week and attending classes on weekends.

- BA, Grove City College, Grove City, 1978

- Certified Toastmaster, 1981
  This credential is shared by the top 12% of all Toastmaster members and is awarded based on evaluated presentations.

RELEVANT PROFESSIONAL AFFILIATIONS_____

- President, Central Alabama Chapter, ASTD, 1997 – 2001

- Vice-President for Professional Development, Pike's Peak Chapter, ASTD, 1996

- President, Cheyenne Toastmasters, 1982

SELECTED PUBLICATIONS IN THE FIELD OF E-LEARNING_____

- With H. Kottler, J. Parsons, and S. Wardenburg, "Knowledge Objects: Definition, Development Initiatives, and Potential Impact," <u>Learning Issues and Trends Report</u>, Alexandria, Virginia, 1998 – 1999

- <u>Distance Learning Resource Handbook</u>, Air Force Distance Learning Office, Cranston Air Force Base, Alabama, October 1998

- <u>Distance Learning Site Managers' Handbook</u>, Air Force Distance Learning Office, Cranston Air Force Base, Alabama, July 1998

Page 3 of 3

JOHN D. MARTIN

5180 Bay Drive
Hide Park, Maryland 21145

Office: 410-386-8105

Cell: 402-905-1964

**Expert in E-Learning and Knowledge Management Strategies and Systems
To Improve Human Performance: Optimizing Employee Success and Driving Profitable Growth**

Recognized leader in the strategic development, design, technological development, marketing, and delivery of advanced technologies to improve human, organization, and financial performance. Successful corporate executive, consultant and entrepreneur with extensive experience in the Global 2000, IT, .COM, software, and systems integration industries.

Thrives in challenging, high-energy start-up ventures, turnarounds, and high-growth organizations worldwide. Characterized as a talented strategist, thought producer, communicator, project leader, and customer relationship manager. Designed and executed creative approaches and innovative marketing tactics to deliver technology-based solutions to complex business demands.

PROFESSIONAL EXPERIENCE:

SENIOR DIRECTOR – GLOBAL SERVICES – ABA SOFTWARE

1999 to 2000

Member of Services Management Team leading this technology venture through organization development, market positioning, and successful IPO (March 2000). Recruited to build consulting practice targeting CEO-level executives as the foundation for the "go-to-market" strategy to introduce enterprise-wide E-learning systems and technologies.

- Instrumental in managing the phenomenal growth of this new services venture, from less than 30 to 100+ business and technology consultants and from six to 50+ customers throughout North America and Europe.

- Recruited experts in knowledge management and learning/training to guide product development, marketing, and service delivery for the Global 2000, education, and government markets.

- Partnered with Big 5 consulting firms such as Smith Consulting and Mada Consulting to create solutions-based offerings and facilitate product/service launch.

- Catalyzed the development of strategy and processes for service delivery.

CONSULTANT & ENTREPRENEUR

1987 to 1999

Twelve-year track record of success pioneering innovations in Business Process Consulting, E-Learning, Knowledge Management, Human Performance, and Organization Development.

- Led strategy, development, and execution of 30+ consulting engagements with Global 2000 firms, start-ups, venture investment firms, and the "Big 5." Created more than $20 million in opportunities.

- Launched several new technology ventures developing first-generation enterprise document management and spreadsheet applications software.

- Assembled and led technology, business, sales, and marketing teams that introduced some of the world's most advanced E learning and human performance improvement technologies.

- Built and managed successful client relationships with Smith Consulting, Bank Trust, Bell Atlantic, Caterpillar, Citibank, Entergy, Ericsson, Federal Express, Gannett Publishing, GE Medical, GM/EDS, Holiday Inn, Merrill Lynch, Microsoft, NYNEX, Ogilvy & Mather, Sprint, USAA, Xerox, and others.

- Consulted with leading venture capital firms to evaluate proposed technology acquisition and development projects.

For an executive in the emerging e-learning field, this resume appropriately focuses on measurable accomplishments from his 25-year career.

JOHN D. MARTIN – Page Two

Notable Projects, Ventures & Achievements:

Interim Director – Capital Development – UBC Trust (1998 to 1999). Retained to work with IT and HR to create and launch a major effort to introduce comprehensive knowledge management practices into major locations worldwide for the 5th largest US Bank.

- Created global strategy for program design/implementation and linked each individual component to improvements in organization efficiency and performance, management capability, client service and retention, and/or profitability.

- Launched several projects, including Lessons Learned Knowledge, Leadership Development Community, Desktop Knowledge Management, Product Knowledge, Risk Management Intellectual Property Protection, and a Virtual University to enable tremendous performance results.

Strategy Advisor to Vice Chairman and Interim Director – Advanced Development for Energy Management Information Strategy – Vitell (1997 to 1998). Led strategic new business venture including direct supervision of partner business unit. Refocused business vision and strategy, designed organization infrastructure, and introduced strategy for market and product development.

- Worked in cooperation with Smith Consulting to create new company and lead team to pursue $100+ million opportunity for international product launch and other strategic global initiatives.

Vice President – VitaQuest Metrics, Inc. (1995 to 1997). Co-Founding Board Member of internationally recognized group of software engineers who consult and train global companies in improving their software development process. Full-time during company start-up with leadership responsibility for strategy, product definition, sales, and marketing. Consulted with management team to guide strategic development of technology-based learning and knowledge systems.

- Instrumental in positioning VitaQuest as one of the world's most preeminent process improvement companies with a clientele including Ericsson, GM, Kodak, Merrill-Lynch, Microsoft, and Sprint.

Director – Advanced Development – PTW Technologies (1992 to 1995). Created new consulting business unit with an engagement strategy focused on human performance. Orchestrated development of embedded performance support technology to dramatically improve measurable individual productivity. Delivered million dollar systems to Federal Express (customer service), GE Medical (sales), Holiday Inn (reservations), and other global corporations with sophisticated transaction-based applications.

- Negotiated and closed over $5 million in new client projects within two years. Positioned PTW as a leader in performance support, E-learning, and knowledge management.

MANAGER – CORPORATE EDUCATION MARKETING – INTEL INSTRUMENTS   1982 to 1987

Recruited to lead INTEL Instruments' nationwide launch into the education market. Challenged to create the strategy and business unit, secure the funding, build the organization, recruit/train the sales team, and deliver the products to create a dominant presence throughout this rapidly emerging market. Competed head-on with ABC Computer and Compu-Tel Computers.

- Built new venture from start-up to over $15 million in sales of learning and computer products.

- Partnered with higher education, K-12, education associations, and government research laboratories (e.g., Stanford, UC Berkeley, MIT, Yale, USC, University of Illinois) to create artificial intelligence workstations and other pioneering knowledge-based systems.

- Co-led the development and launch of the world's then largest corporate distance learning program, characterized as the most successful marketing program in TI's history. Effort impacted more than a hundred thousand people in education, government, and business at thousands of sites throughout North America and Europe. Netted over $70 million in free press and media coverage.

JOHN D. MARTIN – Page Three

VICE PRESIDENT – USBT BANK CORPORATION   1981 to 1982

Associate Director (Chief Operating Officer) and Secretary, Board of Directors for USBT's corporate foundation (10th largest in US). Guided allocation of annual budget (grants targeted to community service organizations, higher education institutions, and public education). Established strategy to guide corporate giving, created high-visibility community based programs, built a fully integrated internal IT function and funded/directed hundreds of programs.

EXECUTIVE DIRECTOR – NATIONAL VOLUNTEER PROGRAM   1976 to 1981

Chief Executive Officer of start-up national non-profit association. Launched PR effort that raised more than $2.5 million for program funding and included direct support from the White House, Congress, state legislators, and labor unions nationwide. Leadership responsibility for budgeting, staffing, program development/delivery, and marketing for a massive volunteer effort.

Early Experience in University Academic/Research and Government Policy Analysis.

EDUCATION:

Ph.D. – Statistics & Education – University of Iowa
M.A. – Education and **B.A. – Liberal Arts** – Ball State University

RECENT PRESENTATIONS & PUBLICATIONS:

- "Value Creation in the New Economy" – work in progress

- "E-business Learning and Value Creating Networks" – Conference Board conference on knowledge management

- "Ten Questions Every Executive Should Ask About Knowledge Management" – self-published as a white paper

WANDA ORTIZ-RIVERA

265 Furlough Drive
Smithtown, NY 11787
(631) 382-2425
wrivera@net.com

ESL TEACHER

Experienced bilingual educator dedicated to fostering education by creating a stimulating, nurturing, and culturally friendly environment for bilingual students. Keen understanding of the importance for student assimilation and the need for respect of their native upbringing. Adhere to new procedures and commissioner regulations for LEP and adequately incorporate these methodologies in a classroom setting to enhance learning.

Highlights of Qualifications:

- **Motivator:** Create a powerful, committed, and sensitive learning environment for bilingual students that promotes personal growth and achievement.
- **Team Contributor:** Natural talent to effectively build administrative and teacher relationships that consistently meet the immediate and long-term needs of the students.
- **Parental Educator:** Keen ability to engage caregivers in the learning process and decrease the learning curve.

EDUCATION AND CERTIFICATION

COLUMBIA UNIVERSITY, Teachers College, New York, NY
Ed.M. in Spanish, Emphasis in Bilingual/Bicultural Education   1998

DOWLING COLLEGE, Oakdale, NY
Master of Business Administration   1992
Bachelor of Art, Natural Science, and Math, Minor: Spanish Literature   1991

New York State Certification, N — 6 with an Extension in Bilingual Education
ESL Teaching Certification

TEACHING EXPERIENCE

Bilingual Resource Teacher, John F. Kennedy, Portchester School District, New York, NY   **1998-Present**

- Designed, created, and implemented innovative teaching curricula for Kindergarten through fourth grade that successfully mainstreamed bilingual students.
- Encouraged parental involvement in their children's education by facilitating interactive workshops.
- Performed, documented, and reviewed evaluations and assessments for student referral and mainstreaming with central staff and parents.
- Integrated reading, math, science, and social studies into learning curricula geared to facilitate mainstream topics and ideas.
- Actively interacted with Title I teachers to create individualized educational plans.
- Utilized knowledge of CALPs and BICS to proactively engage students in the learning process.
- Administered school-wide ESL testing, properly distinguishing students with language barriers.

Bilingual First Grade Teacher, Pine Park, Brentwood School District, New York, NY   **1994-1998**

- Designed unique lesson plans geared to pique students' interests and promote active learning.
- Respected individual learning styles and modified assignments to meet individual objectives.
- Initiated a reading program integrating different reading methodologies and parental workshops.
- Collaborated with parents/guardians through regular telephone communication, workshops, and parent-teacher conferences.

Adjunct Professor, Bilingual Department, Teacher's College, Columbia University, New York, NY   **1995-1997**

- Presented new methodologies to graduate students on how to properly teach first and second language acquisition to bilingual students.

continued...

This is a classic resume for a teacher of English as a Second Language: chronological, accomplishment-focused, and with a strong introduction. The graphic is a nice enhancement.

WANDA ORTIZ-RIVERA

TEACHING EXPERIENCE CONTINUED

Researcher and Tutor, Spanish Bilingual/Bicultural Education Department, Teacher's College
Columbia University, New York, NY — 1994-1997

Student Advisor, Bilingual Department, Teacher's College Columbia University, New York, NY — 1994-1997

Bilingual Elementary Teacher, P.S. 46, Bronx, NY — 1992-1994

Bilingual Math Professor, Kingsborough Community College, Brooklyn, NY — Summer 1993

Elementary Teacher, South Country Summer Program, Bayshore, NY — Summer 1992

TEACHING METHODOLOGIES & ASSESSMENTS

- Woodcok Munoz
- LAB
- BICS
- Supera
- TPR
- CALP
- Terranova
- Gouins
- National Approach (Tracy Terrell)
- Brigance
- ESL assessments

COMMITTEES

- Served on Committee of Special Education (CSE) to determine the future status of bilingual students.
- Assisted in writing grants and proposals for state and federal funding.

HONORS

Fellowship Award, Multicultural Studies, Emphasis Bilingual/Education, 1994

Honor Student, National Dean's List, 1987-1993

Awarded by Columbia University and Fundacion Jose Ortega Y Gasset - Madrid
Presented Methodologies of Teaching Reading to Bilingual Students

Selected by college President and faculty to represent student body at Mediterranean XIII Conference in Barcelona, Spain, 1990

Selected as a Language Translator and Interpreter, Dowling College Symposium for Dr. Camilo Jose Cela, 1989 Nobel Prize Winner In Literature, 1990

RESEARCH

Bilingual/Bicultural Classroom - Teacher's Reflective Practice

PRESENTATIONS

How to Help Your Child with Homework
How to Teach Your Child to Love Reading
How to Help Your Child with Test-Taking
Home and School Connection

PROFESSIONAL AFFILIATIONS

Member, Kappa Delta Pi, 1995-Present
Member, State Association of Bilingual Education (SABE), 1995-Present
Member, National Association of Bilingual Education (NABE), 1995-Present
Member, Statewide School Program, 1999-2000

PAMELA L. WHITFIELD

260 Haverstick Road, Apt. 14 • New Castle, DE 19700
Residence: (302) 326-3980   Office: (302) 297-4661

COMMUNITY HEALTH EDUCATOR

PROFESSIONAL PROFILE

Talented health educator with excellent academic and professional credentials and experience dealing with sensitive healthcare issues. Strong analytical, research, and project management skills combined with expertise in planning community outreach programs. Experienced counselor of at-risk populations. Extensive focus on train-the-trainer development, seminar/workshop design, and creation of educational materials related to STDs and AIDS/HIV. Committed to promote wellness and prevent disease. Strong written and verbal communications, interpersonal relations, needs assessment, and presentation skills. Proficient PC-based computer skills and knowledge of word processing, spreadsheet, and presentation applications. Internet research.

EDUCATION AND PROFESSIONAL DEVELOPMENT & TRAINING

HIV/STD Educator/Trainer Network, Atlanta, GA – 1999-2000

Bachelor of Science, Community Health, INDIANA UNIVERSITY, Bloomington, IN – 1999
• Internship: Student Health Promotion
• Vice President, Education, ETA ETA GAMMA National Honorary Society – 1998-99

Co-op and Internship Accomplishments

➤ Created and developed pamphlets for college campus student health promotions.
➤ Spearheaded marketing campaign on STD awareness, signs, and symptoms and distribution to nearly 13,000 collegians advising of safe-sex techniques, health awareness programs and services.
➤ Evaluated grant proposal targeting eligible women to receive free mammograms.
➤ Researched and created presentation for county health department targeting junior-high-school students on the dangers of unprotected sex, STDs, and pregnancy. Presentation adopted for use within the countywide school systems.

PROFESSIONAL EXPERIENCE

Public Health Educator (10/99 to present)
HEALTH & SOCIAL SERVICES, DIVISION OF PUBLIC HEALTH, Delaware

Recruited to serve as a specialist in preventive education measures, coordinating and implementing health education/risk reduction programs, presentations, and curricula to a variety of populations.
➤ Coordinate and implement health education/risk reduction programs for youth programs and schools, community-based organizations, and counseling and testing sites within the state. Co-facilitate programs at a variety of correctional facilities in collaboration with women's, men's, and youth correctional facilities.
➤ Create public information bulletins that include resource information and prevention messages.

Selecting a different font for the name is a simple yet effective way to enhance the appearance of this neat, well-organized resume for an individual in the community health education field.

Pamela L. Whitfield, Page 2

Professional Experience – *continued*

➤ Collect and analyze data for future assessment and approval of education projects; document completed tasks and contacts with constituents.
➤ Develop training brochures, pamphlets, training manuals, and resource guides.
➤ Implement established procedures and standards to ensure compliance with state public health policies.
➤ Trained and certified over 400 volunteers in the train-the-trainer program.
➤ Assisted with reformatting HIV/AIDS Instructor Certification Course curriculum.
➤ Co-created community outreach survey that targets communication education needs for HIV/AIDS trainings and presentations.

Medical Secretary (6/99 to 9/99)
OCCUPATIONAL HEALTH CENTERS, Indianapolis, IN

Fast-track promotions from Physical Therapy Aide to Medical Secretary for an emergency, immediate-care health facility. Daily contact with outpatient population referred for workmen's compensation emergencies. Accurately annotated patient records. Scheduled physical and occupational therapy sessions with appropriate medical professionals and therapists.

Other work experience: 5 years' experience in customer service and consumer sales.

—————————— PROFESSIONAL CERTIFICATIONS ——————————

➤ Certified HIV/AIDS Instructor/Trainer – American Red Cross
➤ Certified HIV/AIDS Preventive Programming and Counseling and Testing Instructor/Trainer – DE Division of Public Health
➤ Elementary Student *No Smoking Campaign* Instructor – American Red Cross

CYNTHIA M. PEREZ

4 Myerson Way
Seattle, WA 82520

perezcm@aol.com

Day: (307) 449-1401
Eve: (307) 776-1511

PROFILE

Seasoned educational professional and noted expert from MIPS, the largest and most reputable American outdoor leadership school. Expertise in curriculum and program development and education administration. Experienced in creating and executing complex field rationing programs, managing staff, and directing participants.

EMPLOYMENT

MIPS Outdoor Leadership School, Seattle, WA

Chief Rationing Instructor   **1982 to Present**

Direct all facets of the educational program concerning backcountry expedition food planning. Provide instruction to 1,255 students annually on planning rations, ordering rations, and ensuring correct distribution. Conduct extensive training and direction for staff. Process 95,000 pounds of food annually. Manage food intake, labeling, packaging, and storage. Administer a $215K annual budget.

- Coordinate the logistics of providing rations to students and instructors. Conceptualize detailed rationing programs, accounting for smooth operations, variety and versatility of foods, nutritional standards, and budgeting.

- Collaborate with technical experts to design and execute food rationing protocol. The spreadsheet programs compute number of participants, number of cook groups, ration periods, and ration poundages. Direct students and staff in activities including packaging food and planning food for expeditions.

- Conduct public speaking, providing clear, specific, highly detailed, and articulate directions to participants in order to facilitate effective rations preparation within a short time frame.

MIPS PROFESSIONAL TRAINING

- Summer Wilderness Course
- Winter Ski Course
- Wilderness First Responder
- Management
- Supervision
- Communications

INDUSTRY PUBLICATIONS

- The MIPS Food Guide: Editor, 1st edition (1994); Co-author, 2nd edition (1998); Co-author, 3rd edition (1999).
- Subject of an article in *Camping America* magazine, "Cooking with Cynthia," August 1998.

EDUCATION

B.S., Outdoor Recreation, The University of Washington, Seattle, WA, 1981

This resume clearly communicates the expertise that is necessary to stand out in the highly specialized field of outdoor leadership instruction.

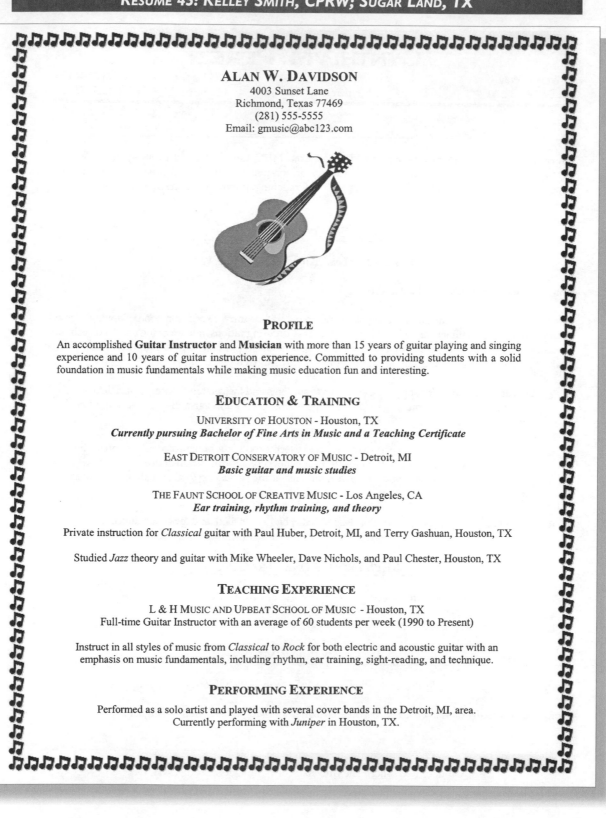

ALAN W. DAVIDSON

4003 Sunset Lane
Richmond, Texas 77469
(281) 555-5555
Email: gmusic@abc123.com

PROFILE

An accomplished **Guitar Instructor** and **Musician** with more than 15 years of guitar playing and singing experience and 10 years of guitar instruction experience. Committed to providing students with a solid foundation in music fundamentals while making music education fun and interesting.

EDUCATION & TRAINING

UNIVERSITY OF HOUSTON - Houston, TX
Currently pursuing Bachelor of Fine Arts in Music and a Teaching Certificate

EAST DETROIT CONSERVATORY OF MUSIC - Detroit, MI
Basic guitar and music studies

THE FAUNT SCHOOL OF CREATIVE MUSIC - Los Angeles, CA
Ear training, rhythm training, and theory

Private instruction for *Classical* guitar with Paul Huber, Detroit, MI, and Terry Gashuan, Houston, TX

Studied *Jazz* theory and guitar with Mike Wheeler, Dave Nichols, and Paul Chester, Houston, TX

TEACHING EXPERIENCE

L & H MUSIC AND UPBEAT SCHOOL OF MUSIC - Houston, TX
Full-time Guitar Instructor with an average of 60 students per week (1990 to Present)

Instruct in all styles of music from *Classical* to *Rock* for both electric and acoustic guitar with an emphasis on music fundamentals, including rhythm, ear training, sight-reading, and technique.

PERFORMING EXPERIENCE

Performed as a solo artist and played with several cover bands in the Detroit, MI, area.
Currently performing with *Juniper* in Houston, TX.

This resume for a guitar instructor was posted on his Web site, distributed to music schools, and used to apply for employment as a high-school music instructor.

Jason Lipman

192-37 35th Avenue
Flushing, NY 11351
718-555-9003

Physical Education Teacher (K-12)

- Eager to bring students into the twenty-first century using a unique combination of high-caliber physical education experience and athletic achievement. Will utilize teaching knowledge and over fifteen years background as successful business owner to parallel the development of athletic abilities with the understanding of real-life skills.

- Dedicated to enthusiastic and dynamic teaching as a means of creating a lifelong love of sports and learning in children and young adults. Create an energizing educational experience that motivates students to enjoy physical, academic, and personal accomplishment.

- Trained for a teaching career, but in response to family need, reluctantly put plans aside and joined family business after college (worked in business from age of five). To stay in teaching, took substitute teaching assignments while running business. After fifteen years of profitable business management, have sold business to teach full-time.

Education and Certification

Post-Graduate Coursework
Currently attending Master's in Elementary Education program
St. Joseph's College, Brooklyn, NY

Three-credit Education Course
State University of New York at Stony Brook

Bachelor of Science in Health and Physical Education
Tennessee State University, Yarrow, TN 1983
(attended on full football scholarship)

Undergraduate Coursework
Jefferson Rangle College, Lincoln City, MD
(attended on full football scholarship)

Certification (Provisional, pending renewal)
NY State Physical Education K-12

Key Qualifications

- Experienced college-level coach; worked for five years as defensive line and strength training coach at Hofstra University. Experienced substitute teacher with ability to motivate students in difficult situations.

- As coach and teacher, incorporate learning modality principles into group and individual instruction. Plan, prepare, and instruct in each skills area using wide variety of motivational and implementation strategies to engage students in active learning and accomplishment.

- Possess unique ability to break down components of athletic training into easily assimilated units. Students struggling with techniques become successful after this instructional coaching.

Athletic Achievements

Played two years of semi-pro football for the Elkin Eagles

Tried out for the Giants and the Buffalo Bills

Defensive Line Coach for Hofstra University Bengals Football Team

Hofstra University Strength Training Coach

College Football:

Azalea Bowl MVP
NAIA National Playoffs
Senior Year Team Captain
First Team, All-American
First Team, All-District

High School Football:

All-American
All-State
All-County
All-Long Island
All-League

This excellent resume incorporates numerous design elements with a high degree of originality. It is well written, well organized, and easy to skim despite being fairly text-heavy.

Jason Lipman   2

Employment in Education

Substitute Teacher (grades 1-12), New York, NY   **1989 to present**

- New York City Schools
- Sewhanaka School District
- St. Kevin's Elementary School, Elmont, NY

Teach academic subjects and all physical education activities including indoor baseball, wiffle ball, basketball, and volleyball. Handle difficult assignments by developing a mutual respect with students and deflecting natural aggression towards substitutes. Utilize personal style of instruction that enhances motivation and reduces opportunities for student disruption. Create an energized atmosphere that generates interest and participation.

Defensive Line Coach for Hofstra Bengals Football Team
Weight Lifting Coach
Hofstra University   **1983 to 1988**

As Defensive Line Coach, taught techniques and form; made up daily practice schedules and routines; set up film appointments for players and graded players by films. Reviewed game plans, incorporating defense and offense. Handled scouting and recruiting for New York and New Jersey teams; wrote scouting reports and attended team meetings. Taught visualization techniques for instinctive, reactive play.

As Weight Lifting Coach, attended NSCA convention; learned and incorporated cutting-edge conditioning strategies into workouts that encouraged college athletes to do total-body conditioning between sets. Developed jump-rope program that dramatically increased athletes' agility.

Student Teaching

Health and Physical Education (grades 7-12)
Johnstown Middle School and High School, Raleigh, ND   **1983**

Offered permanent position; declined due to family responsibilities. As student teacher, instructed students in football, weight training and track. Used motivation and skills coaching to develop shot put ability in student struggling with technique; student qualified for state championship.

Health and Physical Education (grades K-12)
Hopewell School, Hopewell, TN   **1983**

Business Ownership

Owner/Partner/Operator
All-State Carting, Maspeth, NY   **1983 to 2001**

Recently sold business to a major public company in waste management. All-State was a six-partner waste management company with its own transfer station facility and was aggressively involved in the management/disposal of recycling, municipal solid waste, and construction/demolition debris.

Kathleen Lange

**3233 North Bartlett Avenue
Milwaukee, Wisconsin 53212
katlange@aol.com
(414) 962-4224**

**TEACHER AND INSTRUCTOR—
KINDERGARTEN THROUGH ADULT**

Learning-Handicapped, Cognitively Disabled,
and Emotionally Disturbed
Multi-Cultural, Disadvantaged, and At-Risk Youth
Inclusion Instruction
Community-Based Instruction
Curriculum Development and Design
Classroom Management
Multi-Disciplinary IEP Evaluation
Basic Education
English as a Second Language

After an attractive cover page that includes a brief summary of the individual's extensive areas of expertise, the resume goes on to include strong "selling points" in the form of testimonials—placed so that they do not detract from the traditional experience sections of the resume.

Professional Experience

SPECIAL EDUCATION

Milwaukee Public Schools, Milwaukee, Wisconsin	1999 to Present 1990 to 1993

TEACHER, COGNITIVELY DISABLED AND EMOTIONALLY DISTURBED

Instruct twenty, ninth- through twelfth-grade cross-categorical students in math and life skills. Team-teach with regular-ed teacher in an inclusionary setting consisting of regular-ed and special-ed students. Use the Internet and other computer-assistive devices to develop research skills. Establish relationships and coordinate pre-vocational, community-based instruction with technical colleges, hospitals, and manufacturing firms. Prepare individual education plans and conduct multi-disciplinary IEP meetings. Help individuals with personal needs, for example teenage mothers needing parenting advice or home management information.

San Diego School District, San Diego, California   1996 to 1997

RESOURCE SPECIALIST

Assessed learning disabled elementary and junior-high students. Wrote and implemented remediation plans. Chaired child study team.

Los Pueblos High School, San Diego, California   1994 to 1996

TEACHER, SPECIAL EDUCATION

Instructed severely emotionally disturbed young people (ages 13-18) from neighboring schools, group homes, and residential treatment centers. Consulted with mental health professionals in determining individualized instruction and group curriculum. Met jointly with students and/or families to develop and coordinate services or provide counseling.

San Diego Union Schools, San Diego, California   1993 to 1994

TEACHER, SEVERELY HANDICAPPED

Developed curriculum including Reading, Phonics, Life Skills, and Math for severely disabled elementary students.

Bradley Foundation, San Diego, California   1989 to 1990

TEACHER, EMOTIONALLY DISTURBED

Instructed emotionally disturbed and autistic students in basic education courses. Interacted with therapists, psychiatrists, and social workers. Participated in team meetings to review individual students' progress.

"In my work with Kathy, she has proven to be both a dedicated teacher and caring individual. Despite her large number of students and the seriousness and variety of their learning, intellectual, behavior, and emotional difficulties, Kathy has accepted the challenge of providing appropriate individualized and group curricula with enthusiasm. When students or situations required a change in approach, Kathy showed flexibility, creativity, and willingness to coordinate with others. She builds supportive relationships with all of her students, often extending her energies beyond what is expected. As a result, it is no small wonder that many of her students make substantial progress while in her classroom and go on to become productive members of their communities upon graduation."

Barbara Cash, Licensed Clinical Social Worker, San Diego County Department of Mental Health Services.

"You have a deep commitment to teaching and have made a very conscious decision to contribute to people through education . . . Another great strength of yours is the ability to personalize learning experiences for students. . . . You have a tremendous capacity and drive for building positive, personal relationships with each of your students. You are outgoing and relate easily . . . Because of your willingness and desire to involve others in all of your activities, students have more say in their education and an atmosphere of cooperation marks the learning/growing process . . . Your capacity for empathy is unusual and a real gift to those whom your life touches. You can acknowledge and understand feelings, deal direct with them... You are a teacher with a hopeful optimistic attitude toward students . . . Being a resource to your students is another great gift you offer them."

Excerpts from *Urban Teacher Portrait— Kathy Lange* Milwaukee Public Schools

Professional Experience (continued)

ADULT EDUCATION

Work Training Program, San Diego, California   1997 to 1998

JOB COACH

Trained developmentally disabled and mentally ill adults for competitive employment with area businesses. Analyzed and learned jobs required by employers. Acted as liaison between WTP workers and employers—ensured quality control and monitored/corrected behaviors.

San Diego College, San Diego, California   1994 to 1998

INSTRUCTOR, BASIC EDUCATION

Taught Math, English, and Reading to physically and learning disabled adults. Instructed English as a Second Language for immigrant students.

REGULAR EDUCATION

St. Joseph's School, San Diego, California   1986 to 1987

TEACHER

Designed and implemented curricula for junior-high students in Science, Math, English, Reading, and Social Studies. Coordinated Science Fair.

Milwaukee Public Schools, Milwaukee, Wisconsin   1969 to 1976

TEACHER

Taught Urban Education and Title 1 Reading to elementary students.

Education

BS (Elementary Education), California State University
Graduate Coursework—Educational Therapy,
California State University
Graduate Coursework—Remedial Reading & Special Ed.,
Cardinal Stritch University
Graduate Coursework—Special Ed., California Lutheran College

Licenses

Lifetime Kindergarten, 8th Grade, Wisconsin, Illinois
Professional Clear Multiple-Subject K-12 and Adult Ed., California
Professional Clear Severely Handicapped, California
Professional Clear Learning Handicapped K-12, California
Provisional Special Education License, Wisconsin

GIOVANNA MARINA

55 Pheasant Run Drive
Markham, Ontario A2B 3C4
Phone: (905) 666-8899

OBJECTIVE: EDUCATIONAL ASSISTANT / SUPPLY TEACHER

SPECIALIZING IN PROVIDING SUPPORT AND EDUCATIONAL ASSISTANCE
TO CHILDREN OF ALL AGES AND ABILITIES

Patient, caring, energetic, personable, and organized with outstanding interpersonal and communication skills. Recognized for ability to develop effective plans and programs for children. Extensive experience in community support and programming, infant and childhood care, and community outreach. **B.A. in Psychology.**

PERSONAL STRENGTHS

PLANNING / PROGRAM DEVELOPMENT:

- Experience designing, developing, and implementing comprehensive children's programs and activities for daycare and community programs.
- Proven ability to plan and coordinate large community events, designing agendas and coordinating all resources.
- Proficient working independently and developing programs from inception to implementation.

COMMUNITY SUPPORT & OUTREACH:

- 10 years experience in community involvement, including daycare, public school, church, and Girl Guides involvement.
- Extensive volunteer experience working with both children and adults, including developmental and special needs cases.
- Recognized for naturally caring and supportive demeanour, with a reputation for "going the extra mile".

LEADERSHIP AND PERSONAL INTERACTION:

- Held a variety of executive and leadership positions within community, liaising with individuals, parents, and public officials.
- Supervisory and leadership experience, overseeing and developing junior employees and volunteers.

COMPUTER PROFICIENCY:

- Experience working with Excel, Lotus, Internet, and email applications.
- Demonstrated ability to quickly gain proficiency with new and proprietary software programs.

ADMINISTRATION:

- Organized, efficient, and thorough with an ability to manage multiple tasks, work under deadlines, and adapt as situations arise.
- Additional skills include marketing, fundraising, event planning, and bookkeeping.

Note how work and volunteer experience are combined on the second page of this educational assistant's resume. The functional grouping of "personal strengths" on page 1 highlights what she has to offer.

GIOVANNA MARINA   (905) 666-8899   Page 2

WORK / VOLUNTEER EXPERIENCE

Owner / Operator – Home-Base Community Daycare, Markham, Ontario
- Created and marketed a highly successful home-based community daycare – overwhelming community response quickly resulted in waiting lists.
- Developed a comprehensive and child-oriented daycare program designed to provide a healthy, fun, and educational environment for children ages 6 months to 10 years.
- Designed creative activities, crafts, and excursions structured around weekly themes, augmenting activities with materials acquired from local libraries and services.
- Coordinated with parents to provide appropriate support for children with behavioural issues.

Vice-Chair, School Community Council – Randall Wayne Public School, Markham, Ontario
- Currently sitting on Executive Board for new school, responsible for defining roles and responsibilities and liaising between school and community at regular public meetings.

Brownie Leader – Girl Guides of Canada, Markham, Ontario
- Developed entire annual program for local troupe, including all weekly meetings, development activities, fundraising, and outdoor excursions.
- Organized annual Christmas trip to local Senior Citizens residence, organizing shared crafts activities and sing-alongs.
- Oversaw two Junior Leaders and completed all administrative and bookkeeping functions.

Sunday School Teacher – All Saints Anglican Church, Markham, Ontario
- Led weekly 75-minute lessons to 5-15 children aged 3 to 6, following pre-set program guidelines and encouraging participation among children.

Annual Picnic Coordinator – All Saints Anglican Church, Markham, Ontario
- Organized annual picnic for 100 attendees, planning activities and coordinating all resources and six adult volunteers.

Fundraising Committee – Randall Wayne Public School, Markham, Ontario
- Currently contributing to the development and implementation of school fundraising activities.

EDUCATION / TRAINING

Bachelor of Arts (Psychology) – York University, Toronto, Ontario   1989

Sexual Misconduct & Harassment Awareness Workshop – Anglican Church of Canada   2000

PERSONAL INTERESTS

Outdoor activities including canoeing, hiking, and camping.

References available upon request.

WOODROW P. FARNWORTH, III

Ten Old Mill Road   Lake Patten, New Mexico 53409   (505) 612-7690

EDUCATIONAL PHILOSOPHY

Webster surprisingly defines a **Tutor** as a "guardian...to look after, guard, keep." And one who teaches as, "to point out...to impart the knowledge of." I have always looked at instructing others from these perspectives. As a History buff with an **undergraduate degree in History and Minor in Political Science**, these definitions speak volumes of the core teaching approaches I use. Each generation is "entrusted" with the responsibility to pass on the historical truths of its day to the next.

> WE MUST KNOW OUR HISTORY, NEVER FORGET ITS LESSONS,
> AND TEACH PATIENTLY, WITHOUT PREJUDICE.

TRAINING / TUTORING EXPERIENCE

My transferable teaching skills are evidenced by the fact that I have had many opportunities to train employees as a senior customer service manager for several consumer-driven companies. For the past decade, I simultaneously held the role as Lead Trainer. I designed and presented classes on a variety of operational procedures and protocols. Primarily because I thoroughly enjoy empowering others,

> **I found that my employees (especially those in school or college)
> often asked me to mentor them regarding their academic coursework.**

One of the key reasons they felt comfortable with my style of tutorage was my attitude toward their questions. **They always knew their inquiries were welcomed** at any time, in any amount, in any place. Confucius once remarked, "It is better to ask a question and appear a fool for five seconds, than never ask a question and be a fool the rest of your life." **My staff knew I would readily receive their questions** and would think more of them because they had the courage to ask smartly, rather than remain silent foolishly.

SPECIAL RESEARCH PROJECT

My **lifelong interest in History** led me **to co-author a historical compendium of fascinating information on a church's 100-year history**. I thoroughly enjoy ferreting out unique tidbits of trivia and data that shed new light on a particular topic or situation. This talent has proved useful in inspiring students to look more deeply into a subject matter. Leave no stone unturned.

> **"A page of history is worth a volume of logic."** Oliver Wendell Holmes

VALUE OFFERED TO YOUR INSTITUTION

The value I bring to your establishment is my insatiable curiosity. People who know me best would tell you that I am always asking why. When **informally tutoring employees**, I asked them 10 analytical questions, which served as a catalyst to discovering the facts. Then, as we were working side-by-side creating visual product displays or placing produce in the most appealing manner, **I quizzed them to measure their learning retention. Great fun for them and me!**

CAREER TARGET

After a rewarding career in customer relations management and employee training, I am now ready to share my passion for teaching with students in an academic setting in History, Political Science, Philosophy, or English Literature. After acquiring a Bachelor of Arts degree from the University of New Mexico, I completed 18 months of Graduate studies in Specialized History. Furthermore, I also hold a State of New Mexico Teaching Certificate.

This nontraditional resume, written for a businessman who wanted to apply his years of experience in training and tutoring others to an academic setting, contains just about everything a traditional resume has but is written in narrative style as a combination resume/broadcast letter.

CHAPTER **8**

Resumes for Educational Support Professionals

- Librarians/Interactive Media Directors
- Media Educators
- Substitute Teachers
- School Social Workers
- Admissions Counselors
- Guidance Counselors
- School Psychologists
- School Volunteer Leaders
- Technology Coordinators
- Aides/Program Coordinators

MICHAEL MILLER

458 North Western Avenue, Salt Lake City, UT 84117 • Phone (801) 277-5555
E-mail: mmiller237@hotlink.com

INFORMATION SERVICES LIBRARIAN

PROFILE

Articulate, organized Librarian with over 10 years' experience in all facets of Library Science related work. Expertise in utilizing World Wide Web as a tool for research and analysis. Skilled instructor of various workshops including World Wide Web, The Internet, Electronic Databases, and Bibliographic Software. Excellent presentation skills. Advanced computer literacy.

TECHNICAL SKILLS

- Microsoft Office, Word, Excel and PowerPoint • WordPerfect, Lotus Notes
- NOTIS Library System • Arc View, Photoshop, FrontPage, Unix, HTML
- Internet • Voyager Library System • Verity Search Engine
- LEXIS/NEXIS, OCLC

EDUCATION

Master of Library Science, University of Utah (1995)
Graduate coursework in Sociology, University of Phoenix (1993-1994)
Bachelor of Science in Sociology, Utah College (1992)
- Dean's List
- Received Dawson Scholarship (1989)
School of Library & Information Science, Catholic University (1989)

SPECIAL PROJECTS AND ACCOMPLISHMENTS

- Achieved Above and Beyond Peer Recognition Award for Library Service (1993).
- Presenter at Utah State Library Conference for University of Utah College faculty (1996). Topic: Integrating Technology into the Classroom via the Internet.
- Presenter at Utah Educational Research Association Annual Conference (1995).
- Spearheaded retrospective conversion of U.S. Government Documents for University of Utah Acquisitions Department.
- Pioneered Rio Grande Learning Center for homeless mothers. Managed and directed resource selection, furniture, computer needs, and gathered potential funding resources for materials.

A clever graphic combining a large initial with a book is an eye-catching introduction to this librarian resume. The large headline and brief profile clearly communicate his expertise and career interests.

MICHAEL MILLER   Page 2

(Continued)

PROFESSIONAL EXPERIENCE

Salt Lake City Main Library, Salt Lake City, UT   1995-2001
INTERNET LIBRARIAN
- Collaborated with instructors in teaching specialized topics. Prepared and delivered workshops.
- Coordinated reference queries via phone and electronic mail.
- Managed and directed website development for several websites including creation of intellectual content of SLC Library web pages.
- Wrote documentation for Rio Grande Learning Center and facilitated operation.
- Oversaw support staff in departmental area.

Alderman Library, University of Utah, SLC, UT   1994-1995
REFERENCE LIBRARIAN
- Administered direction and answers to reference questions.
- Created Alderman Library website and consulted on development of web based tutorials.
- Prepared study aids and bibliographies.

Huntsman Library, Provo University, Provo, UT   1992-1994
REFERENCE LIBRARIAN
- Maintained e-mail inquiries in reference to cancer.
- Updated and coordinated cancer reference materials and catalog files.
- Troubleshoot and maintain library equipment.

Science and Engineering Library, University of Utah, SLC, UT   1990-1991
REFERENCE PRACTICUM
- Utilized print, electronic medium and online resources to assist patrons with reference questions.
- Conducted on-site instruction for use of various reference resources.
- Oversaw archives, periodicals and circulation.

Cabal Library, Virginia Commonwealth University, Richmond, VA   1989-1990
REFERENCE LIBRARIAN/WEEKEND COORDINATOR
- Managed supervision and training of student employees in Circulation/Reserve Department.
- Coordinated workflow, shelving, and circulation.
- Handled billing procedures.

PROFESSIONAL AFFILIATIONS

- American Library Association
- Utah Library Association
- Task Force member, Salt Lake City Library and Information Network (1997)

Joan M. Sullivan

121 College Drive

Adams, MI 48000

(734) 555-6412

jsullivan@tdi.net

EDUCATION

Master of Library Science, 1990
MICHIGAN STATE UNIVERSITY, East Lansing, Michigan

Bachelor of Arts in English, 1988
ADAMS COLLEGE, Adams, Michigan

EXPERIENCE

ADAMS COLLEGE, Adams, Michigan
Chief Librarian, 1993-Present
Reference Librarian, 1989-1993

Direct the daily operations of campus library with 66,000 volumes, 300+ periodical titles, and seven staff members. Administer $235,000 annual budget. Determine policies and procedures, and plan goals and objectives for the library. Train and direct workers to receive, shelf, and sort materials, and to assist library patrons in locating materials.

PROFESSIONAL ACHIEVEMENTS

- Converted from manual to electronic catalog system. Patrons and students now have quick access to all publications in the Adams County Library System, as well as the college library. Additionally, this technology reduced staffing requirements, saving approximately $28,000 annually.

- Developed and implemented seminars, "Study Smarter, Not Harder" and "Ace That Research Paper," to help students with their study skills and research techniques. These seminars were so successful that the syllabus is being used as a model to develop similar programs at high schools in Adams County.

- Chairman, Committee for Literacy, 1999-2000 term. Spoke to local television and radio stations on behalf of the committee, enhancing community awareness of illiteracy.

- Established a Reading Tutor Program, which allows English and Education majors to earn credits by tutoring high school students who are behind in their reading skills.

- Coordinated cultural workshops presented by the library on subjects such as Classical Guitar, Blues Guitar, Modern Poetry, and Michigan History.

- Coordinator/editor of <u>Adams College Poetry Anthology</u>, 1992-Present.

This resume shows the dramatic impact of an unusual typestyle and graphic. Other than these elements, the resume is simply formatted in Times New Roman. Note the emphasis on achievements that will set her apart from other candidates.

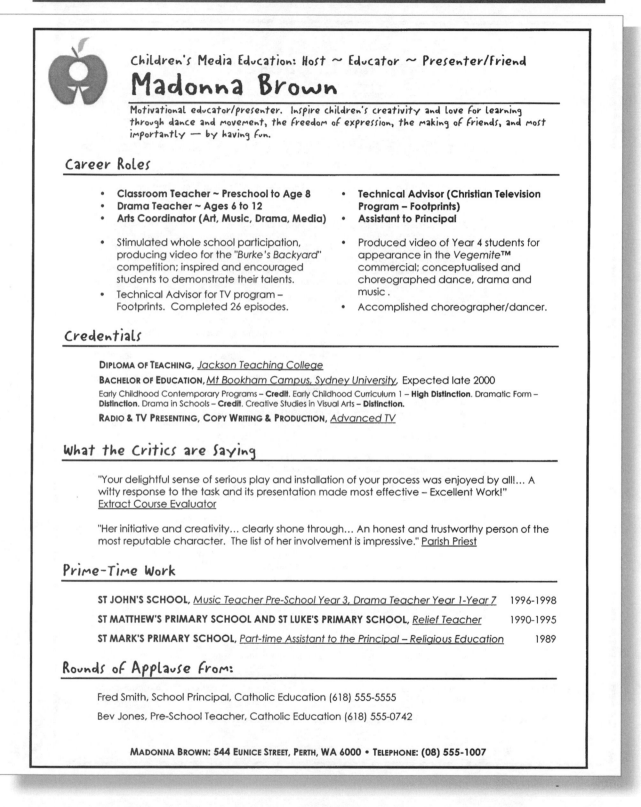

Children's Media Education: Host ~ Educator ~ Presenter/Friend

Madonna Brown

Motivational educator/presenter. Inspire children's creativity and love for learning through dance and movement, the freedom of expression, the making of friends, and most importantly — by having fun.

Career Roles

- Classroom Teacher ~ Preschool to Age 8
- Drama Teacher ~ Ages 6 to 12
- Arts Coordinator (Art, Music, Drama, Media)

- Technical Advisor (Christian Television Program – Footprints)
- Assistant to Principal

- Stimulated whole school participation, producing video for the "Burke's Backyard" competition; inspired and encouraged students to demonstrate their talents.
- Technical Advisor for TV program – Footprints. Completed 26 episodes.

- Produced video of Year 4 students for appearance in the *Vegemite*™ commercial; conceptualised and choreographed dance, drama and music .
- Accomplished choreographer/dancer.

Credentials

DIPLOMA OF TEACHING, *Jackson Teaching College*

BACHELOR OF EDUCATION, *Mt Bookham Campus, Sydney University*, Expected late 2000

Early Childhood Contemporary Programs – **Credit**. Early Childhood Curriculum 1 – **High Distinction**. Dramatic Form – **Distinction**. Drama in Schools – **Credit**. Creative Studies in Visual Arts – **Distinction**.

RADIO & TV PRESENTING, COPY WRITING & PRODUCTION, *Advanced TV*

What the Critics are Saying

"Your delightful sense of serious play and installation of your process was enjoyed by all!... A witty response to the task and its presentation made most effective – Excellent Work!" Extract Course Evaluator

"Her initiative and creativity... clearly shone through... An honest and trustworthy person of the most reputable character. The list of her involvement is impressive." Parish Priest

Prime-Time Work

ST JOHN'S SCHOOL, *Music Teacher Pre-School Year 3, Drama Teacher Year 1-Year 7*	1996-1998
ST MATTHEW'S PRIMARY SCHOOL AND ST LUKE'S PRIMARY SCHOOL, *Relief Teacher*	1990-1995
ST MARK'S PRIMARY SCHOOL, *Part-time Assistant to the Principal – Religious Education*	1989

Rounds of Applause from:

Fred Smith, School Principal, Catholic Education (618) 555-5555

Bev Jones, Pre-School Teacher, Catholic Education (618) 555-0742

MADONNA BROWN: 544 EUNICE STREET, PERTH, WA 6000 • TELEPHONE: (08) 555-1007

This creative resume, written to help a primary school teacher break into children's multimedia education, "marries" the essence of being a performer (dancing, movement, and expression) with television terms such as "prime time" and "what the critics are saying."

Barbara L. Baeker

109 Bonaventure Blvd.
DeLand, Florida 32724
(904) 236-9573
slbaek@mis.net

MISSION

To create, support, and continue a cooperative, stimulating environment that will encourage all children to learn, develop, and succeed.

PROFILE

An enthusiastic and caring educator skilled in building a positive rapport and mutual respect with students. Creates an engaging learning environment featuring thematic units with integrated curriculum, hands-on interactive lessons, and multi-media technology. Structures whole group, small group, and individual instruction to accommodate individual academic levels and learning styles. Encourages parental involvement in the form of home reinforcement and volunteerism.

- Degreed educator with four years of experience teaching children pre-school to grade 12.
- Recognized for superior classroom management techniques.
- Past Director of the Rebecca Caudill Public Library Story Hour program.
- Valuable experience in broad-based, interdisciplinary instruction.
- Contributed to feature article published in Florida's Department Libraries titled *Children's Interactive Program Design*.
- Successfully completed long-term assignment as substitute Librarian assisting pre-school and elementary school students.
- Highly developed written and oral communication skills.
- Self-directed professional, able to work independently or as part of a team.
- Computer literacy includes all popular Microsoft applications and Internet navigation.

EDUCATION

Florida State University – Tallassee, Florida – Dean's List, Magna Cum Laude
Degree awarded – Bachelor of Arts in Education, 1994

State of Florida, Middle School Certification Grades 5 – 8
Social Studies, Language Arts, and Reading, 1994 – 1998

TEACHING EXPERIENCE

1994 – 1998   **DeLand Board of Education**
Substitute Teacher. Assigned to replace staff for both long and short terms. Gained recognition for flexibility, dependability, and organization resulting in much higher than average rate of calls to work. Successfully implemented existing and original lesson plans both inside and outside areas of specialization including library science, language arts, social studies, math, algebra, reading, and art.

COMMUNITY SERVICE

Parent Volunteer, Hendricks Avenue Middle School   1998 – 2000
Volunteer, DeLand Humane Society   1999 – 2000
Den Leader, Boy Scouts of America   1994 – 1998
Volunteer, Salvation Army   1993
Parent Volunteer, Brookview Elementary School   1992 – 1993
Director, Rebecca Caudill Public Library Story Hour Program   1989 – 1991

ADDITIONAL EXPERIENCE

1991 – 1993   **Dexter Real Estate and Insurance Company**
1989 – 1991   **Creech Insurance Agency**
1981 – 1986   **Frazier Insurance Agency**

REFERENCES

Comprehensive portfolio and excellent professional references available on request.

After sending in this resume for a children's librarian position, this individual was called and interviewed the very same week. The book graphic looks particularly attractive printed in color.

Laura Negrete

23373 Moosewood Circle
Deerfield Beach, FL 33433

Phone: (954) 224-2020
Email: Lnegrete@aol.com

Clinical & School Social Worker (LCSW)
Psychotherapist

Adults • Children • Couples • Families • Elderly • Special Ed & Emotionally Disturbed

- Individual & Group Counseling
- Multidisciplinary Staffings & Conferences
- Crisis Intervention
- Family & Teacher Consultation
- Community Resourcing
- Medicare & Medicaid Reporting

- Case Study Coordination
- Social Development Studies
- Child Interviewing
- Psycho-Educational Support Group Leader
- Behavioral Contracting
- Diagnostic Assessment Using DSMIV

PC proficient in Microsoft Word, Lotus, and ClarisWorks (used in schools).

Professional Experience

PSYCHOTHERAPIST   **1998 – Present**
Self-employed, Deerfield Beach, FL

Private social work practitioner serving adult, children, couples, and families in local metro area. Conduct individual therapy sessions with clients. Consult with families to assist emotionally and behaviorally disturbed children. Make service and alternative school placement recommendations to families. Regularly create behavioral contracts for families and children.

- Instrumental in making successful alternative school placement for recent special needs and emotionally disturbed child. Worked extensively with family to ensure child's needs were met within parent's financial constraints.
- Worked successfully with family to place Alzheimer's patient in appropriate nursing facility.
- Provided extensive individual and joint therapy for terminally ill patient and family.
- Currently volunteering on panel to place social workers in the South Florida County schools for *South Florida's Promise – The Alliance for Youth*.

SCHOOL SOCIAL WORKER   **1995 – 1998**
School District A, Chicago, IL

Recruited to serve entire school population (650 students) from K - 8. Conducted group and individual counseling and provided crisis intervention. Served as consultant to teachers and families. Conducted screenings, referrals, and evaluations on regular and special education students. Provided treatment seminars for parents and staff. Developed behavioral plans and developed social developmental studies. Conducted home visits.

- Granted tenure in 1997 for outstanding contributions.
- Developed the following highly successful programs and support groups:
  - *Self-esteem Program* for 2nd and 3rd grade students - Used puppets, stories, and songs to engage students. Program was ultimately duplicated for EMH students.
  - *Peer Mediation Program* - Selected and trained panel of 4-5 students on managing inter-student conflict and delivering consequences.
  - *Divorce Support Group* - Trained teachers to lead student support groups.
  - *Grief Support Group* – Designed program to support children with ill or dying family members.

This effective resume uses key words to emphasize areas of expertise and a combination of paragraph and bullet styles to distinguish accomplishments from responsibilities. The formatting is clean and classic.

Laura Negrete   Page 2 of 2

Field Experience & Internships

EXTERNSHIP   1994 – 1995
Maple Elementary School and Apollo Middle School, Chicago, IL

Provided individual treatment for K – 6 students with behavior disorders and learning disabilities.
Created and facilitated groups with special and regular education students. Collaborated with
multi-disciplinary diagnostic team in screening and staffing. Prepared social developmental
histories and individualized education plans. Administered pre-school screenings and Adaptive
Behavior Scales.

SECOND YEAR FIELD PLACEMENT   1993 - 1994
Family and Community Services, Chicago, IL

Conducted long- and short-term individual, couple, and family therapy. Co-led a single
parent/child support group. Provided crisis intervention, financial counseling, and casework.

FIRST YEAR FIELD PLACEMENT   1991- 1992
Appalachia Mental Health Center, Chicago, IL

Provided long-term and short-term treatment to individuals and couples. Established and co-led
weekly support group for after-care clients. Completed psychosocial assessments.

Education/Certifications/Licenses

Completed Post-Graduate Studies in Social Work
Loyola University, Chicago, IL, 1995, Concentration and Certification in School Social Work

MSW
Loyola University School of Social Work, Chicago, IL, 1994

BA Education (Early Childhood Education Major)
Northeastern Illinois University, Chicago, IL

Licensed Clinical Social Worker (LCSW) in Florida and Illinois

Current Teaching Certificate, K through 9

Type 73 Social Work Certified, Illinois

Continuing Education

Divorce Mediation Institute, 1993 - 40-hour divorce mediation certification program

Loyola University of Chicago Medical Center, Sexual Dysfunction Clinic, 1993
Completed 9-week certification program

Regularly complete 30 hours of continuing education units (CEUs) every 2 years in Florida and
Illinois to maintain LCSW status.

Professional Memberships

- National Association of Social Workers (NASW) – National and Florida Member
- Illinois Association of School Social Workers (IASSW)
- Illinois Society for Clinical Social Work (ISCSW)

Greta Johannsen, M.S.

11815 Junction Lake Boulevard
Eden Prairie, MN 55344 — 320.555.7010

> "Greta is an educational 'welcome wagon' —
> out in the field or within the academic halls.
> Her love for education is contagious among all
> ages and people. She shines as an educator."
> Dr. Gerald Spovin
> MASSCCO President

HIRING ASSETS:

Twelve years' combined experience in college / secondary counseling and admissions roles, complemented by a teaching/coaching background. Sincere commitment to the welfare of the student. Special talent for assessing individual needs. Work cooperatively with students and families, colleagues, and the community.

Competencies: Individual Counseling, Group Counseling, Career Development, Educational Counseling, Measurement and Evaluation, Coordinator of Resources. Admissions. Liaison.

EDUCATION

UNIVERSITY OF MINNESOTA — Minneapolis, MN
M.S. Degree, Applied Psychology; Secondary School Counseling emphasis, 1994
B.E.S. Degree, Emphases: Special Education, Communications, Coaching, 1989

PROFESSIONAL EXPERIENCE

COUNSELING & MENTORSHIP

- Counseled students regarding career, college, and personal choices.
- Guided and implemented career classes for students, grades 9-12.
- Set up and administered standardized testing and advanced placement testing.
- Advised a successful TARGET program.
- Served as Advisor for student IEPs.
- Taught students (K-12) with special needs; coached numerous athletic teams.
- Facilitated groups for career, education, self-esteem and other personal issues.
- Guided freshmen advisees, mentored advising team, and coordinated orientation activities.

ADMISSIONS, PUBLIC SPEAKING & RELATIONSHIP BUILDING

- Recruited students for several colleges through school presentations, informational sessions, and on-campus interviews. Represented collegiate institutions at college fairs.
- Conducted on-site presentations at up to 100 high schools per year regarding post-secondary options.
- MSU Advisory Board, Admissions Student Ambassadors, Interviewed, trained / supervised interns.
- Represented the technical and college system on statewide panels.
- Partnered with college marketing teams; assisted with orientation programs.

CAREER PATH

ANOKA HENNEPIN TECHNICAL COLLEGE — St. Cloud, MN	1998 — present
Admissions Representative	
RIDGEWATER COLLEGE — Hutchinson / Willmar, MN	1997 — 1998
Admissions Representative	
EDEN PRAIRIE HIGH SCHOOL — Eden Prairie, MN	1995 — 1997
Guidance Counselor	
MANKATO STATE UNIVERSITY — Mankato, MN	1989 — 1996
Admissions Representative	
BRECK SCHOOL — Minneapolis, MN	1993 — 1994
Guidance Counselor (Internship)	
MINNEAPOLIS PUBLIC SCHOOLS — Minneapolis, MN	1985 — 1988
Coach / Advisor / Instructor	

PROFESSIONAL LEADERSHIP

- MASSCCO, Minnesota Association of Secondary School Counselors and College Admissions Officers
- NASAA, National Association of Student Activity Advisors
- NACAC, National Association of College Admissions Counselors
- Minnesota School Counselors Association

A strong testimonial, placed prominently in the top-right corner, does a good job of "selling" this individual. Note that her experience is grouped in a functional style, followed by a brief listing of the positions she's held.

S B Steven J. Baker

5836 Woolery Lane
Dayton, OH 45415
Phone: (937) 264-0909

Email: sbaker@prosnet.net

SUMMARY

Seasoned elementary and intermediate school guidance counselor skilled at providing positive direction for students' academic, social, and emotional well being.

- Leader of curriculum tutoring and guidance programs to help students having academic difficulties.
- Creator of new reward, award, and recognition programs as student confidence-builders, subsequently inflating staff morale and promoting a positive atmosphere.
- Active, involved individual participating in numerous student training programs, contributing to academic associations, and upholding high standards of continued education and discipline with students and self.

CAREER SKILLS / KNOWLEDGE

- ❖ Social Block Tutoring
- ❖ Academic Advisement
- ❖ Public Speaking
- ❖ Program Creation / Implementation
- ❖ Testing Standards / Administration
- ❖ Career Counseling

EMPLOYMENT

INSTRUCTOR / OWNER
Dayton Learning Academy, Dayton, OH   2000 – present
Provide educational programs for children: Schedule, administer, and review diagnostic and achievement testing; prepare and design curricula to address specific areas of academic deficiency as well as enhance strengths for personal educational growth; deliver tutoring services for specific subject areas. Monitor and address staffing needs to ensure that qualified, certified tutors are available to meet the academic needs of the learning center and the students.

GUIDANCE COUNSELOR
Monty County Educational Facility, Dayton, OH   1992 – 2000
Addressed academic progress, family dynamic issues, and post-secondary educational student concerns. Provided materials and supplemental resources to students.

- **Plan creation —**
  - ❖ School-Wide Professional Development Plan, Students' Individualized Educational Plans, School Safety Plan, New Student Eligibility Guidelines.
  - ❖ Served on the Building Leadership Team.
- Secured funds for Honor Roll and Birthday ribbons, notified the local press of top student performers, and assisted with Student of the Month Celebrations.
- Scheduled and coordinated in-service critiquing and conferences for administrators, special education staff, teachers, parents, and students and served as an advocate for the benefit of all students.
- Counseled hundreds of elementary students providing daily guidance and counseling for individuals and groups; testing coordination and implementation for grade-level achievement; intervention, writing, and assessment testing.

An eye-catching monogram and diamond-shaped bullets liven up this traditionally formatted resume. Note the key words highlighted in the Career Skills/Knowledge section.

Steven J. Baker   Page Two

FOURTH GRADE TEACHER
Monty County Board of Education, Dayton, OH   1986 – 1992
Taught Basic Social Block (Math, Science, Social Studies, Ohio History) and reading programs. Implemented grade-level curriculum through basal text with trade books; met and exceeded county and state reading guidelines.
- Established a mentoring program, Indian Days, enabling fourth graders to teach and assist kindergarten classes on the academic knowledge gained from the curriculum.
  - Secured donations and materials for an authentic Indian Tribal as a permanently placed structure on school campus.
- **Committee Participation** —
  - Textbook selection committee, HASP Science Training.
  - Served on BLT, BBST.

MEMBERSHIPS / HONORS

Ohio and National Education Associations, *since 1988*
Monty County Reading Association
Ohio Counselor's Association, *since 1995*
Dean's List Auburn University and Troy State University
Monty Area Chamber of Commerce

TRAINING PROGRAMS

Reading Renaissance Training
After-School Tutoring and Discipline Program
Stephen Covey's Seven Habits of Highly Effective People
Play Therapy Training AUM / HASP Training, Monty University
Professional Development Training, Counseling/Education Related Fields
(300+ hrs, 1990-1995 cycle; 900+ hrs, 1995-2001 cycle)

EDUCATION

EDUCATIONAL SPECIALIST
Ohio State University (expected Fall 2002)

MASTER'S, COUNSELING, School Guidance Counseling Certification
Ohio State University, 1994

MASTER'S, EDUCATION
Monty University, 1992

B.S., ELEMENTARY EDUCATION
University of Dayton, 1986

THOMAS C. LANIER

tlanier86@aol.com

1104 East Bel Air Circle
Fox Point, Wisconsin 53112

Cellular: (414) 609-4679
Residence: (414) 353-9854

EDUCATIONAL PSYCHOLOGY PROFILE

A dedicated and creative educational psychologist with professional focus developing and facilitating individual and group sessions for community-based organizations and within school environments. Master of Educational Psychology and completion of comprehensive examination. Proficient using Microsoft Word, Excel, and the Internet. Demonstrated experience in the following areas:

- Program Development
- Classroom Presentations
- Individual & Group Counseling
- Conflict Resolution & Anger Management

- Solution-Based Therapy
- Crisis Intervention & Grief Management
- Family Dynamics
- Multicultural, Diverse Populations

PROFESSIONAL EXPERIENCE

Fox Point Elementary School, Fox Point, Wisconsin   Oct 2000 to Present

Educational Psychologist (Independent Consultant)
Design and implement a new program targeted toward 3rd and 4th grade students: "The Achievers Program." Small groups, meeting twice per week, focus on developing life skills such as motivation, resilience, resourcefulness, goal setting, time management, and decision-making. Mastery of skills evidenced by academic and behavioral improvement.

The Counseling Center of Ozaukee Co., Inc., Mequon, Wisconsin   Oct 1999 to Oct 2000

Prevention Education Coordinator
Developed, organized, and implemented prevention education presentations/activities designed to provide students with information and skills to cultivate and maintain healthy, happy lives. Classroom lessons included self-esteem, decision-making, stress, peer pressure, communication skills, and alcohol/drug avoidance.

YMCA, Milwaukee, Wisconsin   1998

Educational Psychology Intern
Provided individual, family, and children's group counseling to diverse, multicultural population. Developed and facilitated a large group program—Group Works—for children ages 7 through 14. Practiced and strengthened professional counseling skills and increased knowledge and sensitivity in areas of multicultural counseling, dynamics of diverse family compositions, referral networks for community resources, and clinical assessment techniques.

Congress Elementary School, Milwaukee, Wisconsin   1998

Guidance Counseling Intern
Provided individual and small-group counseling sessions and large-group counseling presentations within classroom and guidance office environments. Participated in parent/teacher meetings to discuss and develop emotional and behavioral strategies for students with physical, mental, and emotional challenges.

This is an extremely well-written resume that clearly presents the individual's expertise and broad background in counseling children.

Thomas Lanier Résumé   (414) 353-9854   tlanier86@aol.com   Page 2 of 2

PROFESSIONAL EXPERIENCE (CONTINUED)

Congress Elementary School, Milwaukee, Wisconsin   1998

Volunteer Support Staff
Facilitated in-classroom guidance program (3rd through 5th grade) consisting of anger and grief management, conflict resolution, empathy, and relaxation techniques. Developed program independently using individual creativity and resource materials.

Educational Policy & Community Studies, UW-Milwaukee, Milwaukee, Wisconsin   1996

Program Development Independent Study
Designed an after-school program called "Group Works" that provided an alternative to existing after-school care and incorporated community-mentoring components. Presented program to Boys' and Girls' Club of Ozaukee County, where it was received very positively.

Milwaukee Crisis Center, Milwaukee, Wisconsin   1996

Community Education Intern
Addressed self-esteem, aggression, and anger management issues to preschool and elementary children of cocaine-addicted mothers enrolled in the center's mental health program.

Family After-School Program, Mequon, Wisconsin   1995

Community Education Intern
Observed, participated in, developed, and presented developmentally age-appropriate activities for kindergarten and elementary school.

OTHER EXPERIENCE

Ozaukee Building Products, Inc., Mequon, Wisconsin   1985 to 1995

General Manager
Assisted owner with supervision of employees and business operations of a building supply distributor.

EDUCATION

Master of Educational Psychology, Marquette University—Milwaukee, Wisconsin
- Emphasis: Community Counseling   ■ GPA: 3.87/4.00

Bachelor of Science, Cardinal Stritch University—Milwaukee, Wisconsin
- Emphasis: Educational Policies & Community Studies   ■ GPA: 3.925/4.00

PROFESSIONAL AFFILIATIONS

American Psychological Association, Member

COMMUNITY INVOLVEMENT

- Children in Transition Support Group, Facilitator
- Fox Point School, Classroom Volunteer
- Area Community Center, Parent Education Program Committee Member
- Area Community Center, Campus Management Committee

DIANE A. SMITH

1212 Hacienda Place
Sherman Oaks, CA 91403
818-555-2470 - dianesmith@nownet

Parent Involvement and Volunteer Service Specialist

QUALIFICATIONS:

Parent Involvement:

- Recruited, oriented and encouraged parents to participate in child development programs.
- Assisted in facilitating parent participation in program planning, implementation and evaluation.
- Coordinated, scheduled and wrote materials for parent training in health, mental health, dental and nutrition education.
- Participated with teachers in individual parent conferences to discuss the child's physical, social/emotional and intellectual progress.
- Worked cooperatively with social services, health and handicap component staff to identify and inform parents of available community resources.

Volunteer Services:

- Consulted with administrators and staff to determine the program's need for volunteer services and plans for recruitment.
- Communicated effectively with other community organizations, explaining the Head Start program's activities and role of volunteers.
- Planned, organized and conducted volunteer orientation and training.
- Served as liaison between administration, staff and volunteers.
- Assisted in preparing statistical reports regarding volunteer services.

Management:

- Assisted in planning, organizing and conducting a variety of procedures and activities designed to assess and complete handicap component goals and objectives.
- Organized and established priorities and schedules.
- Established and maintained effective working relationships with adults from diverse ethnic groups.
- Coordinated, scheduled and maintained a staff training calendar.
- Assisted in planning and implementing a cost-effective budget utilizing donated goods and services.

PAGE 1 OF 2

Using a functional format to group qualifications under key areas, this resume presents a strong and cohesive picture of diverse volunteer experience.

DIANE A. SMITH

EDUCATION:

1999   M.A., Education
        Pacific Baptist Theological Seminary, Encino, CA

1992   B.S., Family Relations and Child Development/Early Childhood Education
        University of California at Los Angeles, CA

CERTIFICATION:

California: Preliminary Multiple Subject Credential

Nevada: General Provisional Teacher of Young Children

Provisional Kindergarten and General Provisional Elementary

RELATED PROFESSIONAL HISTORY:

1993-1994   Educational Consultant, Child Study Center, Culver City, CA

1993-1994   Nutritionist Aide, Culver Health Department, Culver City, CA

1993-1994   Kindergarten Teacher, Encino Independent School District, Encino, CA

HONORS:

Scholarships: ESTARL/California; WMU/California; ABWA/Nevada.

MEMBERSHIPS:

American Association of University Women

Yearbook Chairman/Family Life Education Chairman

National Association for the Education of Young Children

International Association for Childhood Education

Melissa Ballentine

2316 Diamond Drive ▪ Ames, IA 50010 ▪ (515) 233-9874 ▪ melib@aol.com

OBJECTIVE: DISTRICT TECHNOLOGY COORDINATOR

PROFILE

Qualified technology instructor with desire to use advanced education in Curriculum and Instructional Technology to promote excellence in the classroom. Proven problem-solving abilities with both students and faculty. Passion for continuing education in the area of technology motivates and excites others.

- Recognized for technological instruction and mentoring.
- Solicited textbooks, software, and supplies to supplement tight budget constraints.
- Wrote successful grant applications for funding.
- Interacted with and developed rapport with diverse population from multicultural backgrounds.

EDUCATION

Ph.D., Curriculum and Instructional Technology, Iowa State University, Ames, IA, 5/01 (anticipated)

M.S., Curriculum and Instructional Technology, Iowa State University, Ames, IA, 5/98
- GPA: 3.69/4.0
- Thesis: *Student usage and perceptions of portable computers: The portable computer learning project*
- Worked full-time to finance education

B.S., Elementary Education, Iowa State University, Ames, IA, 5/95
- Dean's List

EXPERIENCE

Mentoring Program, Iowa State University, Ames, IA, 2/00 – Present
- Tutor faculty members on computer literacy and specific software programs depending on their ever-changing needs.

Teaching Assistant/Research Assistant, Iowa State University, Ames, IA, 8/96 – Present
- Teach computer lab for undergraduate pre-service teachers.
- Install software for Technology in Learning and Teaching Center.
- Provide mentoring, instruction, and computer problem-solving to faculty and students.
- Instruct pre-service teachers on computer incorporation in the classroom.

Tutor, Educational Resources, Ames, IA, 5/96 – Present
- Tutor students of various ages with extended educational needs.

Science Teacher (6th and 8th Grades), Clear Creek Independent School District, Clear Lake, TX, 10/95 – 5/96
- Successfully solicited textbooks, software, and supplies from various vendors; wrote grants for additional funding.

Student Teacher (3rd and 5th Grades), Aldine Independent School District, Houston, TX, 1/95 – 5/95

COMPUTER PROFICIENCY

IBM and Macintosh platforms: Adobe PhotoShop, Microsoft Word, Excel, PowerPoint, Claris FileMaker Pro, Claris Home Page, Hypertext applications, and AVI

This resume, for a young woman with lots of education and enthusiasm but very little experience, uses a shadowed box to showcase her passion for educating others in the area of technology.

LAURA VICARRO
298 Temple Street • Orlando, FL 33221 • 407/555-7070

PROFILE

- Extensive experience gained working with children in private child care and volunteer settings, creating and leading activities that enhance and enrich their lives.
- Background in Social Services that has included department and case management of Public Assistance, Medicaid and Food Stamps programs.
- Management of staff and restaurant operations.
- Diverse skill base that includes exceptional competency in:

Organization	Patience	Customer Service
Interpersonal Relations	Tactfulness & Diplomacy	Dedication
Communication	Confidentiality	Project Management

WORK HISTORY

Cafeteria Aide: GENEVA ELEMENTARY SCHOOL - Geneva, FL   *1996-2001*
- Prepared and served lunch to students, teachers and staff — approximately 500 meals daily. Participated in annual health and nutrition seminars. Trained in all cafeteria functions.

Child Caregiver: SELF-EMPLOYED - Orlando, FL   *1990-1995*
- Provided care in my home to children ages 8 weeks to 10 years on a year-round basis. Led children in organized activities, including art and music. Prepared meals.

Senior Social Welfare Examiner: ORANGE COUNTY, DEPARTMENT OF SOCIAL SERVICES - Orlando, FL
- *[1985-1989]* Promoted to this position reporting directly to the Principal Welfare Examiner. Supervised six welfare examiners and support staff of two with an approximate caseload of 900. Maintained a working understanding of and interpreted state regulations in the management of Public Assistance, Medicaid and Food Stamp programs. Verified accuracy of case documentation. Approved/denied welfare requests. Attended training sessions specific to each program and trained staff.

Social Welfare Examiner
- *[1979-1985]* Managed a caseload of 80+. Determined Medicaid eligibility for individuals requiring long-term care in skilled nursing or health related facilities through interviews with patients and their family members. Interacted with Health Department professionals to monitor care and determine methods of meeting other needs. Visited health facilities to ascertain level of care for recertification. Participated in various training sessions, including abuse identification and awareness.

Manager: CREPES 'N THINGS - Orlando, FL   *1978-1979*
- Oversaw restaurant operations including staff scheduling and supervision, food purchasing, weekly payroll, and food preparation. Assisted with food preparation.

Server: THE WATERFRONT RESTAURANT - Orlando, FL   *1976-1978*

Stocks & Securities Assistant: PEOPLES STATE BANK - Groveland, FL   *1974-1976*
- Provided administrative support to the Trader. Produced purchase orders, communicated with security advisors and liaised with stockbrokers in an environment requiring high levels of timeliness and accuracy.

COMMUNITY INVOLVEMENT

Camp Counselor • Cub Scout Den Mother • Sunday School Teacher • Vacation Bible School Coordinator/Teacher
Organized/Hosted Young Mothers' Program • PTA Member & Parent Volunteer • Youth Group Leader
Church Elder • Church Financial Receipts Secretary • Chaperone, Children's Choir

EDUCATION

Coursework in Sociology and Social Work: University of Central Florida; 1980-1982
Liberal Arts Coursework: University of Orlando; 1972-1974
50 hours earned towards Associate's Degree

This individual used an expansive profile to pull together her diverse work and volunteer experience. Note the inclusion of "soft skills" (patience, tactfulness and diplomacy, confidentiality, dedication) that are important though not easily measured.

NATALIE C. TOPEL

25 Tomkins Way
Las Vegas, Nevada 89117

(702) 222-9411

PROFESSIONAL PROFILE

EDUCATOR / PROGRAM COORDINATOR

✓ Practical training, experience and demonstrated achievements in the areas of:
  - Program Development, Coordination and Implementation
  - Classroom Teaching and Curriculum Development
  - Student Assessment, Evaluation and Mentoring
  - Disadvantaged and Minority Student Services

✓ Superb communication, presentation, coordination, research and problem-solving abilities; interact effectively with people of diverse ethnic/economic backgrounds.

✓ **Verbal/written fluency in Italian and Spanish; conversant in French and Portuguese.**

✓ Proficient with Windows, Microsoft Office, WordPerfect, and SPSS research software.

✓ **Sincerely enjoy motivating students and fostering academic enrichment.**

EDUCATION

WESTERN UNIVERSITY, COLLEGE PARK, INDIANA
Master of Arts: Political Science - August 1998
Thesis: "Political Tolerance to Immigrants in the USA"
Conference Attendance: 1998 International Mentoring Association Conference

DELTA UNIVERSITY at NORTH RIDGE, NORTH RIDGE, INDIANA
Bachelor of Science, with Honors: Sociology major, Political Science minor - May 1992
Grants/Scholarships:
  Peer Mentor Award, Spring 1992
  Indiana Higher Education Award/SSA, Spring 1989
  Indiana University at North Ridge Dean's Scholarship, Spring 1989
  Supplemental Educational Grant, Spring 1989
  Pell Grant, Spring 1989
Memberships and Activities:
  Alpha Kappa Delta International Sociology Honor Society
  The International Host Programs, 1990-92
  Sociology Club, 1989-92
  University Division Peer Mentor Program, 1989-92
  Student Alumni Council, 1991
  Columnist for The Slate (student newspaper), 1990-92
  - Wrote a weekly column focusing on current social issues for the Student Government Association, 1991-92
  - Served as **Senator** and **Parliamentarian** (paid positions)
Honors/Distinctions/Academic Presentations:
  Listed in Who's Who Among Students in American Universities & Colleges, 1992
  Alumni Council Honors (Dean's List), 1991.
  Invited to present "Violence in the American Male" at the 1991 Midwest Student Sociological Conference; presented "The Feminization of Poverty" at the 1990 conference.
  Invited to present "A Political View of Venezuela" at the 1989 International Comparative of Political Science Conference.

To highlight strong academic qualifications and play down limited professional experience, this resume includes an extensive education section on page 1. The Professional Profile includes a lot of information in an easily read format.

NATALIE C. TOPEL

PAID/STIPEND POSITIONS

1993-2000   WESTERN UNIVERSITY, COLLEGE PARK, INDIANA

Program Coordinator — Student Services, Division of Minority Affairs, 1996-00
- Devised and implemented a student survey to determine student study habits, classroom/ learning experiences, and why students were failing classes.
- **Designed and implemented an instructional program, based on the Thriasman Model, which resulted in all program members passing their classes with a grade of B or higher.**
- Planned and coordinated support programs for Math and Science students.
- **Instrumental contributor in writing the grant and related evaluations that led to three more years of funding for the Student Services program.**
- Facilitated freshman orientation programs for students, mentors and staff members.

Upward Bound Program Instructor — Division of Minority Affairs, 1996-98
- Taught a "Multi-cultural Ethnic & Race Relations for the Social and Political Arenas" class to high school students. Developed course curriculum and exams.

Visiting Faculty Liaison — Medieval Institute, 1995
- Received visiting faculty arriving from worldwide locales: distributed room assignments, itineraries and food tickets; assisted with transportation arrangements and special requests; escorted visiting faculty to conferences and special events.

Teaching/Research Assistant and Student Advisor (Graduate Assistantship) — Department of Political Science, 1993-95
- Taught "Introduction to Political Science" one day per week.
- Conducted research — for four professors — pertaining to various topics such as NAFTA, congressional activities, and the economies of South American countries.

1989-1992   DELTA UNIVERSITY at NORTH RIDGE, NORTH RIDGE, INDIANA
Peer Mentor for Freshman Orientation/Student Advisor for Undergraduates
- Interviewed students to ascertain their academic interests and goals; recommended appropriate pre-requisite courses and assisted students with class registration.

Christine A. Corrigan

1400 East Greenwood Drive
Mount Prospect, Illinois 60056
Home: (847) 398-5021
Work: (847) 718-7044

— PROFESSIONAL PROFILE —

- Assist teaching staff of public schools by performing any combination of tasks in classroom.
- Hold Bachelor's Degree in Elementary Education.
- Specialize in Upper Elementary and Junior High Language Arts and Social Studies.
- Excellent skills in identifying educational requirements.
- Dedicated to enthusiastic and dynamic teaching as a means of creating and nurturing a lifelong love of knowledge in children.
- Computer literate. Knowledgeable in Macintosh software, Microsoft Word, Claris Works, spreadsheet, database, and word processing.

— EDUCATIONAL EXPERIENCE —

Wheeling High School, Wheeling, Illinois
Writing Lab Supervisor — August 1977 - Present
Tutor and assist students in the development of writing assignments by checking for grammar, organization, and proper mechanics using computer software programs. Also train faculty in the use of new software computer programs.

District 214, Arlington Heights, Illinois
Summer School Coordinator — June 1997 - August 1997
Communicated and trained school personnel on summer school procedures, data entry, and word processing.

John Hersey High School, Arlington Heights, Illinois
Summer School Clerk — May 1996 - August 1996
Registered students, processed attendance, and communicated with staff, administrators, and parents.

Barrington Middle School, Barrington, Illinois
Student Teacher — August 1995 - December 1995
Developed thematic unit, used Reading / Writing Workshop Program, participated in staff meetings to assess students, participated in Parent / Teacher conferences, involved in team teaching, attended school board meetings, and supervised class field trips.

Olympia Middle School, Stanford, Illinois
Intern — March 1995 - April 1995
Worked with 30 students in eighth grade classroom. Developed and taught Language Arts unit, observed students' behavior, and assisted students individually.

This individual is qualified for a broad variety of education-related jobs and uses a Professional Profile to detail her relevant qualifications. The pencil-shaped bullets and informal headline font give this resume an appropriate playfulness.

CHAPTER 9

Resumes for University Educators

- College and University Faculty
- Adjunct Faculty
- Clinical Instructors
- University Education Coordinators

HARRY LEE MORRISON

235 Round-About Way ➤ Pacific Beach, California 90245

hlm@ucsd.org
858.525.3269

CAREER OVERVIEW

Innovative educator skilled in building positive rapport with students and colleagues. Experienced in teaching at the secondary and college level. Proficient in developing effective and innovative curriculum and authentic assessment models. Demonstrated leadership ability with capacity to align groups in whole system change. Specialize in developing outdoor/experiential programming to foster individual and group learning. Experience working in multicultural environments. Develop, direct, and implement programs focused on assisting students to recognize their ability to succeed. A master team builder and team sports coach.

SELECTED ACCOMPLISHMENTS

➤ Key member of team that created charter high school proposal including developing philosophy, curricula, and teaching methods.

➤ Coordinated teaching and learning activities with local charter school in successful partnering enterprise.

➤ Recipient of grant for designing a curriculum activities project for Mira Costa College's Community Resource Center.

➤ Co-developed and taught Gender-Responsible Leadership course to students.

KEY QUALIFICATIONS

➤ Effective **teaching, advising,** and **assessment** skills in an academic setting.

➤ Ability to create **innovative programs** and conduct support workshops for colleagues and students to maximize performance outcome.

➤ **organizational development skills** including whole systems, redesign, strategies, planning, process reengineering, and total quality management.

➤ **Proactive leadership skills,** positive coaching and motivational practices.

➤ Strong **interpersonal relations,** effective oral and written **communication abilities.**

➤ **Decision-making skills** and problem-solving capabilities.

CREDENTIALS

CALIFORNIA DEPARTMENT OF EDUCATION   1995
   STANDARD SECONDARY TEACHING CERTIFICATE

EDUCATION

UNIVERSITY OF CALIFORNIA, SAN DIEGO   San Diego, CA
   ED.D.: Educational Leadership and Change   March 1998
   MASTER OF ARTS DEGREE: Human and Organizational Development   March 1997

UNIVERSITY OF SAN DIEGO   San Diego, CA
   BACHELOR OF ARTS DEGREE: Secondary Education and Social Studies   1995

PORTLAND COMMUNITY COLLEGE   Portland, OR
   Liberal Arts   1992

COMMUNITY AFFILIATIONS

CENTRAL SAN DIEGO COUNTY YOUTH	Current	San Diego, CA
Key member of sub-committee, designing programs directed at teen-related health and education issues.		
BIG BROTHERS/BIG SISTERS ORGANIZATION	1996 to 1998	San Diego, CA
Volunteer		
SAN DIEGO COUNTY HEALTH DEPARTMENT	Summer 1995	San Diego, CA
Youth Tobacco Educator		

This resume for an experienced university educator combines many elements of the traditional CV with sections such as Career Overview, Selected Accomplishments, and Key Qualifications that are typically used in resumes.

EXPERIENCE

UNIVERSITY OF CALIFORNIA AT SAN DIEGO — San Diego, CA
FACULTY - Education Department — 1998 to current
➤ Education Coordinator for Skyview Charter School — official "lab school" for education students.
➤ Courses taught: Curriculum Design, Educational Psychology, Small Group Dynamics.
➤ Proficient at cross-curriculum instruction.
➤ Work closely with students in setting personal and academic goals.

FACULTY - Adventure Education Department — 1996 to 1998
➤ Courses taught: Foundations of Adventure Education, Outdoor Education and Recreation, Alpine Mountaineering, Backcountry Skiing, Gender Responsible Leadership.
➤ Taught outdoor leadership, technical and education skills.

TOP PERFORMERS — Colorado Springs, CO
TEAM BUILDING FACILITATOR — 1998 to current
➤ Design and implement action programming for corporations and organizations.
➤ Facilitate and support the client's learning objectives.
➤ Analyze performance outcomes and apply situational interventions that enhance group problem solving capacity.

CHULA VISTA UNIFIED SCHOOL DISTRICT — Chula Vista, CA
SUBSTITUTE TEACHER — 1995 to 1996
➤ Prepared materials in accordance with lesson plans, improvised creatively when no lesson plans were available; effectively maintained a positive learning environment.

CAHUILLA INDIAN RESERVATION — Anza, CA
INSTRUCTOR — Summer 1994
➤ Designed and taught a summer education program; created a culturally relevant, interdisciplinary curriculum; coordinated educational outdoor trips.

OUTWARD BOUND SCHOOL — Portland, OR
CHIEF INSTRUCTOR for Alpine Mountaineering Courses — 1990 to 1993
➤ Developed and implemented safe adventure, outdoor learning experiences and curriculum for urban, at-risk students in the Cascade Mountains.
➤ Trained, directed and monitored staff, coordinated land agency permits, and facilitated employee meetings.

PROFESSIONAL DEVELOPMENT

Continuing Education/Workshops/Seminars
➤ Assessment and Instruction: Infusing Brain Research, Multi-Intelligences, Learning Styles, and Mind Styles — Phoenix, Arizona, February 1999
➤ Whole System Change in Education — San Diego, CA, November 1998
➤ The Hendricks Institute: Corporate Transformation Training — Santa Barbara, CA, October 1996
➤ Covey Leadership Center: First Things First: Leadership Training — San Francisco, CA, August 1996
➤ Teaching to ADHD students — San Diego, CA, March 1995
➤ Integrated Thematic Instruction — San Diego, CA, September 1994

Presenter/Trainer
➤ UCSD Senior Management Team: Presenter: System Thinking and Organizational Change — San Diego, CA, 1998
➤ Association for Experiential Education Conference: Presenter Relationship as Hero: A New Approach to Outdoor Leadership — San Diego, CA, 1997

HARRY LEE MORRISON
- page two -

235 Round-About Way ➤ Pacific Beach, California 90245
hlm@ucsd.org ➤ 858.525.3269

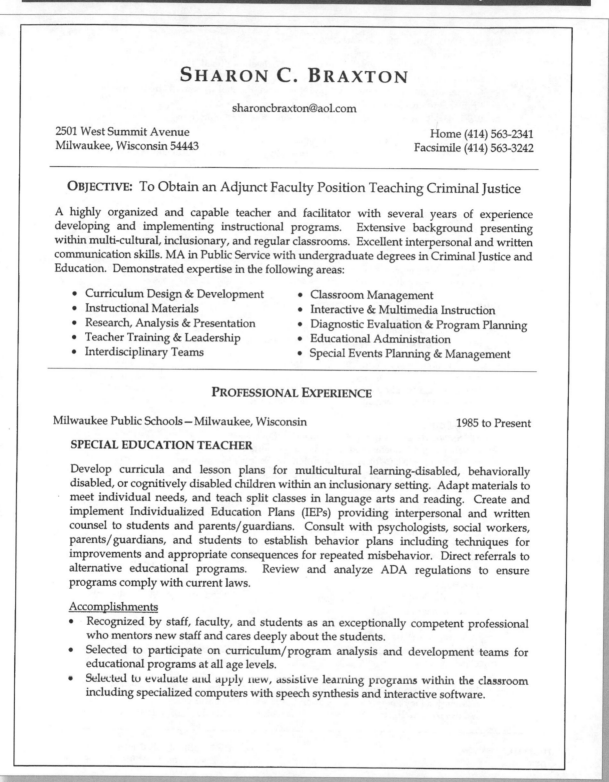

SHARON C. BRAXTON

sharoncbraxton@aol.com

2501 West Summit Avenue
Milwaukee, Wisconsin 54443

Home (414) 563-2341
Facsimile (414) 563-3242

OBJECTIVE: To Obtain an Adjunct Faculty Position Teaching Criminal Justice

A highly organized and capable teacher and facilitator with several years of experience developing and implementing instructional programs. Extensive background presenting within multi-cultural, inclusionary, and regular classrooms. Excellent interpersonal and written communication skills. MA in Public Service with undergraduate degrees in Criminal Justice and Education. Demonstrated expertise in the following areas:

- Curriculum Design & Development
- Instructional Materials
- Research, Analysis & Presentation
- Teacher Training & Leadership
- Interdisciplinary Teams

- Classroom Management
- Interactive & Multimedia Instruction
- Diagnostic Evaluation & Program Planning
- Educational Administration
- Special Events Planning & Management

PROFESSIONAL EXPERIENCE

Milwaukee Public Schools — Milwaukee, Wisconsin   1985 to Present

SPECIAL EDUCATION TEACHER

Develop curricula and lesson plans for multicultural learning-disabled, behaviorally disabled, or cognitively disabled children within an inclusionary setting. Adapt materials to meet individual needs, and teach split classes in language arts and reading. Create and implement Individualized Education Plans (IEPs) providing interpersonal and written counsel to students and parents/guardians. Consult with psychologists, social workers, parents/guardians, and students to establish behavior plans including techniques for improvements and appropriate consequences for repeated misbehavior. Direct referrals to alternative educational programs. Review and analyze ADA regulations to ensure programs comply with current laws.

Accomplishments
- Recognized by staff, faculty, and students as an exceptionally competent professional who mentors new staff and cares deeply about the students.
- Selected to participate on curriculum/program analysis and development teams for educational programs at all age levels.
- Selected to evaluate and apply new, assistive learning programs within the classroom including specialized computers with speech synthesis and interactive software.

The strengths of this resume are its attractive, highly readable format, comprehensive list of key words, and emphasis on accomplishments as well as responsibilities.

SHARON C. BRAXTON résumé   sharoncbraxton@aol.com   Page 2 of 2

PROFESSIONAL EXPERIENCE (continued)

University of Wisconsin Milwaukee—Milwaukee, Wisconsin   1995 to Present

EDITORIAL ADMINISTRATIVE ASSISTANT

Assist editor (Professor John Kindberg) of the *Teaching Special Education Professional Journal* with pre- and post-publication activities. Solicit throughout professional community for articles. Receive articles and submit manuscripts for peer review. Prepare journal for publication.

EDUCATION

MASTER OF ARTS IN PUBLIC SERVICE (specialty Administration of Justice)   2000
Marquette University—Milwaukee, Wisconsin

BACHELOR OF SCIENCE IN CRIMINAL JUSTICE (National Dean's List 1995)   1995
University of Wisconsin—Milwaukee, Wisconsin

BACHELOR OF ARTS IN EDUCATION   1978
Mississippi State University, Jackson, Mississippi

TECHNOLOGY SKILLS

Proficient with Microsoft Word, Excel, and PowerPoint—Windows and Macintosh

COMMUNITY ACTIVITIES

Black Women's Network—Co-Chair & Committee Head for Annual Recognition Award Dinner
Miss Black Wisconsin Scholarship Pageant—Recruiter & Mentor for program participants
St. Cecilia's-Lakeside—Tutor & Mentor for underprivileged children

PUBLICATIONS AND RESEARCH PROJECTS

- "The Impact of the Use of Advanced Technology in the Criminal Justice System," August 2000. Independent Research Project.
- "Pseudofamilies in Prison: Advantages and Disadvantages," June 2000. Correctional Management and Policy Analysis.
- "Project S.T.O.R. (Schools Teaching Options for Reconciliation) Proposed Evaluation," May 2000. Research, Program Planning, and Evaluation in Criminal Justice.
- "The State of Incarceration: Where We Are Today," July 1999. Independent Research Project.

JESSICA L. O'HARA
5725 OAK STREET
RALEIGH, NC 34874
(919) 544-9175

PROFILE

Successful health care professional with administrative competence and over sixteen years of hands-on experience in patient-driven environments. Self-motivated and positive attitude to meet or exceed goals as a team member and in the team leader role. Organized, detail-minded problem solver. Excellent analytical skills with the ability to develop and implement new programs. More than seven years of demonstrated clinical instruction expertise.

PROFESSIONAL EXPERIENCE

TEACHING

CLINICAL INSTRUCTOR   August 1992 – Present
SOUTHEASTERN TECHNICAL COLLEGE, Raleigh, NC
Coordinate full clinical and didactic instruction for 72 students at one out-of-state and four in-state colleges using a live interactive television curriculum.

Areas of Responsibility
- Participate as a member of a self-directed work team that provides administrative responsibility for the entire shared program model.
- Use surveys and evaluation tools to determine retention, employer feedback, program graduate competencies, and student performance.
- Develop curriculum and effective teaching techniques for distance education instruction.
- Explore new partnerships with other colleges to provide dental hygiene instruction across the country with a goal of providing instruction to learners where there is a shortage of qualified dental hygienists.
- Serve as a consultant to the American Dental Association Commission of Dental Accreditation.
- Seek out grant opportunities and write effective grants.

Teaching Assignments

1998 – 2000	Periodontology 2/Clinic 3, Lead Instructor, Dental Hygiene Transition Into Practice, Dental Hygiene Advisory Committee
1997 – 1998	Periodontology 2/Clinics 2 & 3, Lead Instructor, Dental Hygiene Transition Into Practice, Dental Hygiene Student Club Advisor
1995 – 1997	Periodontology 2/Clinics 2 & 3, Lead Instructor, Dental Practice Management, Dental Hygiene Student Club Advisor
1994 – 1995	Periodontology 2/Clinical Dental Hygiene
1993 – 1994	Oral Anatomy & Histology/Clinical Dental Hygiene
1992 – 1993	Dental and Oral Anatomy/Clinical Dental Hygiene (Curriculum merger with Oral Histology)
1992	Spring Clinical Dental Hygiene (volunteer basis)

For this educator, detailed listings of professional-development courses are important to show she is up-to-date in the field. The Profile describes an accomplished individual with broad areas of expertise.

JESSICA L. O'HARA
Page 2 of 3

PROFESSIONAL EXPERIENCE – *Continued*

CLINICAL EXPERIENCE ———————————————————————————————

DENTAL HYGIENIST   July 1986 – Present
- ROBERT NORTHFORK, D.D.S. (1996 – present, summer vacations)
- FAMILY DENTAL ASSOCIATES, GLEN BRENNER, D.D.S.
  DENNIS HAMPTON, D.D.S., M.S. (1987 – 1997)
- KLEIN DENTAL OFFICES, ADRIAN KLEMP III, D.D.S. (1992 – 1994)
- PEDIATRIC DENTAL CLINIC OF ASHEVILLE,
  GENE REDDING, D.D.S., M.S. (1988 – 1991)
- SOJKA DENTAL CLINIC, PAUL SOJKA, D.D.S. (1986 – 1987)

EDUCATION

MASTER OF SCIENCE – VOCATIONAL EDUCATION, December 1996
UNIVERSITY OF WISCONSIN – STOUT, Menomonee, WI

BACHELOR OF SCIENCE – BIOLOGY, December 1991
UNIVERSITY OF WISCONSIN – STEVENS POINT, Stevens Point, WI

ASSOCIATE OF APPLIED SCIENCE – DENTAL HYGIENE, May 1986
SOUTHEASTERN TECHNICAL COLLEGE, Raleigh, NC

PROFESSIONAL DEVELOPMENT
- How to be an Effective Team Leader, May 2000
- International Alliance for Learning (Presenter): Annual Conference on Accelerated Learning and Teaching, Atlanta, GA, January 2000
- Assessing and Improving Learning: Staying on the Right Track, WTCS Conference on Assessment, November 1999
- ADA CODA Site Visit, April 1999
- St. Louis Community College Consultant Visit, Forest Park, July 1999
- WEAC – Brain-Based Learning, IPD/QUEST Conference, Eric Snyder, February 1999
- WTCS/WIDS Online Learning Project, Intralearn Training, Phil Mecagni, February 1999
- International Alliance for Learning: Annual Conference on Accelerated Learning and Teaching, Houston, TX, January 1999
- Appointment beginning October 1998, American Dental Association Council on Dental Accreditation – Dental Hygiene Program Site Examiner
- Central Regional Dental Testing Service (CRDTS) Faculty Calibration, June 1998
- American Association of Dental Schools, Poster Presentation, Minneapolis, MN, March 1998
- Consortium of Community Colleges Workshops, Ann Arbor, MI, November 1997
- SETC, Dental Hygiene Program – Lotus Learning Space Workshop, May 1998
- SETC, Dental Hygiene Program – Accelerated Learning Workshop, May 1997
- SETC, Dental Hygiene Program – Teamwork, Communication Workshop, May 1996
- Numerous professional development workshops and seminars, 1992 – 1996

JESSICA L. O'HARA
Page 3 of 3

CERTIFICATIONS

- WTCS Certification, May 2001
- State of North Carolina Local Anesthesia Certificate, January 2000
- State of North Carolina Dental Hygiene License, August 1986 – Current
- American Heart Association, CPR certification, 1984 – Current
- Mentoring/Professional growth calibration for clinical instruction

AREAS OF SPECIAL COMPETENCE

- Periodontics
- Pedodontics
- Comparative Anatomy
- Vocational Education
- Physiology
- Microbiology
- Histology
- Biochemistry
- Ethics
- Jurisprudence
- CPR Certified
- Alternative Delivery/Methodology

CONTINUING DENTAL HYGIENE EDUCATION COURSES

- Anti-Infective Periodontal Therapy Seminar, April 2000
- Local Anesthesia Training, Waukesha County Technical College, November 1999
- PerioChip Usage, Techniques and Placement, October 1999
- Pharmacology Update for the Dental Team, September 1999
- Empowering the Dental Team to Deliver Quality Periodontal Care, S. Low, March 1999
- Periodontal Therapy for a New Millennium, Driscoll, November 1998
- Periodontal Update and Treatment Strategies, Driscoll, University of Minnesota, April 1998
- Numerous continuing dental hygiene education courses, 1986 – 1998

References upon Request

Michael J. Smith

4321 Storm Barn Way
Morgantown, WV 26501
(304) 555-5512
Email: mjsmith@hotmail.com

Career Profile

University Level Telecommunications Instructor / Distance Education Coordinator

**Media Relations ◈ Radio/Studio Production ◈ Project Management
Computers ◈ State-of-the-Art Telecommunications Equipment**

Results-oriented telecommunications instructor able to orchestrate and manage challenging projects—providing quality instruction and training. Chaired major projects on campus introducing the university to the benefits of distance education, web-based learning, and a radio station.

Professional Experience

Distance Education Coordinator & Telecommunications/Journalism Instructor
West Virginia University, Morgantown, West Virginia   1992 to 2001

Distance Education Coordinator—Title III Distance & Continuing Education Program
- Successfully implemented a Distance Education Learning program from the ground floor. Created a marketing initiative to convince teachers that distance education would greatly enhance their work using cutting-edge technology.
- Consulted with faculty and staff to develop web and video-based curriculum. Guided development of web and video-based courses and programs.
- Effectively trained faculty on techniques and methodologies of web-based curriculum development and telecourse video instruction. Operated high-tech equipment to tape/transmit courses.
- Reviewed and recommended current off-the-shelf web development products and telecourses.
- Co-Chaired the Campus Information Technology Committee.

Full-Time Instructor
- Taught 12 credits a semester to sophomores, juniors, and seniors: News Writing and Reporting, Broadcast Management, Television Production and Programming, Introduction to Radio Production and Programming, and Television Performance. Developed curriculum and class syllabi and administered tests.
- Academic advisor for 12 assigned students each semester.
- Editor of the departmental newsletter *Views,* 1994 to 1999.
- Faculty Coordinator of the campus closed-circuit Media Center. Faculty Advisor to campus media organization. Supervised the campus television weekly newscast.

Because this individual was most interested in distance education, he emphasized this in the profile and led off the Professional Experience section with the most relevant of his activities and accomplishments.

Michael J. Smith   Page 2

Project Manager/Student Radio Station

- Envisioned, created, built, equipped, and completed the first-ever university campus radio station (WHWK-AM) to serve the student population.

- Received a budget of $160K and coordinated all phases of the project including initial planning, design, building renovation, equipment procurement, and installation. The project took 10 months to complete and the radio station is fully operational with three studios—one digital and two analog. Trained student programmers and announcers.

Media Arts Instructor

Ohio State University, Columbus, Ohio   Summer 1996

- Faculty liaison for the Ohio State University Committee for the Olympic Games. Taught courses and directed media-based instruction for student participants in the OSU-Host Broadcast Training Program—designed to employ student workers in fulfilling the International Broadcast of the 1996 Summer Olympic Games.

Technical Skills

Adult Learning Programs/Development & Delivery	PowerPoint	Multimedia Distance
Education Tools Web Course Development Software	WebCT	Microsoft FrontPage 98
Closed-Circuit Cable Transmission	HTML	Microwave Link Satellite
Windows NT System	T1 Lines	Picture-Tel
Microsoft Word	CUseeMe	

Education

Master of Arts in Broadcast Journalism, University of California, 1991
Internship: Assistant Photographer, Gary News Service
Bachelor of Arts in Communications, Ohio State University, 1988

Notable Awards

Outstanding Man of the Year, Men in Communications, 1994

EVELYN A. REYER

5300 Spring Mountain Road
Las Vegas, Nevada 89146

(702) 222-9411
evelynreyer@aol.com

PHYSICAL EDUCATION TEACHER
with special expertise in Adaptive Physical Education (APE)

PROFILE

✓ Graduate degree, ten years' experience, and demonstrated competencies in: Curricula Development ... Course Evaluation ... Program Design/Implementation ... Student Advocacy and Counseling ... Marketing/Networking/Community Resourcing ... Recruiting and Supervising Program Volunteers ... Sports Team Coaching.

✓ Outstanding facilitation, presentation, research, needs assessment, and organizational skills; effectively interact with and support faculty, administration, and students.

PROFESSIONAL EXPERIENCE

1994-2000   RED MOUNTAIN UNIVERSITY, REDLANDS, CALIFORNIA
Physical Education Instructor

Taught Beginner, Intermediate, and Super Circuit Weight Training as well as Adaptive Physical Education (APE) courses, i.e., Adaptive Fitness and Sports Education.

✓ Developed course descriptions, curricula, written exams, and schedules.

✓ Taught, motivated, and evaluated students; prepared IEPs; arranged for additional assistance and intervention as deemed necessary.

✓ Liaised with local rehabilitation centers, advocacy groups, and community organizations to increase APE program awareness.
— Successfully cultivated and recruited new students.
— Designed educational literature and marketing materials.

✓ Wrote and implemented the APE peer tutor training manual; recruited, scheduled, trained, and supervised 30+ volunteer peer tutors.

✓ As member of the Disabled Student Services Committee:
— Served as an APE Program Liaison and Student Advocate.
— Delivered presentations to the college administration regarding program results and augmentation.

✓ As member of the Physical Education Committee:
— Participated in developing and improving physical education curriculum.
— Researched, reviewed, and incorporated federal funding regulations and the latest APE information into programs and procedures.

Page 1 of 2

This resume for a college-level physical education instructor is extremely readable, thanks to a large, clear typeface and well-organized layout.

EVELYN A. REYER

1990-1993   GRAMBLE COMMUNITY COLLEGE, REDLANDS, CALIFORNIA
Assistant Coach — Women's Basketball Team

✓ Coordinated game schedules, developed strategies, and monitored students' academics.

✓ Counseled students in academic and personal issues.

EDUCATION

FRESNO STATE UNIVERSITY, FRESNO, CALIFORNIA
Master of Arts: Physical Education; Adaptive Phys. Ed. Specialty — 1993

RED MOUNTAIN UNIVERSITY, REDLANDS, CALIFORNIA
Bachelor of Arts: Physical Education; Adaptive Phys. Ed. Specialty — 1990

VOLUNTEER ACTIVITIES

FRESNO STINGRAYS, FRESNO, CALIFORNIA
Head Coach — Wheelchair Basketball Team, 1990 to 1992

✓ Instructed and motivated team members.

✓ Scheduled season practices, games, and transportation.

ROBERT PARISI

540 Hawthorne Street, Apt. 5C, Tarrytown, NY 10591   (914) 555-1234
rparisi@westnet.com   fax (914) 777-4321

SUMMARY

- Goal: A challenging teaching position utilizing my advanced education and 13 years of experience contributing to a liberal arts college setting.
- Qualified by demonstrated competencies in teaching, writing, research, customer service, and international relations.
- Specialize in the influence of international politics on commerce and finance. Strong interest in Middle Eastern studies and oil politics.
- Conversant in Spanish. Ability to read Spanish, Italian, Romanian, Portuguese, and French.
- Formal diversity/multicultural training.

EDUCATION

Master of Arts, History   2000
New York University, New York, NY
GPA: 3.9, President's List Honors

Certificate in International Affairs   2000
New York University, New York, NY

Bachelor of Arts, Education/Social Studies   1982
Marymount College, Tarrytown, NY

RELATED EXPERIENCE

Adjunct Professor of History   2001-Present
Iona College, New Rochelle, NY

- Teach a weekly class in American History.

Guest Lecturer   1996-1998
Marymount College, Tarrytown, NY

- Delivered class lectures in West European and Middle Eastern History. Consistently invited by colleagues because of graduate studies and known interest in these subjects.
- Authored prospectus for History 254, "Geopolitics of the Modern Middle East."
- Advised History Department on new classes upon request.

Teacher   1985
Carnegie High School, New York, NY

- Taught five classes of Economics and Honors History (Western Civilization and American). Prepared students to pass Regents examinations.

Note the Related Experience section on page 1 that allows this individual to put his strongest experience front-and-center while relegating less-relevant experience to page 2.

ROBERT PARISI   PAGE TWO

ADDITIONAL PROFESSIONAL EXPERIENCE

Bursar   1987-2001
Marymount College, Tarrytown, NY

- Managed 1000+ accounts averaging $7,000,000 USD annually. Accounts tripled during tenure.

- Expanded billing program to accommodate increased enrollment, new academic offerings, and the addition of summer and music programs for the community at-large.

- Fostered an environment where students and families could discuss educational financing, payment plans, and options.

- Introduced processes and systems to improve service: Coordinated pro-rated billing for ESL students and streamlined registration for the returning education program.

- Served as the primary liaison among the college, students, and their sponsors. This often required communication with embassies, consulates, international banks, and corporate sponsors.

- Supervised and trained student workers in the practices of the business office.

- Facilitated communication among the administration, registrar, and financial aid. Ensured seamless transitions during Business Office staff changes. Prepared and delivered presentations as required.

- Initiated increased involvement in campus life as member of committees for new academic programs. Contributed understanding of the impact of program changes on billing.

- Edited the college catalog annually and the staff handbook as needed.

Account Manager   1986-1987
Marine Midland Bank, White Plains, NY (now HSBC)

- Managed international purchases and cardholder accounts. Management implemented suggestion that these accounts be treated separately for improved customer service.

- Investigated and analyzed cardholder queries to provide resolution of issues.

- Researched account histories for the security department.

- Composed internal and external correspondence for the department.

Researcher   1985-1986
Citibank, N.A., New York, NY

- Prepared Letters of Credit based on research using the department's microfilm library.

- Researched transactions and queries on Letters of Credit and Foreign Exchange.

- Communicated with banks in Europe and Africa to document and process drafts/checks to be cleared by the Federal Reserve Bank of New York.

CURRENT MEMBERSHIPS

Celtic League American Branch   1989-Present
West Hampton Historical Society   1996-Present

Susan T. Shields, M.S.N., D.A.C.B.F.N.

90 Merriam Drive • Fairfield, CT 06430
Phone: 203/975-2009

NURSING MANAGEMENT PROFESSIONAL

Nursing Instruction & Teaching • Program Management • HR & Administration

Master's-prepared genetics/perinatal nurse offering 20+ years' clinical management experience and extensive qualifications for a teaching/nursing faculty, health services program management, or human resources/administrative position. Team-based leader with proven ability to drive forward process improvement and organizational change to achieve common goals. Extraordinary communication and listening skills; highly self-motivated and tenacious in completing projects. Demonstrated expertise in:

- Nursing Management/Administration
- Pediatric, Obstetrical & Neonatal Nursing
- Family Advocacy & Bereavement Counseling

- Nursing Instruction, Teaching & Mentoring
- Program Development & Management
- Health Promotion & Preventative Health Issues

EDUCATION & CREDENTIALS

M.S.N., Perinatology and Genetics, Summa Cum Laude
University of New York – New York, NY – 1992

B.S.N., Nursing, Magna Cum Laude
University of Connecticut – Hartford, CT – 1979

A.S., Nursing
Webster Community College – Chicago, IL – 1974

B.S., Sociology/Psychology/Social Work
Central Illinois University – Deerfield, IL – 1971

Certifications & Licensing

Clinical Nurse Specialist (CNS), Perinatology and Genetics
Certification and Diplomate, American College Board of Forensic Nursing (DACBFN)
Certified Basic Life Support Instructor (BLSI) • Certified Bereavement Counselor and Coordinator
Connecticut Nursing License #098765 • New York Nursing License #256430

PROFESSIONAL HIGHLIGHTS

Teaching & Nursing Instruction/Patient & Staff Education

- Instructed nurse interns in a classroom setting for the past 12 years, teaching courses and lecturing on neonatal genetics, maternity unit care, and neonatal grief counseling. Facilitated nursing students' learning and coordinated patient-care activities in collaboration with nursing faculty members.
- Spearheaded funding and development of an in-service training program covering issues involved in supporting parents coping with death of an infant or birth of a severely physically challenged infant.
- Performed pre-JCAHO inspection of educational programs; isolated areas for improvement and recommended changes that enhanced quality of staff orientation and patient educational counseling.
- Served as educational staff development officer; exceeded goals and achieved 95% compliance in an in-service and skill verification program for medical staff at an internal medicine clinic. Researched and briefed nurse educators on disease management and preventative clinical care strategies.
- Fielded thousands of urgent care and triage telephone calls on a medical triage line serving a population of 30,000+. Instructed patients in appropriate self-care techniques; measurably improved resource management and decreased patient care costs $50,000 in just 7 months.

This resume for an experienced nurse/educator includes teaching experience on page 1 because that is her career target. If she were interested in a nurse manager position, she could easily swap the order of her experience.

Susan T. Shields, M.S.N., D.A.C.B.F.N.   Page 2

Nursing Management & Administration

- Led a 30-person staff of RNs and technicians in a regional referral, high-risk neonatal intensive-care/newborn nursery serving 80-100 infants each month. Attained recognized status as a level III NICU. Oversaw 18 nurses/providers in an internal medicine clinic with 2,500 outpatients each month.

- Directed, supervised, and evaluated medical technician/nursing staffs composed of up to 22 medical professionals on obstetrical units with up to 5 labor rooms, 33 postpartum beds, and 20 cribs, handling an average 2,000 deliveries annually and coordinating care with 12 providers.

- Cost-effectively managed budgets exceeding $160,000 annually and state-of-the-art medical equipment valued at more than $490,000. Investigated and devised cost saving initiatives, including a low-tech infant security system that saved $68,000 by eliminating the need for specialized equipment.

- Planned, implemented, evaluated, and directed delivery of high-quality, cost-effective nursing services for 1,200 pediatric patients monthly. Executed quality improvement initiatives and developed comprehensive operating guidelines for all patient care, ensuring focus on preventative care.

- Initiated and headed development of cutting-edge programs, including a grief support and outreach program, breast cancer awareness luncheon, and a working group concerned with Advanced Directives and Durable Power of Attorney for patients. Led development of associated policies and procedures.

- Contributed to the development and implementation of process and quality improvement initiatives based on quantitative and qualitative data collected as a member of several multidisciplinary committees, including the Utilization/Quality Management, Infection Control, and Health Promotion Committees.

- Coordinated the smooth relocation of an obstetrical unit and the subsequent assimilation of a second obstetrical/infant care and neonatal intensive care unit. Developed policies to meet quality of care standards. Created a staff orientation program that eased the transition and improved morale.

CAREER HISTORY

U.S.A.F. Adams Medical Facility, Adams A.F.B., MI, 1996 – Present
Medical Telephone Triage Nurse (Feb 2000 – Present)
Facilitator/Coordinator, Women's Health Initiative (Dec 1998 – Feb 2000)
Nurse Manager, Primary Care Management Clinic (Mar 1998 – Dec 1998)
Nurse Manager, Pediatric Clinic (Sep 1997 – Mar 1998)
Newborn Nursery Nurse Manager, Obstetrical Unit, Labor & Delivery (Aug 1996 – Sep 1997)

Baker Hall Medical Center, Corona A.F.B., CA, 1992 – 1996
Nurse Manager, Maternity Unit/Newborn Nursery – Mother/Infant Recovery

Armistead Medical Center, Armistead A.F.B., NY, 1984 – 1992
Nurse Manager/Asst. Nurse Manager, Internal Medicine Clinic (Nov 1990 – Jul 1992)
Nurse Manager/Asst. Nurse Manager/Staff Nurse, Neonatal Intensive Care (Feb 1984 – Nov 1990)

Berlane Regional Medical Center, Berlane A.F.B., IL, 1981 – 1984
Nurse Manager/Staff Nurse/Flight Nurse

PROFESSIONAL AFFILIATIONS

Member, American Association of University Women (AAUW)
Member, Association of Women's Health, Obstetrical and Neonatal Nurses (AWHONN)
Former Chairperson and current Member, AWHONN Research Review Committee
Diplomate, American College of Forensic Nurses (DACFN)
Member, International Society of Nurses in Genetics (ISONG)
Member, National Association of Neonatal Nurses (NANN)
Member, National Bereavement Alliance – known as Resolve Through Sharing (RTS)
Member and Adams State University Nominating Board, Sigma Theta Tau – national nursing honor society

CHAPTER 10

CVs (Curriculum Vitae)

- Secondary and University Educators
- International Educators

EDMUND J. SCIBILIA

P.O. Box 110, Middletown, CT 06457
(860) 347-0011 • fax (860) 347-0012
escibilia@snet.net

PROFESSIONAL SUMMARY

- Highly motivated and accomplished teaching professional with more than 20 years of exemplary experience; outstanding command of the general science curriculum with special expertise in developing and implementing comprehensive curriculum enhancements.
- Utilize dynamic, synergistic style in collaborating with other educators in a team-teaching approach; considered a catalyst with keen strategic planning skills and a pragmatic, resourceful approach to responsibilities.
- Lifelong advocate of continued learning and advancement; very effective in influencing the grasp of knowledge and love of learning in others.
- High energy level complemented by demonstrated ability to reach learners at all levels and incite them with a thirst for learning to the maximum extent possible.
- Dedicated and involved community volunteer with demonstrated leadership; Vice Chair, Board of Education.

EDUCATION

SOUTHERN CONNECTICUT STATE UNIVERSITY • New Haven, CT
- *Sixth-Year Professional Diploma of Advanced Studies as Secondary Science Specialist* (1988)

SOUTHERN CONNECTICUT STATE UNIVERSITY / YALE UNIVERSITY / MIT
- *Fellowship through Institute for Science Instruction and Study* (1985)

EASTERN CONNECTICUT STATE COLLEGE • Willimantic, CT
- *Master of Science, Elementary Science Education* (1977); Dean's List Standing

CENTRAL CONNECTICUT STATE COLLEGE • New Britain, CT
- *Bachelor of Science, Education* (1971); Dean's List Standing

PROFESSIONAL EXPERIENCE

1972–Present **NORTH BRANFORD MIDDLE SCHOOL** • North Branford, CT
Grade 6 Science and Reading Teacher (Science, 1975–Present; Reading, 1998–Present)
Utilize well-honed skills in planning, preparing, delivering, and assessing. Promote a positive environment for in-classroom learning complemented by ability to bring real-life examples to instruction, both in science and reading. Teaching style reflects a continual effort to innovate and excite students. Consistently complement curriculum through nontraditional methods in teaching; incorporated team-teaching concepts working with students identified as learning disabled a full decade before the inclusion approach was embraced. Implemented variety of hands-on modeling techniques for reading students in absence of curriculum; created rubrics designed to foster performance-based assessment. Provide exposure to examples of excellence in literature, adult nonfiction, historical accounts, and classics as catalyst for creative discussions and response journal writings.

Salient Accomplishments ...
- Appointed to serve as Chairman of Curriculum Development Committee, fully rewriting science curriculum at all grade levels consistent with the Connecticut State Department of Education's Science Curriculum Framework (1994–Present); previously contributed extensively to two comprehensive rewrites of science curriculum between 1972 and 1990.
- Macintosh consultant, presenting workshops for CEUs to professional staff and educators; expertise in Microsoft Word, Claris, Lotus, Quicken, FileMaker Pro, and MacSchool grading programs (1987–Present).
- BEST Mentor (1990); certified by State of Connecticut as cooperating teacher and mentor for new and beginning teachers; mentor to teacher on performance review (1999).

This CV starts off with a strong summary. After page 1, it follows a standard format of simply listing activities, credentials, memberships, and so forth.

EDMUND J. SCIBILIA   Page Two

PROFESSIONAL EXPERIENCE *(cont'd.)*

NORTH BRANFORD MIDDLE SCHOOL • North Branford, CT
Grade 6 Science and Reading Teacher (Science, 1975–Present; Reading, 1998–Present)
• Member, Guilford Middle School Building Committee (1999); preparing specifications for new 5–6 Middle School addition.
Grade 6 Honors Science (1988)
Grade 6 Social Studies (1991–94)
Grades 6 and 7 Science Teacher (1973–75)
Grade 6 Science and Math Teacher; Grade 7 Science Teacher (1972–73)

1971 **FARM HILL SCHOOL** • Middletown, CT
Grade 4 Classroom Teacher

1969–71 **MIDDLESEX COMMUNITY COLLEGE** • Middletown, CT
Lab Assistant and Teaching Assistant / Purchasing Agent

PROFESSIONAL AFFILIATIONS

• **National Science Teachers Association (NSTA)** • Member
• **National Education Association Representative Assembly Delegate** (Orlando, FL, 1999)
• **NSTA Convention Participant** (New Orleans, LA, 1997; Portland, ME, 1988; Hartford, CT, 1976; Providence, RI, 1970)
• **Connecticut Science Teachers Association (CSTA)** • Member
• **Connecticut Association of Boards of Education** • Member
• **National Education Association, Connecticut Education Association, North Branford Education Association** • Member
• **Connecticut Education Foundation, Inc.** • Volunteer

DISTINCTIONS

• **Who's Who in America** (2000)
• **Who's Who in Science and Technology** (1999)
• **Who's Who in the East** (1999, 1998)
• **Who's Who Among American Teachers** (1996)
• **Nominee, Presidential Award for Excellence in Secondary School Science and Mathematics Teaching** (1991)

CONTINUING PROFESSIONAL DEVELOPMENT

• Strategic Planning Core Values & Expectations Committee (1999)
• Strategic Planning Renewal and Action Team Member in Association with Cambridge Associates (1997)
• Core Institute for Support Teachers (1991); Mentor, newly certified first-year teacher (1997–Present)
• Connecticut Association of Boards of Education; Public School Policy Development (1996)
• Project Learn A Time For A Change; Alternative Scheduling (1996)
• Investigation of a Middle School Model; Education of the Blind (1996)
• Educator's Role in Helping Children with Grief; Suicide Prevention, Referral Process & Procedure (1996)
• Connecticut College Regional Inservice Enhancement Center for Science / Physics Refresher (1995)

EDMUND J. SCIBILIA   Page Three

CIVIC / COMMUNITY INVOLVEMENT

- **Middletown Board of Education** (1996–Present)
  - Vice-Chair/Secretary (1997–Present)
  - Member (1996–Present)
  - Chairman, Policy Committee
  - Chairman, Tolerance Committee
  - Member, Curriculum Committee
  - Member, Transportation Committee
  - Member, Building and Grounds Committee
  - Member, Communications Committee

- **North Branford Education Association** • Vice President (1994–Present)
  - Middlesex County Council (1999–Present)
  - CEA Summer Leadership (1998)

- **Association of Connecticut Fairs** (1981–Present)
  - Delegate
  - Chairman, Scholarship Committee
  - Premium Book Chairman

- **Guilford Fair Foundation, Inc.** (1997–Present)
  - Founder, 1997
  - Treasurer (1997–Present)
  - Secretary (1995–97)

- **Mt. Ascutney Property Owners Association** (1987–Present)
  - Member, Executive Committee (1989–Present)
  - President (1998–99)

- **Guilford Agricultural Fair Association, Inc.** (1979–98)
  - Honorary Member (1989) • Awarded for exemplary voluntary service
  - Treasurer/Coordinator of Exhibits
  - Advance Sales
  - Superintendent of Gates
  - Chairman, Scholarship Committee
  - Member, Constitution Committee

- **Middletown Town Committee** • Treasurer (1993–Present); Member (1982–Present)
- **Church of the Epiphany** • Treasurer/Vestry Member/Junior Warden (1985–94)
- **Middletown Zoning Board of Appeals** • Vice-Chairman (1983–89; elected position)
- **Connecticut Public Television Volunteer** (1986–87)
- **North Branford Community Television** • Board of Directors/Founder (1974–80)

Curriculum Vitae

William Allan

26 Fairfield Crescent
Hillsborough
Auckland

Phone (09) 625 7588 (home)
Phone (025) 156 291 (cellular)

This CV, for a client in New Zealand, conforms to the expected style and length for an education professional's CV in that country. The layout allows the interviewing panel to make annotations in the margins.

Curriculum Vitae

William Allan

Personal Details

Name:	William Alexander Allan
Address:	26 Fairfield Crescent, Hillsborough, Auckland
Telephones:	(09) 625 7588 (home), (09) 621 9780 (work), (025) 156 291 (cellular)
Email:	wil.al@xtra.co.nz

Interests: Golf, running, tennis, swimming, family time, sporting activities, gardening, reading, studying, and computers

Presentations: Keynote speaking engagement at Technology Conference, 1999

Publications: Papers on the development of technology and technology education

Career Objective

To continue my career as a Lecturer specialising in technology within a higher education establishment, where I can utilise my core competencies and experience to add value and make a measurable contribution.

Personal Attributes

Extracts from references:

- "William is **hardworking**, **extremely focused** and very **task oriented**. His work has been characterised by **thoroughness**, effective use of a variety of media, and planned down to the last detail. William is very **creative** and **professional** in his approach, and the materials he produces for workshops and presentations are of high quality. He is **innovative** and experimental and highly skilled in the use of a variety of media… Feedback from his schools has invariably been positive and full of praise for his approach and professionalism."

- "William is a **dynamic** and **effective leader**… I would wish to place most emphasis on his staff direction, his **inspirational dynamism**, his ability to think laterally in the solving of problems… The credit for all (William's) achievements … I believe … (are) two outstanding characteristics: his **prodigious work effort** and **drive**, and his total **professionalism**. … William's work is characterised by **careful** and **thoughtful** planning. He has the rare ability to look ahead as well as to attend to the day-to-day detail…. His immediate staff are inspired by his depth of knowledge and his **perceptive leadership** … He is an **exceptional man,** a real professional whose skills and standards never fall below a level that most craftsmen find unattainable. With that goes an **unusual warmth** and **kindness**, a **dedication** to this job and the welfare of students, and an **unsurpassed measure of integrity**."

These references may be cited in an interview.

Curriculum Vitae

William Allan

Core Competencies

DESIGN AND TECHNOLOGY
- Strong in the use of computer technologies for design.
- Impressive imaginative flair and creativity.
- Excellent background in the use of visual media and marketing (graphic and design fields in both business and schools).
- Confident in using electronic and visual media equipment and programs; consistently use a wide range of visual presentation systems.

MULTIMEDIA
- Possess considerable multimedia skills especially in the development of Internet and LAN-based instructional and flexible learning-based materials – have reinforced and initiated learning programmes through the development of online resources and courses.
- Extremely skilled in web design, multimedia and publishing on the Internet.

PEOPLE DEVELOPMENT
- Possess an innate talent for developing and coaching people
- Sincere attitude to help and serve people
- Ability to enhance the performance of others

PROGRAMME MANAGEMENT
- Ability to mobilise people and resources to achieve planned objectives.
- Strong grasp of programme management methodologies.
- Ability to adapt and integrate different technical disciplines, methodologies, and industry knowledge to ensure best possible solutions.

PROJECT MANAGEMENT
- Confident in managing projects at all levels of education including primary, intermediate, secondary, and tertiary (evidenced in my contract work and Taranaki Polytechnic).
- Worked as a Contract Facilitator.
- Confident in the coordination of contract work – successfully led, coordinated and managed one of the most successful "Information Technology for Teachers" programmes in the country for Telecom NZ.

TEACHING
- Demonstrated talent for motivating, encouraging, and leading students in a positive direction for better learning
- Co-produced a very successful Internet website as a teacher resource (www.hasslefree.co.nz)

EDUCATION
- Experience in leveraging information technology to enhance education
- Have a sound knowledge of the processes involved in curriculum development in schools

Curriculum Vitae

William Allan

Career Profile

1999 – 2000	Dunedin College of Education
	Senior Lecturer of Technology Education

- Developed and directed a video on technological practice and benefits of links with community resources.
- Wrote a resource on "Design" for the Ministry of Education.
- Organised and delivered professional development programmes for schools on computer graphics, multimedia and web production techniques.
- Developed an Internet website and a programme of learning for a group of Manoia School students who come to DCE for their technology education.
- Developed graphic material which promoted and identified the technology education department.

2000 – present	New Zealand Qualifications Authority
	Member of the National Assessment Panel

- Meet with the National team of panel members to develop the style of assessment that can be expected in the year 2002.

1999 – 2000	Employed by a variety of schools
	Consultant

- Advised on property design and development issues for technology education - creative environments.
- Liaised with school administration boards to establish needs.
- Provided information on professional development related to technology education.
- Developed concepts of spatial design possibilities to accommodate and deliver an effective technology education.
- Compiled a plan of action and brief for architectural firms to undertake the development of these facilities.
- Provided a service accommodating change management.

1998 – 1999	Christchurch Polytechnic
	Tutor for the Commercial Computer Graphics Course

- Wrote and delivered units of work in Graphic Design, Time-Based Media, Digital Imaging, Visual Imaging, Computer Reprographics and Web-Based media.
- Assisted in the preparation of material for the application of a Course in Bachelor of Visual Arts.

1998	Ministry of Education
	Contract

- Wrote the guidelines for Property Management in Schools for Technology Education. Contracted to various schools to provide advice for property development and work with architects in the creation of plans for technology blocks.

Curriculum Vitae

William Allan

Career Profile *(continued)*

1998	New Zealand Qualifications Authority
	Regional Moderator

- Moderated Graphics and Design Unit Standards.
- Coordinated the moderation activities of allocated local moderators.
- Checked moderate samples of provider assessment material.
- Confirmed that judgements were consistent with National Moderation Standards.
- Reported on check moderation process and assessment material.
- Resolved disputes and undertook the process of mediation.

1996 –1998	Albany University College of Education
	Contract Facilitator of Technology

- Provided leadership in the professional development of teachers in technology education throughout Albany and Auckland areas.
- Provided guidance to principals and boards of trustees about the implementation of technology.
- Worked collaboratively with teachers and other advisers to develop positive teaching and learning environments for technology.
- Worked with schools on developing integrated programmes of work and negotiated the structure of curriculum policy statements.
- Regional coordinator for National Technology Association.
- Maintained links and co-ordinated Technology Education in (over the two and a half years) 70 primary schools and 9 secondary schools.
- Developed strategies for the positive assessment and reporting of technology education.
- Developed a help line.
- Responded to milestone report requests

1996 – 1998	New Zealand Qualifications Authority
	Writer

- Writer of Unit Standards, training manual, and assessment guide; moderator for Graphics and Design Unit.
- Coordinated Unit Standards information from a variety of sources.
- Wrote assessment guide material.
- Moderated schools' Unit standard material.
- Provided professional development workshops.

1995	The University of Auckland
	Consultant

- Organised, produced, and delivered design presentations for technology curriculum development.
- Created a full multimedia production to provide an historical and informative presentation on Design and how it fits into the technology curriculum.
- Delivered the presentation in three major areas of the Auckland Region.

Curriculum Vitae

William Allan

Career Profile *(continued)*

1991 – 1994	Maree Campbell College, Auckland
	HOD Information Technology and Applied Art & Design

HOD Information Technology:
- Developed learning activities based on computer applications.
- Coordinated access to computer resources.
- Ensured computer network and classroom resources were maintained and provided future analysis about direction the school should proceed when upgrading.
- Prepared and monitored a budget for computing.
- Evaluated the effectiveness of classroom programmes.
- Developed individualised in-service training programmes for teachers.

HOD Applied Art and Design:
- Ensured the schemes of work met the National Syllabus requirements.
- Ensured objectives met the local needs and the abilities of the students and that the necessary teachers' resources were managed with care.
- Ensured the budget was adhered to and funds wisely used.
- Provided a constant link with the updated technology involved in this area of study.
- Constantly consulted with teachers to advise and evaluate classroom activities.
- Teacher in charge of implementing Technology.
- Provided information to staff and Board of Trustees about Technology and the proposed implementation procedure.
- Ensured well-documented information on proposed expenditure and expected budget.
- Investigated the necessary resources required for implementation.

1988 – 1991	Hillsborough College, Auckland
	Assistant Teacher in the Graphics and Technology Department

- Updated the Graphics and Design Technology Curriculum.
- Produced a series of Modules for future Senior Graphics and Technology education.
- Managed personnel and many departmental programmes.
- Taught Technology and Graphics in levels three to seven.
- Ran a peer support programme with the third form students.

1982 – 1987	New Terrace High School, Auckland
	HOD Applied Art and Design

- Instrumental in developing the Technology and Graphics Departments from a low status in 1987 into one of the most sophisticated technology departments in the country.
- As a result of the above achievement:
  "Air New Zealand, in the last two years, has employed more apprentices from this school than any other."
  "Trainee Teachers in the Technology course at Auckland College of Education virtually queued to obtain an appointment here and lecturers now conduct tours of students through the workshops."
- Instrumental in developing electronics and robotics as secondary schools based programme.

Curriculum Vitae

William Allan

Qualifications

Certificates and Diplomas

- Masters in Education Degree, 1998

- Higher Teachers Diploma, 1991

- Quality Management Certificate, 1993

- Trained Teacher Certificate, 1983

- Teacher Diploma, 1981

- Projectionist Certificate, 1981

Courses

- Graphic Presentation and Photography, 1979

- Computer Awareness (Mac), 1986

- Advanced Computer (Mac), 1987

- Photography, 1987

- Design, 1989

- Graphics and Technology, 1989

Referees

Verbal referees available at an interview.

Curriculum Vitae

LAWRENCE ALLEN CAMBRIDGE, PH.D.

P.O. Box 11990 ▪ Dallas, Texas 75700
972-999-7777 (Residence) ▪ 972-997-8888, Ext. 555 (Office)

EDUCATION

HARVARD UNIVERSITY – Cambridge, Massachusetts
THE UNIVERSITY OF TEXAS via SREB – Austin, Texas

Postdoctoral Study

STATE UNIVERSITY OF IOWA – Iowa City, Iowa
Ph.D., Psychology (Educational/Experimental)

UNIVERSITY OF WISCONSIN – Madison, Wisconsin
M.S., Educational Psychology and Science Methods

FISK UNIVERSITY – Nashville, Tennessee
A.B., Zoology

CREDENTIALS

Diplomate in School Psychology, American Board of Professional Psychology, Inc.
Fellow, American Association on Mental Deficiency (since 1969)
National Postdoctoral Fellow in Educational Research
Licensed Psychologist, Louisiana Board of Examiners for Practicing Psychologists

SELECTED PROFESSIONAL HIGHLIGHTS

- Selected as **1st Postdoctoral Fellow** of Southern Association of Colleges and Schools (SACS).
- Appointed **Vocational Expert/Psychological Consultant** – Bureau of Hearings and Appeals of the Social Security Administration (25 years).
- **Initiated/implemented Graduate Program** at Grambling State University.
- Elected as **1st Chairman of Graduate Council.**
- As **President,** led Wiley College to **highest enrollment in two decades** and **greatest improvement of facilities ever.**
- **Coordinator** of **Louisiana Consent Decree Program. Generated $53 million revenues** to Grambling State University.
- **Developed/implemented/negotiated/signed contracts for International Faculty/Student Exchange Programs.**
- **Attained Fulbright Scholar-in-Residence** (India) and **Fulbright Study Abroad Program** (Columbia, S.A.).
- **Successfully accomplished fund-raising and student-enrollment goals** through extensive Caribbean travel.
- **Authored/directed** numerous federally funded grants/projects. **Published/presented** myriad of articles and papers.
- Acquired **multicultural/multilingual (French/Spanish)** familiarity through extensive study and international travel.

PROFESSIONAL APPOINTMENTS/DISTINCTIONS

Chairperson, Louisiana Board of Regents' Resource Task Force on Cultural Diversity in State Universities and Colleges
(1990–1992)
Member, Council of Fellows Executive Committee – American Council on Education (1987–Present)
Member-at-Large, Executive Committee – Conference of Louisiana Colleges and Universities (1987–1992)

In this traditional CV for a college provost, impact is created by the extensive listing of professional credentials. There is no "sales pitch" and very little descriptive information.

LAWRENCE ALLEN CAMBRIDGE, PH.D.   Page 2 of 6

PROFESSIONAL APPOINTMENTS/DISTINCTIONS (Continued)

Member, Committee on Ethnic Minority Affairs, Division 16 of School Psychology – American Psychological Association (1985–Present)

Member, Board of Directors – The Academic Year in New York City (1984–1990)

Coordinator, Grambling State University's Six-Year Consent Decree Program (1981–1988)

Member, Board of Regents' Committee on Off-Campus Instruction (1981–1988)

Member, Board of Regents' Advisory Committee on Developmental Education (1981–1992)

Vice Chairman, Committee on Research and Special Projects – SACS (1973–1982)

Presenter – International Symposium in Saltillo, Coahuila, Mexico regarding National Identity and Cultural Implications of North American Free Trade Agreement (NAFTA) (1992)

Initiator/Leader – Successfully developed/implemented International Faculty/Student Exchange Programs in India, China, and Thailand (1982, 1987); traveled to all countries to make presentations and negotiate/sign contracts

Author/Director, 5-Year Title III–Strengthening Developing Institution grant designed to demonstrate model for enhancing educational quality and control (1986–1991)

Opening Faculty Conference Speaker – Alabama State University, Montgomery Alabama (September 1986)

Member, Title III–SDIP External Evaluation Teams, Joffre T. Whisenton and Associates (1979–1985)

Member, Louisiana Attorney General's Advisory Committee on School Desegregation (1973–1977)

Author/Co-Author/Director, Federally funded Research and Program Grants (see Publications section)

Reviewer/Evaluator, Federal Proposals – U.S. Office of Education (1967–Present)

Author/Director, Special Education Teacher Training Grants (six) (1960–1965)

Research Associate – The American Association of State Colleges and Universities – Resource Center for Planned Change (1976–1990)

Chairperson/Author – Chaired Steering Committee for and prepared mandated **Role, Scope and Mission Report** for presentation by Grambling State University to the Louisiana Board of Regents (Fall 1975)

Initiator – Shared Authorship of successfully funded application for Minority School Biomedical Support (MSBS) Program (**$386,000 grant** to Grambling State University) (1972)

Visiting (Evaluation) Team Chairman, Commission on Colleges – Southern Association of Colleges and Schools (Each Year, 1971–Present) (see attached list of SACS Consultations)

Institutional Self-Study Consultant, Commission on Colleges and Schools, Atlanta Georgia (1972–1993)

Initiator/Author – Authored and acquired funding for Grambling State University phase of Positive Futures, incorporated (programs in Community Development and Criminal Justice). Chaired committee that was successful in obtaining approval from both governing bodies to implement A.S. Degree in Criminal Justice

Initiator/Author – "Basic Theme" Project of the Emergency School Assistance Agency (ESSA) Program of the U.S. Office of Education in North Louisiana; authored and served as consultant to several similar projects

Staff Psychologist – Emory University's Project Southside, Atlanta, Georgia (1970)

Evaluator of Grant Applications in Special Education, U.S. Office of Education (1968–1973)

Presenter – Presented paper, "A Review of Competency Assessment in Louisiana," at National Conference on Competency Assessment in Teacher Education: Making It Work, University of Kentucky (1980)

Member, Board of Directors – Black Educator Council for Human Services (BECHS) (1973–1975)

Consultant/Psychologist – Headstart Project – Ouachita Parish Community Action Program, Monroe, Louisiana (1972–1978)

Psychological Consultant/Vocational Expert – Bureau of Hearings and Appeals – Department of Health and Human Support (1964–1990)

Consultant – Academic Administration Program – United Board for College Development, Atlanta, Georgia (1974–1976)

Consultant, Educational Resource Center for School Desegregation – Tulane University (1968–1970)

Author/Director – Authored proposal; negotiated grant terms; traveled to Africa to direct T.S.U. Peace Corps Africa Graduate Program (1970–1971)

Professor of Psychology (part-time)/Psychological Consultant – Graduate School of Education and Project LIFT – Northeast Louisiana University (1967–1969)

Initiator – Conceived the plans, co-authored the proposal, and led the efforts which resulted in the **$1.5 million HUD project** and completion of **$3 million challenge grant** at Wiley College (1993–1996)

LAWRENCE ALLEN CAMBRIDGE, PH.D.   Page 3 of 6

PROFESSIONAL EDUCATIONAL EXPERIENCE

DALLAS COLLEGE – Dallas, Texas
Provost/Vice President for Academic Affairs (1996–Present)

WILEY COLLEGE – Marshall, Texas
President (1993–1996)

GRAMBLING STATE UNIVERSITY – Grambling, Louisiana
Special Advisor to the President/Executive Director of Total Quality Management (TQM) (1992–1993)
Provost/Vice President for Academic Affairs/Eminent Professor of Psychology/Education (1991–1992)
Vice President for Academic Affairs and Research/Professor of Psychology/Education (1977–1991)
Associate Dean for Administration and Research/Professor of Psychology/Education (1971–1976)
Professor of Psychology and Education/Director of the Center for Institutional Research (1965–1969)
Professor of Psychology and Education/Director of and Psychologist for Special Education Diagnostic Center (1961–1965)
Associate Professor/Director of and Psychologist for Special Education Diagnostic Center (1958–1961)
Instructor/Assistant Professor of Biological Sciences/Coordinator of Human Growth Courses (1952–1956)

LOUISIANA STATE UNIVERSITY – Baton Rouge, Louisiana
American Council on Education Postdoctoral Fellow in Higher Education Administration – Offices of the President
    and Chancellor of Louisiana State University-Baton Rouge (1976–1977)

TEXAS SOUTHERN UNIVERSITY – Houston, Texas
Dean of Faculties/Professor of Psychology/Education (1970–1971)

MOREHOUSE COLLEGE – Atlanta, Georgia
Distinguished Visiting Professor of Psychology/Education (1970)

COMMISSION ON COLLEGES, Southern Association of Colleges and Schools – Atlanta, Georgia
National Postdoctoral Fellow in Educational Research (1969–1970)

GALLAUDET COLLEGE FOR THE DEAF – Washington, D.C.
Research Assistant (Summer 1957)

STATE UNIVERSITY OF IOWA – Iowa City, Iowa
Research Assistant – College of Education, Bureau of Research and Statistics (1956–1958)

DISTINGUISHED HONORS

Who's Who in America, 41st Edition, Volume 1 (1980–1981)
Who's Who Among Black Americans, 3rd Edition (1980–1981)
Who's Who in the South and Southwest, 14th Edition (1975–1976)
International Scholars Directory (1973)
Dictionary of International Biography, Part I (1973)
American Men and Women of Science, 12th Edition, Volume I (1973)
Outstanding Educators of America (1972)
Recipient of **Bronze Service Star and Unit Citation** – "Red Ball Express" for service in France/Belgium
Platoon Sergeant in European Theater

LAWRENCE ALLEN CAMBRIDGE, PH.D.   **Page 4 of 6**

PROFESSIONAL AFFILIATIONS

Fellow, American Association on Mental Deficiency (since 1969)
Diplomate in School Psychology, American Board of Professional Psychology, Inc.
Member, American Association for Higher Education
Member, American Council on Education
Past Chapter President, American Association of University Professors
American Educational Research Association
American Psychological Association
Past Vice President, Louisiana Association for Higher Education of the LAE
Past President, Grambling Chapter of LAE
Louisiana Board of Examiners for Practicing Psychologists
Louisiana Psychological Association
National Society for the Study of Education
Phi Delta Kappa Professional Fraternity
Prince Hall Mason – Elected to Thirty-Third Degree
Member, American College of Forensic Examiners

PROFESSIONAL PUBLICATIONS/RESEARCH/PRESENTATIONS

Cambridge, Lawrence A. "Role Expectations for Beginning Professors," Chapter in Part I of *The Art and Politics of College Teaching: A Practical Guide for the Beginning Professor*, by Sawyer, Prichard and Hostetler, published by Peter Lang Publishing House, New York, NY, 1992.

Cambridge, Lawrence A. "Educational Quality Assurance: The Mandate, Aim and Risk at Historically Black Colleges and Universities," PEN – *Postsecondary Education Network*, a publication of Division J., American Educational Research Association, October/November 1990.

Cambridge, Lawrence A. "Improving Academic Skills: The Grambling State University Model," Chapter III in *Handbook for Minority Student Services*, by Charles Taylor, Editor, PRAXIS Publications, Inc., Madison, Wisconsin, 1990.

Cambridge, Lawrence A. "Grambling State University Comprehensive Developmental Education Program," **Featured Presentation** at the Ninth Annual Conference on Learning in Higher Education, June 1-2, 1989, University of Wisconsin-Parkside, Kenosha, Wisconsin.

Cambridge, Lawrence A. "Conceptual Note: The Mandate, Aim and Risk of Educational Quality Assurance at Historically Black Colleges and Universities," *Journal of Social and Behavioral Sciences*, Volume 34, No. 4, Fall 1988.

Cambridge, Lawrence A. "Catch the Vision: The Real Meaning of Comfort," **Featured Address** to First Annual Banquet, Commanders of the Rite of Louisiana, United Supreme Council, 33, Ancient and Accepted Scottish Rite Freemasonry, Price Hall Affiliation, Shreveport, Louisiana, August 27, 1988.

Cambridge, Lawrence A. "Inside the Narrow Gate: A Look at You and The Competition," **Featured Address**, Honors Convocation, Jarvis Christian College, Hawkins, Texas, April 26, 1986.

Cambridge, Lawrence A. "Educational Quality Assurance at Historically Black Colleges and Universities," **Featured Address**, 1986–1987 Opening Faculty Conference, Alabama State University, Montgomery, Alabama, September 2, 1986.

Cambridge, Lawrence A. "Developmental Education in Perspective: A Retrospective View by a Pioneer in the Field," **Featured Address**, Faculty Annual Conference, Louisiana Association of Developmental Educators (LADE), Lafayette, Louisiana, November 15, 1985.

Cambridge, Lawrence A. "Standards for Achieving Quality Education," **Featured Address**, Pre-School Conference, Southern University-Shreveport, August 16, 1984.

Cambridge, Lawrence A. "Using State Fiscal Policy to Promote and Recognize Quality," **Panel Presentation**, Conference of Louisiana Colleges and Universities, Louisiana State University-Shreveport, Louisiana, February 25, 1982.

LAWRENCE ALLEN CAMBRIDGE, PH.D.   **Page 5 of 6**

PROFESSIONAL PUBLICATIONS/RESEARCH/PRESENTATIONS (Continued)

Cambridge, Lawrence A. "Blacks Taking Care of Business for Blacks," **Featured Address**, Annual Meeting, Louisiana Chapter of Frontiers International, Inc. Opelousas, Louisiana, December 5, 1981.

Cambridge, Lawrence A. "A Review of Competency Assessment in Louisiana," in *Competency Assessment in Teacher Education: Making It Work*, edited by Sharon G. Boardman and Michael J. Butler, published by the American Association of Colleges for Teacher Education and the ERIC Clearinghouse on Teacher Education, Washington, D.C., August 1981.

Cambridge, Lawrence A. and Hensley, Oliver D. "An Attack on Impediments to Cross-Cultural Teaching," Chapter 14, *Problems of Disadvantaged and Deprived Youth* by John C. Cull and Richard E. Hardy (editors), Charles C. Thomas Publishers, Springfield, Illinois, 1975.

Cheers, Arlynne Lake, and Cambridge, Lawrence A. *Teaching and Learning in the Model Classroom*. Jericho, New York: Exposition University Press, 1974.

Cambridge, Lawrence A. "The Morale Problem Among Black Educators in Louisiana," *The Journal of the Louisiana Education Association*, November 1972, 3.

Cambridge, Lawrence A. "Response to Re-Focusing on the Future," *Proceeding of the Fortieth Conference of Academic Deans of the Southern States*, November 30, 1971, 15-18. (**Address delivered** to the 40th Conference of Academic Deans of the Southern States, Deaville Hotel, Miami Beach, Florida, November 30, 1971).

Cambridge, Lawrence A. and Hensley, Oliver D. "An Attack on Impediments to Effective Cross-Cultural Teaching," *Children*, 1971, 18, No. 1, January-February, 19-22.

Cambridge, Lawrence A. and Goodwin, Louis C. "Professor in the Small Colleges," *Improvements of University and College Teaching*, 1970, 18, No. 4, 258-60.

Cheers, Arlynne Lake, and Cambridge, Lawrence A. *Toward the Professional Preparation of Elementary School Teachers*. (In conjunction with U.A.O.E. Research Project #2390, Contract #OE-6-10-125), Grambling State University, Division of Research, Grambling, Louisiana, 1969.

Cheers, Arlynne Lake, and Cambridge, Lawrence A. *A Comparison of Two Groups of Teacher Trainees Whose Professional Experiences Differ in Organization, Scope and Sequence*. U.S.O.E., Project $2390, Contract #OE-6-10-125, DHEW, Office of Education, Bureau of Research, Washington, D.C., 1969.

Cambridge, Lawrence A. "Administrators and Self-Orientation: A Backdrop for Development of Educational Leadership," *Bulletin of Arkansas Teachers Association*, Volume 38, No. 2, December-February, 1968, 12-14.

Cambridge, Lawrence A. and Dorsey, Phillip. "Coping With Troubled Behavior," *The Pointer*, 1968, Volume 13, No. 2, 18-20.

Cambridge, Lawrence A. and Dorsey, Phillip. *Mentally Slow Children: Their Characteristics, Needs, and Education*, Grambling State University, Grambling, Louisiana, 1967.

Cambridge, Lawrence A. "Application of Learning Theory to Classroom Instruction," *Journal of Louisiana Education Association*, 1964, 42, No. 26-27.

Cambridge, Lawrence A. and others. "Comparison of Two Methods of Teaching Remedial English to College Freshmen," *Cooperative Research Branch*, U.S. Office of Education, 1963.

Cambridge, Lawrence A. and Stroud, J.B. "Inhibition Phenomena in Fast and Slow Learners," *Journals of Educational Psychology*, 1961, 52, No. 1, 30-34.

Cambridge, Lawrence A. "Interrelationships Among Memory, Rate of Acquisition and Length of Task," *Phi Delta Kappa (Epsilon Bulletin)*, 1959, 34, 14-16.

LAWRENCE ALLEN CAMBRIDGE, PH.D.   Page 6 of 6

SELECTED COC-SACS CONSULTATIONS

Consultant – Le Moyne-Owen College, Memphis, Tennessee – **Institutional Self-Study Program for Re-affirmation of Accreditation** (February 1993)

Consultant – Paul Quinn College, Dallas, Texas – **Institutional Self-Study Program for Re-affirmation of Accreditation** (September 1992)

Chairman, COC-SACS Re-affirmation Committee – Alabama State University, Montgomery, Alabama (March, 1990); Clark College, Atlanta, Georgia (March 1988)

Chairman, Off-campus COS-SACS Visiting Committee for Spud Center – Bethune Cookman College, Daytona Beach, Florida (March 1987)

Chairman, COC-SACS Substantive Change Committee – Alabama State A&M University (March 1986)

Consultant – Texas College, Tyler, Texas – **Institutional Self-Study Program for Re-affirmation of Accreditation** (February 1994)

Member/Chairperson of Standard III – Educational Program Sub-committee, SACS – Commission on Colleges Re-affirmation Visit to Wiley College, Marshall, Texas (April 1982)

Consultant – Institutional Self-Study for COC-SACS Re-affirmation of Accreditation – Rusk College, Holly Springs, Mississippi (March 1982)

Chairman – Commission on Colleges – Re-affirmation Visiting Committee for the Southern Association of Colleges and Schools to Saint Augustine's College, Raleigh, North Carolina (April 1981)

RESUME 73: NANCY KARVONEN, CPRW, CEIP, IJCTC, CCM; GALT, CA

TEDRA ORGAMANI

Curriculum Vitae

4702 Logan Court
Kellerton, Iowa 50133

(641) 461-9611
orgamani@aol.com

EDUCATION

Doctoral Candidate	University of Dublin, Dublin, Ireland	In progress
LLM	Iowa State University, Ames, Iowa	1993
MSW	Iowa State University, Ames, Iowa	1991
LL.B./JD	University of California, Northridge, California	1989
BBA	University of California, Northridge, California Management	1981

LICENSURE AND CERTIFICATION

Master of Social Work, Addiction Counselor   1999
National Board of Addiction Examiners, Des Moines, Iowa

Certified Criminal Justice Specialist   1999
National Board of Addiction Examiners, Des Moines, Iowa

Licensed Professional Counselor   1998
Board of Health, Des Moines, Iowa

TEACHING APPOINTMENTS

Iowa Children and Family Services Agency (CFSA), Des Moines, Iowa   1996-Present
Training Specialist
Train staff in family and child welfare practice. Develop curriculum in relevant
areas in field.

Missouri State University School of Social Work, Kansas City, Missouri   1994-1996
Assistant Professor/Instructor
Collaborated with Kansas City School System to bring drug awareness program to
primary schools. Partnered with MSU and community organizations to develop and manage
homeless coalition program to reduce effects of substance abuse in Kansas City.
Subjects taught:
- Social Welfare Policy
- Social Work Practice
- Human Behavior
- Social Work and the Law

Des Moines Community College, Des Moines, Iowa   1993-Present
Instructor
Subject taught:
- Business Law

University of Iowa, Training Resource Associates, Des Moines, Iowa   1993-Present
Instructor
Subjects taught:
- Human Behavior
- Ethics for Substance Abuse Counselors

(Continued on Page Two)

This concise, two-page CV details the qualifications for a college professor and training specialist in the field of social work.

TEDRA ORGAMANI
C.V. Page Two

TEACHING APPOINTMENTS (Continued)

University of Iowa, Ames, Iowa (Lamoni, Iowa Campus)	1993-Present

Instructor

Subjects taught:
- Ethics for Professionals
- Professional Development
- Constitutional Law
- Business Law

PROFESSIONAL EXPERIENCE

Iowa Children and Family Services Agency (CFSA), Des Moines, Iowa	1996-Present

Substance Abuse Specialist

Formulated substance abuse resources for CFSA. Originated pilot projects for women and children.

City of Des Moines Human Resources Administration, Des Moines, Iowa	1985-1994

Social Work Supervisor/Social Worker Staff Analyst/Fair Hearing Officer

Initiated substance abuse treatment and prevention program for birth parents. Provided individual, group, and family therapy in field. Created and enlisted community substance abuse services providers in city.

HONORS AND AWARDS

Four-year Academic Scholarship for Undergraduate Study	1998
Social Work Award, AFL-CIO Local 563, Des Moines, Iowa	1991

PRESENTATIONS

Child Welfare System and the Impact of Substance Abuse Ahmed Rasheesh Foundation, Des Moines, Iowa	1990
United Nations and the Convention of the Rights of the Child California State University, Northridge, California	1995

COMMITTEES AND COMMUNITY INVOLVEMENT

Member	Des Moines, Iowa Drug Court Development Committee	2001-Present
Trainer	Train Superior Court Judges on substance abuse issues and community resources	2001-Present
Board Member	Fighting Back Initiative, *Substance Abuse Program* Roberts Wood Johnson Foundation	1999-Present
Member	Served on review panel to draft drug status report Drug Strategies, Inc., Des Moines, Iowa	1999
Trainer	Foster Parents and Drug-Exposed Infants	1998-Present

AFFILIATIONS

Member	The Association of Legal Writing Specialists	1998-Present
Member	Association of Trial Lawyers of America	1997-Present

CHAPTER 11

Resumes for Educational Administrators

- Assistant Principals
- Principals
- Athletic Directors
- University Student Activities Directors
- Public School Administrators
- Superintendents of Schools
- Campus Coordinators
- Directors of Education
- Educational Materials Coordinators
- Daycare Licensing Administrators

George Themeles, CAGS, M.Ed.

62 Anderson Street
Cumberland, RI 02808

(401) 454-7854
gthemeles@worldnet.att.net

Objective: Key position in educational administration

PROFILE

- Strong academic background combined with graduate degree in education, advanced degree in administration and a record of achievement in classroom teaching
- Massachusetts Certified Teacher, Social Studies, grades 5-9 and 9-12
- Massachusetts Certified Principal/Assistant Principal, grades 5-9 and 9-12
- Well-developed oral and written communication skills and interpersonal abilities
- Natural leader and team builder, with practical administrative-level experience
- Member, Phi Delta Kappa

EDUCATION

UNIVERSITY OF MASSACHUSETTS LOWELL, Lowell, MA
- Certificate of Advanced Graduate Study in Educational Administration, Planning and Policy
- Master of Education in Curriculum and Instruction, June 1993

BOSTON UNIVERSITY, Boston, MA
- Bachelor of Arts in International Relations & Political Science (double major), January 1990

PROFESSIONAL EXPERIENCE

NORTH REGIONAL SCHOOL DISTRICT, Cumberland, RI   08/98 - Present
Assistant Principal – Nathan Hale Middle School
Provide general and specific program management assistance in support of an effective and productive learning environment for students and staff. Areas of focus include:
- Special education: Schedule, coordinate, and chair all meetings. Oversee the implementation of IEPs.
- Staff development: Facilitate the evaluation, selection, and promotion of professional development activities, including courses and conferences. Evaluate teachers.
- Student support and management: Established a homework hotline to improve school/home communication. Handle all student disciplinary matters. Act as liaison between teachers and parents.
- Budgeting: In-depth support of the budgetary process with the school principal. Recommend programs and staffing provisions for the following year.
- Special programs: Established an "Odyssey of the Mind" team to foster participation in widely recognized competition designed to encourage and develop cooperative problem solving.

JEFFERSON MIDDLE SCHOOL, Groton, MA   1993 - 1998
Teacher, Grade Seven
Developed objectives and created age/ability-appropriate lessons in accordance with curriculum guidelines, employing a variety of methods to meet multiple intelligences and diverse learning styles. Monitored and evaluated performance and progress. Sections included social studies (3), math (1), and science (1). Completed 300-hour administrative practicum involving budgeting, staff evaluation, day to day administration, and leadership activities.

An unobtrusive yet appropriate apple border gives visual appeal to this resume for a middle school assistant principal. The resume is well organized and easy to skim, so the reader can quickly pick up important information.

George Themeles, CAGS, M.Ed.   Page Two

(Jefferson Middle School, continued)

Participated in a variety of leadership and administrative activities:

- Building-Based Support Teams: Trained in strategy and implementation of peer-based assistance designed to expand resources available, facilitate problem solving, and build relationships among staff.
- Social Studies Task Force: Reviewed state guidelines and curriculum in preparation for revisions and development. Suggested goals and curriculum standards.
- Professional Development Committee Co-chair: Oversaw the designing, planning, implementing and evaluating of professional development courses and in-services system-wide.
- Student Government Advisor Co-chair (1996-97): Coordinated student group designed to foster leadership through charitable community activities.

HUNTINGTON LEARNING CENTER, Andover, MA   1995 - 1996
Tutor
Designed individual programs in reading and math for students across the spectrum of ages, development, and abilities, including assistance with regular classwork as well as enrichment activities.

LAWRENCE HIGH SCHOOL, Lawrence, MA   Winter/Spring 1993
Student Teacher
Taught U.S. History (1877-present), Government, and Sociology courses to junior and senior classes. Employed debates, role plays, and other action centered methods to increase student interest. Provided one-on-one tutoring in the Transitional Learning Center.

JOHNSON MIDDLE SCHOOL, Tewksbury, MA   1990 - 1992
Moderate Special Needs Teacher
Taught all subjects to special needs students with both emotional and physical handicaps. Met regularly with other classroom teachers to support and contribute to individual educational plans. Coordinated closely with other special needs teachers, guidance counselors, and school psychologists to ensure that mainstreaming goals were met.

Substitute Teacher
Taught all subjects to middle school students. Also functioned as a permanent substitute teacher in life science, physical science, and pre-algebra classes.

References available upon request

Bonnie Gregg

1325 – 19th Street
Annwald, WA 98001
(360) 555-2727

Dedicated and successful **ELEMENTARY SCHOOL PRINCIPAL** with proven ability to:

- Advocate and sustain a school culture conducive to continuous improvement for students and staff.

- Develop and monitor procedures and practices that promote a safe school environment.

- Assist instructional staff in development and implementation of curriculum, instruction, and assessment aligned with state and local learning goals.

- Manage human and financial resources to accomplish student achievement goals.

- Communicate with colleagues, parents, and community members to promote student learning.

EXPERIENCE

Principal, Annwald Elementary School, Annwald, Washington   1996–present
- Perform duties of Principal:
  Supervise, hire, and direct staff of teachers, educational assistants, and administrative support—Provide fiscal management—Observe and evaluate Certified Staff—Implementation of Special Education Inclusion—Administer student discipline.
- Implemented student discipline program resulting in 50% reduction of student referrals for discipline.
- Implemented Interdisciplinary Team Organization—Site-Based Management—Curriculum Development.
- Implemented "Success for All" reading program—increase of 35% in students reading at grade level.

Principal, American Tribal School, Flower, Washington   1994–1996
- Performed duties of Principal, and:
  Selected and assigned personnel, providing orientation for new and returning employees—Provided in-service with input from staff—Participated in Curriculum Planning and Development—Implemented and maintained Curriculum—Established and maintained budget for all programs—Observed and evaluated Certified and Classified staff—Directed USDA food service, transportation, facilities, operation, and maintenance of school.
- Implemented Site-Based management—Work Sampling System, including Portfolio Assessment—"Reading Recovery" program.
- In response to needs, implemented All-Day Kindergarten.
- Served on Science Textbook Selection Committee, Cultural Planning Committee, Discipline and Attendance Planning Committee—Attended conferences, including IASA, Goals 2000, NISBA, and NIEA.

Vice Principal, American Tribal School, Flower, Washington   1992–1994
- Performed duties of Vice Principal, and:
  Oversaw student discipline, parent and community relations—Conducted school board meetings—Participated in teacher observations and evaluations—Set up and managed school budgets—Led self-esteem programs—Participated in selection and assignment of staff members.

"...one of the finest leaders in our school system today..."

"...instrumental in creating learning environments that allow every student to be both challenged and successful..."

"...works with teachers, students, and parents to achieve a climate of positive and appropriate behavior..."

"...an outstanding individual whose talents and efforts make her an admirable and respected principal."

Teachers,
Annwald Elementary

Continued next page...

This resume shows clear career progression and a solid list of achievements. The testimonials are unobtrusive yet highly effective.

Bonnie Gregg

Page 2

EXPERIENCE CONTINUED

Teacher, American Tribal School, Flower, Washington, 1989–1992

Taught all subjects to 4th, 5th, and 6th grade students—Taught 7th and 8th grade Math, Science, Social Studies, Art, Health, English, and P.E.

Student Teacher, Daly Elementary School, Flower, Washington, 1989

Observed, planned, and taught 5th grade class—Planned and taught units in Reading, Math, and P.E.—Participated in parent conferences and staff meetings—Participated in and used Cooperative Learning while teaching in the school for the 21st Century

EDUCATION

M.Ed., School Administration, Western Washington University, 1995
B.A., Education, University of Northern Colorado, 1989
Initial Elementary Principal Certificate, 1995

CONTINUING EDUCATION

Seattle Pacific University, 30 hr, Spring 1999: CEU 1276 Management of Behavior Problem Children
Salish Kootenai College, 4 CEU, Spring 1996: CEN 180 The Heart of Leadership

PROFESSIONAL DEVELOPMENT

Enhancing Your Effectiveness as an Elementary School Principal	Bureau of Education and Research	Winter 1999
Using Discipline with Dignity	NBI, Inc., Otter Pond Institute	Winter 1999
Nonviolent Crisis Intervention	Annwald School District	Winter 1998
Processes and Practices of Staff Evaluations	Annwald School District	Fall 1998
Success for All Reading Program	Annwald School District	Fall 1998
Summer Reading Institute	Northwest ESD 189	Summer 1998
Incorporating Essential Learning	Northwest ESD 189	Spring 1998
Kinderroots Training	Annwald School District	Winter 1997
Family Support Team	Annwald School District	Fall 1997
Building Principal as Instructional Leader	Northwest ESD 189	Fall 1997
Success for All Reading Program	Annwald School District	Fall 1997
Special Education and the Law	U.W. Law Division	Fall 1997
School-Wide Positive Discipline	Northwest ESD 189	Spring 1997
Pre-employment Interviewing	WSPA Olympia ESD 114	Spring 1997
Working with High-Risk Kids	Recovery Foundation	Spring 1996
Staff and Community Relations	American Tribal School	Spring 1995
Assertive Discipline	American Tribal School	Fall 1994

PROFESSIONAL MEMBERSHIPS

National Association of Elementary School Principals (NAESP)
Association of Washington School Principals (AWSP)
American Association of School Administrators (AASA)
Association for Supervision and Curriculum Development (ASCD)
National Indian School Board Association (NISBA)
National Indian Education Association (NIEA)

SPECIAL INTERESTS

Reading — Golf — Skiing — Swimming — Aerobics — Music

Jacob D. Simmons

8118 Cresskill Road
Asheville, North Carolina 28804

Home: (828) 252-9569
Office: (828) 274-7264

Athletic Director — Higher Education or Preparatory School

Twenty-year career as collegiate and high school athletic administrator, coach, and recruiter. Consistently successful in introducing innovative administrative systems, athletic and recruitment programs, and student services. Strong leadership, communication, and student and institutional advocacy skills. Frequently conducted high school and college football clinics. Committed to holistic student development and learning. Core competencies include:

- Departmental Leadership
- Player Recruitment & Admissions Support
- Budgeting & Fundraising
- Collegiate Athletic Operations
- Facility Renovation
- Hiring & Staff Development

Professional Experience

FLETCHER COUNTRY DAY SCHOOL — Asheville, North Carolina   1995–Present

Athletic Director

Direct interscholastic athletic program for this private school — grades 7 to 12 — composed of 60 teams (16 sports, 700+ participants) and more than 60 coaches. Coordinate all scheduling, team travel and transportation, and procurement and care of uniforms and equipment. Recruit, hire, and develop coaching staff. Manage $750,000 in annual operating/administrative budgets and a $170,000 Booster Club budget.

Scope of responsibility encompasses operation and maintenance of 11 athletic fields, a 2,500 seat stadium with an eight-lane rubberized track, two gymnasiums, 10 tennis courts, weight room, wrestling room, and two training rooms. Supervise staff of 22, including 16 varsity head coaches and three certified athletic trainers. As Vice President of five-school conference, schedule all league contests.

❑ Won Wachovia Cup three consecutive years (1996-1998); recognized as the top private school athletic program in North Carolina.

❑ Spearheaded planning for new $16 million athletic facility. Focused department's mission and initiated allocation of resources (delivered formal group presentations and currently assist in fund-raising) to enhance program quality and increase student participation. Initiated architect search.

❑ Instituted a strength and conditioning program for all sports teams. Established strength/conditioning coach position.

❑ Created Hall of Honor, a recognition structure to acknowledge past students, coaches, and administrative staff who have contributed significantly to the school's athletic program. Established a 12-member selection committee and drafted selection criteria.

❑ Instituted a harmful substance abstinence pledge system — an education program — for all athletic team members.

❑ Established Sports Information Director position to coordinate dissemination of all athletic information to local media. Also developed a web page for the athletic program.

❑ Upgraded athletic department computer system providing an integrated network link with all departments.

❑ Directed the installation of an eight-lane rubberized track and a $170,000 renovation of a four athletic field complex. Also coordinated $86,000 stadium lighting renovation project.

❑ Developed a leadership program including a 12-member Captain's Council (students), a 10-member Athletic Advisory Council (senior coaches and athletic administrators) to promote student involvement, reduce management costs, and improve program efficiencies.

❑ Drafted a coaches' handbook and produced a parents' athletic department handbook.

Because much of a coach's success is proved by a winning record, this resume starts off the list of accomplishments with this important information. The key words included in the summary show multiple areas of expertise.

Jacob D. Simmons   page 2

UNITED STATES NAVAL ACADEMY — Annapolis, Maryland   1978-1995

Assistant Football Coach (1978-1995)

Served initially as Junior Varsity Assistant Coach (12/78-12/82), then as Varsity Assistant Coach (1/83-6/95). Traveled throughout New England and upstate New York to identify and recruit top talent within region. Coached Division I varsity and junior varsity running backs, place kickers, receivers, defensive backs, and special teams.

❑ During my tenure, Navy played in three Bowl games. Ground game ranked within the top five nationally, seven of eight years as running back coach.

Office Manager (12/78-6/93); Recruiting Coordinator (12/78-12/85)

Maintained broad-based organizational, administrative, and athletic office responsibilities for 14 years. Also directed staff of 16 (13 recruiters, three support) and managed a $250,000 annual budget. Managed nationwide recruiting activities, including coordination with admissions support program (1500 liaison/reserve officers) and an internal talent scout network. Maintained liaison between Navy Football Office and Annapolis Admissions Office, assisting in decision-making process. Planned and organized recruiting weekends for recruits and their families.

❑ Designed and launched a multi-faceted football recruitment program, including high school visitations, in-home presentations, 48-hour campus visitations, one-day open houses and targeted direct mail. **Results:** Navy played in its first two Bowl (Cherry, 1983, and Peach, 1984) games.

❑ Directed conversion from manual to automated data management system for football office in 1982.

THE PEMBROKE SCHOOLS — Richmond, Virginia   Fall-Winter 1978

Physical Education Teacher/Senior English Assistant Teacher/Coach/Advisor

PREVIOUS EXPERIENCE:

Sales Representative, Procter and Gamble, Baltimore, Maryland   Spring 1978

Education

LONG ISLAND UNIVERSITY, C. W. Post College — Long Island, New York

❑ M.S., Counseling, 1981

UNITED STATES NAVAL ACADEMY — Annapolis, Maryland

❑ B.S., Engineering, 1972

Professional Affiliation

National Interscholastic Athletic Administrators Association

Community Activity

Member & Football Team Representative, Fellowship of Christian Athletes (1983-1995)

Professional Development

Independent School Management Athletic Director Workshop (40 hours), 7/96

CONFIDENTIAL

CHARLOTTE KRONIG

8888 Norwood Drive
Collinsburg, Alabama 36100

[334] 555-5555 (Home – Central Time)
[334] 555-6666 (Office – Central Time)

WHAT I CAN BRING TO LAWRENCE COLLEGE AS YOUR NEWEST DIRECTOR OF STUDENT ACTIVITIES

❑ The **leadership** to develop and implement effective student life programs,

❑ The **wisdom** to guide, counsel and support students, and

❑ The **integrity** to earn the trust of every constituency.

EDUCATION

❑ Pursuing M.S., **General Counseling**, Alabama State University, Montgomery, Alabama. *Expect graduation in the Fall of 2000.*

❑ B.S., **Social Work**, Tuskegee University, Tuskegee, Alabama, 1989. *Dean's List virtually every semester. Earned this degree while working up to 30 hours a week.* **Honors.**

RELEVANT WORK HISTORY WITH SELECTED EXAMPLES OF SUCCESS

❑ **Coordinator of Student Activities**, Green State University, Collinsburg, Alabama
1992 – Present
GSU is an historically black university with approximately 1,600 students, 1,000 living on campus.

Directly responsible for activities of up to 65 Greek, professional, and honor student organizations. Assistant coordinator of student activities reports directly to me.

Transformed our underfunded, stagnant student activities program. Built strong staff, faculty, and student support campus-wide. Then expanded and integrated our programs as part of a rigorous curriculum. *Outcomes:* **More than doubled** the number of activities each academic year. **Student turnout soared** and stayed high.

Sought out high-risk students others had tried, and failed, to integrate with our student body. Earned their trust by soliciting their ideas, then placing them in accountable leadership positions. *Outcomes:* All **improved academically and socially**. Nearly all graduated.

Increased public relations impact of Miss ASU pageant by winning support of local businesses—a first. *Outcomes:* Winning **students** now **work confidently** with schools, churches, charities, and nursing homes. **Great payoff** for our university.

Established my office's reputation as a place students can turn for help solving tough problems. *Outcomes:* Recently "rescued" a student who fell through the cracks of the financial aid system. Turned young person ready to quit into a successful graduate.

❑ **Independent Consultant**, Collinsburg, Alabama
1983 – 1992

Guided small, inward-looking, disorganized SGA to improve the academic year's kickoff event. Led them to triple their representatives in the student body in just three days. Showed them how to cut planned expenses in half. *Outcomes:* **400** students **turned out**—a great start for all our students.

More indicators of performance ➲

CONFIDENTIAL

The resume for this administrator shows capability in a support position with two constituencies: the school and its students.

CONFIDENTIAL

Charlotte Kronig   **Director of Student Activities**   [334] 555-6666 (Office)

Work history (continued):

❑ **Founder** and **Manager**, Keep Entertaining Everyday People (KEEP), Collinsburg, Alabama
1981 – Present
KEEP is a non-profit organization that has established rotating partnerships with local schools. With its 28 volunteers, it provides leadership and personal development activities for up to 125 at-risk children at a time.

Built this organization with no money, no support, and no name recognition. Found and filled the needs of underprivileged children by asking them what they wanted. Then got high-visibility venues to showcase their talents. *Outcomes:* **Strong, continuing community support** lets us feature 140 community performers before SRO audiences of 1,200 — **every year for 15 years.**

SELECTED CONTRIBUTIONS TO MY COMMUNITY _____

❑ List of audiences of at least 400 addressed in 1999 as a featured speaker:

D.A.R.E.	Black Caucus Conference	Urban League of Nebraska
National Tots and Teens Convention	African American Women's Conference	Black Awareness Observance, United States Air Force
Coalition of Alabamians Reforming Education	Alabama Young Authors' Conference	National Voting Rights Museum

❑ University coordinator for these key events:

Student Voter Registration Drive, 1996 – 1999

Student Organizations Leadership Workshops, 1994 – 1999

Campus and Community Black History Month Programs, 1990 – 1999

❑ Service on these academic support committees:

Fall Convocation, 1994 – 1999	Honor's Day, 1994 – 1999
Founder's Day, 1994 – 1999	Homecoming, 1994 – 1999
Graduation, 1994 – 1999	

❑ Advisorships:

Miss GSU and Court, 1994 – 1999	Voices of Praise Choir, 1994 – 1999
Founder, Office of Student Activities Assistance Team, 1997 – 1999	Student Government Association, 1995 – 1997

PROFESSIONAL ASSOCIATIONS _____

❑ Alabama Counseling Association

❑ Business and Professional Women's Club of Collinsburg

CONFIDENTIAL

Page two

Ellen DeLeon, M.Ed.

5710 4TH Street, Apt. 1909
Lubbock, Texas 79416

806.799.2822
e_deleon@hotmail.com

ADMINISTRATION / DIAGNOSTICIAN / TEACHER

Over 15 years' experience in public school management, assessment, and teaching. Certifications include Mid-Management, Educational Diagnostician, Elementary Teaching, and Special Education. Earned a Master of Education Degree in Special Education and Learning and Behavior Disorders as well as 49 additional hours beyond a Master's Degree in Mid-Management and Assessment. Teaching levels vary from pre-school to junior high; worked successfully within large and small school districts in 4 states. Excellent leadership, communication, management, and human relationship skills. Core competencies include:

- ☑ Department/Divisional Leadership
- ☑ Special Education Specialist/Teacher
- ☑ Educational Assessment
- ☑ Budgeting & Planning
- ☑ Organization & Management
- ☑ Oral & Written Communications

EDUCATION

Mid-Management, Wayland Baptist University, Plainview, Texas   1999
- ☑ Completed 36 hours of graduate work in 1999 with a 4.0 GPA.

Student Assessment, Texas Tech University, Lubbock, Texas   1995
- ☑ Completed 13 hours of graduate work in assessment.

Master of Education, University of Louisville, Louisville, Kentucky   1992
- ☑ Special Education and Learning and Behavior Disorders

Bachelor of Science in Education, Southeastern Oklahoma State University, Durant, Oklahoma   1981
- ☑ Elementary Education major and English minor.

Credentials and Certificates
- ☑ Mid-Management
- ☑ Educational Diagnostician (Grades PK – 12)
- ☑ Generic Special Education (Grades PK – 12)
- ☑ Elementary Self-Contained (Grades 1 – 8)

PROFESSIONAL EXPERIENCE

Lubbock Independent School District (LISD), Lubbock, Texas   1996-Present
Five years' experience in LISD education includes mid-management internship, educational diagnostician, department chairperson, resource specialist, compliance officer, and teaching in the elementary and junior-high levels. Extensive experience working with special-needs and at-risk students from severe/profound to learning-disabled, ethnically diverse populations and LEP/second-language learners. Supervised a variety of special programs.

- ☑ Supervised and trained a department of 8 staff and 150 students.
- ☑ Advised and provided ideas and strategies for working with students.
- ☑ Led over 300 Individual Education Plan meetings yearly with parents, staff, and students.
- ☑ Chief compliance officer for Evans Junior High School; kept accurate and complete records.
- ☑ Selected testing materials and assessed individual students for placement in special programs.
- ☑ In mid-management internship, assisted with the campus improvement plan, budgeting, disciplining students, supervising field trips and school activities, and attended administrative and school board meetings.
- ☑ Taught reading and English in summer school.
- ☑ Budgeted and selected materials.
- ☑ Opened an Academic Adjustment Unit for 15 students.
- ☑ Evaluated students for Limited English Proficiency.

Committees
— Campus Performance Objectives
— Language Proficiency Assessment

This detail-rich resume uses check-mark bullet points to confirm key qualifications.

Ellen DeLeon, M.Ed.   806.799.2822
Page 2   e_deleon@hotmail.com

PROFESSIONAL EXPERIENCE, continued

Plainview Independent School District (PISD), Plainview, Texas   1992-1996
  Over 4 years with PISD as a Special Education Resource teacher and a Content Mastery teacher. Worked effectively with parents, staff, and students.
  - ☑ Assessed all students at the beginning and the end of the school year to monitor progress.
  - ☑ Successfully implemented a combination multi-sensory and novel studies approach to teaching reading and writing with 10% of students advancing to regular classes.
  - ☑ Worked with staff on social skills training and peer mediation.

Bullitt County Schools, Shepherdsville, Kentucky   1988-1992
  Classroom Teacher (Grades 4-5) and Special Education Resource Teacher (Grades K-7)

Rehabilitation Center, Clarksville, Indiana   1987-1988
  Assistant Education Director/Teacher for handicapped preschool and toddler

Hanna Public Schools, Hanna, Oklahoma   1982-1987
  Fourth-Grade Teacher

Stidham Public Schools, Stidham, Oklahoma   1981-1982
  Kindergarten Teacher

PRESENTATIONS

— "The Umbrella of Special Education," education classes, Texas Tech University, 4 times yearly.
— "Confidentiality & Overview of Special Education," Evans Junior High staff, yearly.
— "Assessment & Modifications," Evans Junior High staff and Haynes Elementary staff, 2000.
— "Functional Assessment & Modifications," LISD district staff professional development, 1999, 2000.
— "Modification for Successful General & Special Education," Lubbock Reading Conference, 1998.

CONTINUING EDUCATION

— Mentoring Day for Educational Diagnosticians: Case Studies in Assessment, 2000
— Interpretive Options & Report Writing with the WJ-III, 2000
— WISC-III as a Process Instrument, 2000
— Training on the Leiter and Kait, 1999
— Statewide Assessment Project Conference, 1999
— Reading & Writing — Moving from Assessment to Intervention, 1999
— Professional Development and Appraisal System, 1998
— Instructional Leadership Training, 1998
— Professional Development and Appraisal System, 1998

— Texas Educational Diagnostician Association Conference, 1998
— Leadership Collaboratives — Leveraging the Process for Students of Poverty, 1997
— Learning Disabilities Association of Texas Conference, 1995
— Technology Camp, 1995
— Learning Disabilities Association Conference, 1994
— Caprock Area Writing Project, 1994
— Multi-sensory Teaching Approach, 1993
— Council for Exceptional Children International Conference, 1992

ASSOCIATIONS & COMMUNITY SERVICE

— Council for Exceptional Children
— Learning Disabilities Association
— Texas Educational Diagnosticians

— Church choir, women's missionary organization, and church social committee
— Taught adult and children Bible studies
  Planned and organized vacation Bible school

JOHN P. NORTON

Route 5, Box 99, Sparta, Wisconsin 54656
Home (608) 269-1515 — Office (608) 269-3908 — E-mail: john-norton@one.net

SUPERINTENDENT: SPARTA AREA SCHOOL DISTRICT

PHILOSOPHY OF ADMINISTRATION

The primary purpose of educational administration is to provide an environment in which individuals can work together cooperatively to serve the needs of students through accomplishing the goals of the institution. Administration should be a democratically oriented process designed to foster an atmosphere in which staff members assist one another, plan together, and freely exchange ideas. A structure must be developed that allows people to participate in the decision-making process. People grow as they attempt to solve problems and seek answers to questions. Administrators should encourage staff participation to increase the possibility of many people being able to secure the kind of interaction through which they share and grow through interchange of ideas. Relating to subordinates in a democratic manner fosters the development of high staff morale and creates the group cohesiveness necessary for the educational improvement of a school district.

CAREER HISTORY

Superintendent of Schools	Sparta Area School District, Sparta, WI	1990-Present
	Truman Community Schools, Truman, MN	1986-1990
	Winnebago Community Schools, Winnebago, MN	1981-1986
	East Greene Community Schools, Grand Junction, IA	1979-1981
	Ringsted Community Schools, Ringsted, IA	1978-1979
Principal	Des Moines Christian School, Des Moines, IA	1976-1978
Guidance Counselor	Calvert County Schools, Prince Frederick, MD	1974-1976
Teacher	Bradford Area Schools, Bradford, PA — Sixth Grade	1971-1974

EDUCATION

Doctor of Education	University of South Dakota, Vermillion, SD Major: Educational Administration	1986
Educational Administration	Iowa State University, Ames, IA Non-degree program	1978
Master of Science	Saint Bonaventure University, Saint Bonaventure, NY Major: Guidance and Counseling	1974
Bachelor of Science	Bryan College, Dayton, TN Major: Elementary Education	1971
Credentials are on file at:	Teacher Placement Office Saint Bonaventure University, Saint Bonaventure, NY	

Rather than detail job duties and accomplishments, this resume leads off with a Philosophy of Administration and follows with a CV-style listing of employment and experience.

RENE HARBOR

23515 Oak Tree Drive, Newhall, California 91321   661-259-7990

ASSISTANT PRINCIPAL / DEAN OF STUDENTS / COORDINATOR / EDUCATOR / TRAINER offering expertise in the development and teaching of educational programs designed to meet a broad cross-section of learner needs. Experience in teaching, project development, and behavioral management. Counseling and training abilities. Excellent administrative, interpersonal, and communication skills, as well as expertise in identifying instructional requirements and developing effective course curriculum. Positive motivator skilled in educating both student and adult learners. Conversational Spanish.

EDUCATION AND CREDENTIALS

Master of Arts, Educational Administration, University of Southern California.
Bachelor of Arts, History, minor in Spanish, University of California, Los Angeles.

Certifications: **Administrative Services**
                    Standard Supervision (Life)
                    General Secondary (Life)

ACCOMPLISHMENTS

- **Focus on Learning Pilot WASC Accreditation Process.** Interpreted guidelines set by the state of California, analyzed process, developed methodology and materials to implement these guidelines, provided individualized training to staff, students, and parents. Currently providing training, guidance, and materials to a second district high school.

- **Coordinator for Categorical Programs** (Gifted and Talented Education/Advanced Placement/ESL). Guided programs successfully through a period of tremendous growth in quality, enrollment, and curriculum.

- **Expanded and refined school curricula.**

- **Directed significant increase in staff development activities,** including the concept of "teachers training teachers."

PROFESSIONAL EXPERIENCE

Assistant Principal — DALE HIGH SCHOOL, Dale United School District, Newhall, CA   1989 - Present
Curriculum/
Instruction
- Supervise instructional goals and objectives. With staff, develop new course offerings in areas of foreign languages, science, math, social studies, ESL sheltered classes, and instructional teaming.
- Direct staff, manage operational budgets, and coordinate activities for GATE, ESL, SB 1882 Staff Development, Advanced Placement, Summer School, and SASI administrative computer system.
- Recently directed development of the Dale High *Vision, Beliefs,* and *Expected School-wide Learning Results.*
- Develop Master Schedule.
- Supervise Library Services
- Actively interview, evaluate, and recruit instructional staff.
- Serve as committee member to select Dale District Mentor Teachers.

Given the lengthy listing of job duties needed to fully describe the scope of responsibility in each position, accomplishments are set off in a separate section to ensure that they don't get overlooked.

RENE HARBOR   Page Two

Staff Development

- Use site-based management principles to support teachers' participation in the decision-making process and assume ownership for school results.
- Work closely with teachers to instill the confidence necessary to perform effectively.
- Provide common planning time for staff to better coordinate curriculum.
- Conduct regularly scheduled performance reviews for certificated and classified staff.
- Supervise and coordinate work of chairpersons of staff development committees.

Plant Management/Daily Operations

- Supervise maintenance and custodial staff; redefined performance standards for custodial staff.
- Schedule all facility utilization.
- Handle all repair and maintenance requests and supervise plant manager in their implementation.
- Oversee School Master Calendar, key distribution, telephone system, daily bulletin, marquee, and printing.
- Regularly publish a newsletter to keep parents informed about school activities, events, and general information. Facilitated technological upgrade in presentation.

Guidance Services

- Supervise counseling staff.
- Manage all Registrar's office functions, ROP Program, and Career Center.
- Member, Crisis Intervention Team.
- Coordinate all school-site testing programs.

Instructor — UNIVERSITY OF LAVERNE, LaVerne, CA   1990 - Present
Teach course entitled Field Work in Educational Administration.   (Concurrently)

Prior to 1989
Assistant Principal — Sierra Madre Junior High School, Wm. S. Dale U.H.S.D., Canyon Country
Dean Of Students — Voyota High School, Dale United School District, Saugus
Dean Of Girls — Dale High School, Dale United School District, Newhall
Dean Of Girls — Grant High School, San Fernando Valley, Los Angeles Unified District
Social Studies Teacher — Grant High School, San Fernando Valley, Los Angeles Unified District
Social Worker — All Nations Neighborhood Center, East Los Angeles

PROFESSIONAL AFFILIATIONS

Phi Delta Kappa
Women in Educational Leadership
USC Educational Alumni
Association of California School Administrators,
    Santa Clarita Chapter — Staff Development Award
Dale District Management Association — Past President,
    Vice President, Secretary, Salary and Benefits Chairperson

Member, WASC High School Accreditation Teams
    Montebello High School, Montebello
    Troy High School, Fullerton
    Bishop School, La Jolla
    Granite Hills High School, San Diego

COMMUNITY ACTIVITIES

Assistance League, Santa Clarita Valley   UCLA Alumni Association

LAWRENCE S. COSTNER

Home: (407) 380-1654
Office: (407) 381-5413

2764 Gray Fox Lane
Orlando, Florida 32826

ACADEMIC ADMINISTRATOR

Accomplished professional with a diversified background in academic administration and secondary education. Consistently successful in introducing strategic marketing and operational plans, athletic programs, and student services to increase enrollment, enhance the student experience, and strengthen competitive market position. Strong leadership, communication, student, and institutional advocacy skills. Areas of expertise include:

- Finance / Capital Development
- Curriculum Development
- Fundraising

- Enrollment
- Student Affairs
- Public Relations

- Financial Aid
- Team Development
- Foundation Management

PROFESSIONAL EXPERIENCE

SAINT PETER'S HIGH SCHOOL, Orlando, Florida   1991 to Present

Principal

Senior Academic Administrator with full autonomy and financial accountability for a private high school. Challenged to turn around this distressed school on the brink of closing. Scope of responsibility was diverse and included all phases of administration and management, strategic planning, capital and budget development and administration, foundation management, fundraising, staffing and personnel functions, curriculum development and implementation, and public relations. Direct a staff of 25 teachers, one business manager/bookkeeper, and four administrative staff. Led improvements within all areas returning school to financial stability.

Management / Finance
- Reversed a deficit budget within five years and currently manage a $2 million budget with a surplus.
- Improved discipline, morale, and the entire campus environment, elevating integrity and esteem.
- Established a collaborative administrative council to analyze and improve the curriculum and academic program.
- Led a capital campaign to establish two new science laboratories and numerous renovations throughout the school.
- Introduced new technology systems throughout the administrative offices and classrooms.

Curriculum
- Instituted a gifted program and eight Advanced Placement classes. Improved the foreign language and science programs.
- Established a Curriculum Development Committee to consistently review and upgrade course offerings.
  Results: 98% of the students now go on to higher education, and students consistently score above the State and National averages on standardized tests.

Athletics
- Led a complete upgrade of the Athletic Program and developed teams which now compete in state championships.
- Doubled the Co-curricular Athletic Program.

Admissions & Enrollment
- Built enrollment to record highs (from 230 to over 350), producing the largest freshman and graduating classes ever. Increased enrollment by 33%.

Breaking down a long list of accomplishments into subsections is a good way to increase their impact and ensure nothing gets overlooked.

LAWRENCE S. COSTNER

Page 2

SAINT PETER'S HIGH SCHOOL (Continued):

Foundation Management/Financial Aid
- Restored shattered relationship with foundation donor and merited an additional $1 million in foundation funds.
- Increased financial aid from $70,000 to $130,000 annually.
- Elevated overall student education scores attracting over $2 million in scholarships for over half of the 60 graduating students (1998).

Fundraising
- Raised over $250,000 annually, in a low-income community, to supplement the school's operating budget.

Public Relations
- Initiated articulation meetings with principals and teachers from feeder schools to better coordinate and improve total academic program.
- Established a Student Ambassador Program to assist with public relations and fundraising functions and represent school throughout the community.

ORANGE CATHOLIC COLLEGE PREPARATORY, Princeton, New Jersey   1970 to 1991

Assistant Principal, Student Affairs (1987 to 1991)
Athletic Director (1972 to 1987) — Teacher, Social Science (1970 to 1987)

Transitioned through all phases of academic administration for this 650-student private college preparatory school. As Assistant Principal of Student Affairs:

- Held management positions including Dean of Students, Director of Student Activities, Student Government Moderator, and Core Administrator responsible for daily operations.
- Served on the Advisory Board and several committees, including Finance, Admissions, Planning, and Curriculum Development.
- Appointed Summer School Principal with full responsibility for academic program and curriculum.

As Athletic Director, held responsibility for the supervision of 35 interscholastic teams and 56 coaching personnel. Managed athletic budget and equipment, student eligibility, coach hiring and evaluations, and individual/team records.

- Elevated the total athletic program to one of the top programs in New Jersey.
- Doubled the size of the girls' program.

As Social Science Teacher, taught U.S. History, Civics (Mock Convention), World History, South East Asian History, Geography, Street Law (Mock Trial), Contemporary Issues and Leadership.

EDUCATION

Masters, Educational Administration	Stetson University, DeLand, Florida, 1989
Administrative Services Credential	Stetson University, DeLand, Florida, 1985
Florida State Teaching Credential (Standard Lifetime)	State of Florida, 1975
History, Physical Education	
B.A., History	Princeton University, Princeton, New Jersey, 1970

PROFESSIONAL AFFILIATIONS

National Association of Secondary School Principals
Florida Association of School Administrators
Association for Supervision and Curriculum Development

Gwendoline J. Tober

Confidential Resume

442 Georgetown Drive, Lake Erie, Ohio 43460 • 419.667.9999
Email: gjt_eriehs@lakeerie.edu

SECONDARY ADMINISTRATOR / EDUCATOR

Education administrator with over 20 years' experience leading faculty and students. Expertise in development and implementation of school improvement and curriculum programs that impact accomplishment of district-wide strategic planning goals. Lifetime commitment to quality education programs that emphasize the personal development of students. Ability to apply creative thinking skills toward short- and long-range goals.

AREAS OF ADMINISTRATIVE STRENGTH

Community Involvement & Leadership ~Administrative & Board Relations ~Block Scheduling
Curriculum & Program Development ~Staff Training & Development ~Outcomes Accreditation
Strategic Planning ~Budget Analysis ~Student Needs Assessment ~Special Education Programs
Grant Writing ~Continuous Education ~Staff Development & Training ~Contract Negotiations

CAREER PROFILE

Erie High School (Lake Erie School District), Lake Erie, Ohio   1988 – Present
High School Principal

Located in NW Ohio, Lake Erie School District consists of 2,200 students with 725 enrolled in grades 9-12. The mission of the high school is based on a partnership with the community that emphasizes the personal development of each student through a unified academic program promoting life-long learning skills and enhancing social responsibility and employability.

Guide and direct all aspects of administration and instruction at the high-school level. Promote a team-building atmosphere and delegate through a staff comprising assistant principal, department chairs, 50 full-time certified instructors, guidance counselors, and education support staff. Work closely with school psychologist, food service, transportation and building and maintenance staff. Charged with full budget responsibilities for high school and athletic complex.

- Gained marked improvement in student ACT scores with increases being recorded 6 years in a row. Currently scores are at their highest level.
- Direct strong curriculum and instruction programs resulting in increased student performance on state proficiency tests at an accelerated rate compared to similar schools in the state.
- Facilitated successful program development to achieve Outcomes Endorsement from North Central Association in 1997.
- Spearheaded development and implementation of a block-scheduling program that has been in successful operation since 1996.
- Oversee and monitor grant programs such as Pacesetter, Venture Capital, and Systemic Improvement.
- Coordinate and supervise student teachers in liaison with two local universities.

After retiring from the school district where she spent 12 productive years, this administrator used this resume to land a senior administrative position with a school district in another state.

GWENDOLINE J. TOBER... continued

SCHOOL ACHIEVEMENTS & HIGHLIGHTS

- Erie High School was the first school in NW Ohio to pursue advanced accreditation status from North Central Association known as the Outcomes Endorsement.
- First school in NW Ohio to institute a successful block scheduling program.
- Highlighted twice in local newspaper for one of the most successful and aggressive School Improvement Programs in the state.
- Erie High School nominated for Ohio's Best Award.

PERSONAL CAREER ACHIEVEMENTS & HIGHLIGHTS

- Elected to serve as member of the Ohio State Committee for North Central Association of Colleges and Secondary Schools 1998-2001.
- Invited to share knowledge and expertise regarding the Outcomes Endorsement process and challenges with other school accreditation teams throughout the state.
- Frequently invited to make presentations and facilitate programs at school and education group functions in Ohio concerning school improvement efforts.
- Recipient of Lake Erie School District's "Golden Apple" award.
- Orchestrated development of district-wide Health Team & Safety Plan.
- Member of District Strategic Planning and Continuous Improvement Teams.

BURLINGTON HIGH SCHOOL – Deer Run, Ohio   1983 – 1988
Associate Principal / Director of Student Activities

BAYSIDE HIGH SCHOOL – Bayside, Ohio   1980 – 1983
Assistant Principal
Athletic Administrator / NHS Advisor / Senior Class Advisor / Yearbook Business Manager

Note: Prior experience as a Secondary Social Studies Instructor is available upon request

EDUCATION / ADDITIONAL TRAINING

Bowling Green State University, Bowling Green, Ohio ~Post Graduate Work
Additional hours in Administration and Supervision / Ohio CEUs (1981-Present)

Bowling Green State University, Bowling Green, Ohio ~Master of Education (1980)
Major: Administration and Supervision

Miami University, Oxford, Ohio ~Bachelor of Arts (1978) ~Major: History ~Minor: Education

Participated in numerous educational training and leadership seminars.

LICENSES / CERTIFICATIONS

Ohio Certification in: High School Principal – through 2005
Comprehensive Social Studies (7-12) – Permanent

PROFESSIONAL MEMBERSHIPS

Ohio Association of Secondary School Administrators
North Central Association of Colleges & Secondary Schools
Phi Delta Kappa Education Honorary ~Phi Alpha Theta History Honorary

SARAH A. BALLARD

1210 Burkland Road – Goodlettsville, Tennessee 37072

Home: (615) 532-8064
Email: SBallard@aol.com

PROFESSIONAL OVERVIEW

- Over 20 years' combined experience in the areas of **TEACHING, COUNSELING, STAFF AND PROGRAM DEVELOPMENT,** and **ADMINISTRATION.**

- Flexible and easy-going with the ability to quickly develop a good rapport and put students – of all ages – at ease.

- Strong ability to teach, motivate, and counsel children and adults – in a training, tutorial, or classroom environment – to excel in both personal and professional development.

- Well-versed and proficient in the design and development of instructional programs and curriculum to meet organizational goals and student needs.

- An accomplished change agent with an established track record in getting positive results working with students, parents, faculty, administrators, and community.

ACADEMIC BACKGROUND

Doctor of Philosophy – Program and Staff Development – 1995
Middle Tennessee State University – Murfreesboro

Master of Arts Degree in Education – Emphasis: Guidance Counseling – 1982
Tennessee State University – Nashville

Teacher Certification in Grades K-12 – 1977

Bachelor of Science Degree in Secondary Education – Emphasis: History – 1977
Belmont University – Nashville, Tennessee

PROFESSIONAL EXPERIENCE

PRINCIPAL / TEACHER Grades 7/8 – 1991 to Present
The Hightower School – Nashville, Tennessee

Effectively manage daily operations of private elementary school with a population of 150 students in grades K-8. Hands-on involvement with faculty and staff development, curriculum development, ordering textbooks and materials, budget, and fundraising. As Head Teacher, taught 7th-8th grade combined class of 26-30 students. Subjects included social studies, science, 8th grade math, and Bible.

- Enrich the quality of education by identifying and nurturing the needs of individual students. Challenge their abilities and encourage them to set higher goals.

- As member of Building Committee, gained valuable experience in planning and designing state-of-the-art elementary school aimed at effectively combining the space needs of both students and teachers, and which ultimately served as a model school for other districts.

A distinctive headline font is used to add interest to the Times New Roman font used for the rest of the resume. This is a clear, well-organized, easy-to-absorb resume for an experienced administrator.

SARAH A. BALLARD

Page 2

PROFESSIONAL EXPERIENCE (CONTINUED)

ASSISTANT PROFESSOR OF EDUCATION – 1982 to 1991
University of the Midwest – Dubuque, Iowa

Developed highly successful pilot program to train student teachers how to efficiently organize and present all subjects to grades 1-8 in a one-room school setting. Established a one-room lab school used in training and evaluation.

- Significantly raised the percentage of student teachers that stayed with the teaching district (from 78% to 95%).

- After receiving national media exposure, the lab school became a model one-room school for rural school districts nationwide.

TEACHER Grades 6-8 – 1977 to 1982
Belmont Junior Academy – Nashville, Tennessee

Taught 7th-8th grade social studies and English (1980–82). Taught 6th grade self-contained classroom (1978–80). Supervised homeroom for 6th grade and taught 6th-7th-8th grade social studies (1977–78).

- Reached and motivated academically challenged students and turned them around by providing one-on-one attention.

PROFESSIONAL AFFILIATIONS

Association of Supervision and Curriculum Development – 1986 to Present

Nashville Area Chamber of Commerce – 1991 to Present

PERSONAL INTERESTS

Visiting historical sites … Genealogy and family history … Reading … Spectator sports.

LOIS A. TAYLOR
517 Yorkshire Court
Jersey City, New Jersey 08533
(201) 332-0213

PROFESSIONAL OBJECTIVE

Seeking a school administrator position.

PROFILE

Acting Principal / Learning Disabilities Teacher / Consultant with 20+ years in education, including more than five years as Acting Principal. Solid decision-making and problem-solving skills. A resource to colleagues, supervisors and parents. Multi-cultural and at-risk teaching experience.

CAREER HISTORY

Stafford Township School District, Manahawkin, NJ (1988-Present)

Acting Principal, Child Study Team Coordinator / Learning Disabilities Teacher–Consultant

As <u>Acting Principal</u>:
- ❑ Manage crisis situations; intervene with local authorities, state agencies, and referral services.
- ❑ Promote staff attendance at educational workshops and conferences hosted by outside agencies and colleges.

As <u>Child Study Team Coordinator / Learning Disabilities Teacher - Consultant</u>:
- ❑ Vital to district implementation of a computerized IEP program.
- ❑ Trained all staff, including administration, in the use of IEP software and continue to function as troubleshooter.
- ❑ Pioneered the introduction of word processing, with spell-check capabilities, into classrooms with special needs students.
- ❑ Developed curriculum designed to improve kindergarten readiness of special needs, pre-school children.
- ❑ Developed monitoring procedures, strategies, and tools for case status and evaluation process.
- ❑ Directed and chaired meetings on innovative teaching tools and methodologies to both administration and faculty.
- ❑ Identified and introduced mainstreaming trends and proposed reading and writing programs designed to optimally meet the needs of special needs students.
- ❑ Write behavior management programs; well versed in behavior management techniques.

As a <u>staff member</u>:
- ❑ Chaired the Building Advisory Committee and the Sick Building Committee, working in concert with PEOSCH.
- ❑ Facilitated grade-level meetings involving retention of students.
- ❑ Introduced Light's Retention Scale.
- ❑ Served as Senior Association Representative on the local education association and as a member of the Negotiations Committee.

Note how job titles are grouped together, then functional responsibilities and achievements are highlighted under subheadings.

RESUME 84, CONTINUED

LOIS A. TAYLOR   **Page Two**

CAREER HISTORY, continued

Manchester Township School District, Manchester, NJ (1986-1988)

Learning Disabilities Teacher / Consultant, Pre-K - Fourth Grades

- ❑ Assisted Administration in establishing pre-referral procedures and staffing initiatives (prior to the establishment of Pupil Assistance Committee mandates).
- ❑ Pioneered modification guidelines for the administration of district-wide tests to classified children (prior to state-mandated criteria).
- ❑ Succeeded in raising teacher awareness of proactive teaching strategies by presenting Teacher Effectiveness and Student Achievement (TESA) inservices.

Ocean County North Shore Joint Commission, Lavalette, NJ (1984-1986)

Learning Disabilities Teacher / Consultant, Pre-K - Eighth Grades

- ❑ Established pre-referral interventions (prior to PAC mandates)
- ❑ Provided inservices on instructional strategies and mainstream interventions.
- ❑ Played a role in the completion of state-wide special education reports for individual districts.

Georgian Court College, Lakewood, NJ (1983)

Learning Disabilities Clinic Evaluator

- ❑ Evaluated and determined specific areas of learning disabilities and provided recommendations to be implemented by clinicians.

Lakewood School District, Lakewood, NJ (1970-1984)

Elementary School Teacher, Second, Fifth, Third Grades

- ❑ Established and promoted throughout New Jersey a reading program for 10-, 11-, and 12-year-old students who were reading below second grade level.
- ❑ Instructed teachers and administrators in the application of the Read / Write Project.
- ❑ Served as PTA Vice President and Senior Association Representative for the local education association.

EDUCATION / CERTIFICATIONS

Georgian Court College, Lakewood, NJ

> **Supervisor / Principal Certification**
> **Learning Disabilities Teacher / Consultant Certification**
> **Master of Arts, Elementary Education**

College of New Jersey, Trenton, NJ

> **Bachelor of Arts, Elementary Education (K-8)**

REFERENCES

Furnished upon request.

Sandi Palmer

1202 Coolidge Drive • Atherton, IA 50010 • (515) 297-3904 • sandi1436@aol.com

Objective

A position as Director of Education at Sylvan Learning Center that will fully utilize strong leadership abilities, innovative organizational skills, and sound instruction and learning techniques that motivate children to become independent, life-long learners.

Professional Profile

Personal Motto: "Classroom management is the key to successful teaching."

- Organized, take-charge education professional with strong follow-through ability and excellent management skills; able to plan and oversee projects from concept to successful conclusion.
- Motivated, high-energy educator with strong track record fostering student creativity and responsibility while enhancing learning.
- Effectively prioritize a broad range of responsibilities in order to consistently meet deadlines.
- Develop excellent rapport with individuals at all levels – strong interpersonal skills.
- Provide individualized instruction based on student's need as the situation dictates.
- Actively supervise and mentor numerous block students and student teachers.

Experience

Lower Elementary Teacher
Atherton Community School District, Atherton, IA, 1970 – present

Teach full academic curriculum at first, second, and third grade levels. Strong emphasis on reading, writing, and mathematics. Write curriculum, assess and evaluate student performance, design report cards, and maintain excellent communication with students, parents, and staff.

Instruction

- Encourage students to make responsible choices by teaching consequences. Consistency of follow-through is key.
- Provide classroom training, performance evaluation, and motivation as a mentor to student teachers completing college requirements for an education degree.
- Develop and integrate classroom enrichment activities such as research projects in the library, Internet research, reading to younger children, and playing games related to regular curriculum.
- Motivate students through rewards system – earn play money or fines to be used in various ways. Earn opportunity to e-mail family or friends about successes.
- Integrate computer technology into the classroom; designed two unique web pages; established e-mail accounts for communication needs between students, parents, and teacher.

continued on page two

This resume uses a subtle watermark of a desk and apple to distinguish this administrator from other candidates. She made it through two intense interviews to become a finalist for the position described in the Objective.

Sandi Palmer

Experience *(continued)*

Analysis/Planning

- Appointed by administration for lengthy terms on reading and math curriculum teams. Developed, validated, and enhanced curriculums for both subjects.
- Served three-year term on Building Level Team. Represented staff in site-based management approach; evaluated and implemented new ideas presented by staff; planned staff development days and faculty meetings.
- Designed three diverse report cards that reflected school philosophy and needs of staff.

Education

Bachelor of Arts, University of Northern Iowa, Cedar Falls, IA (formerly State College of Iowa) Major: Education with emphasis on math.

Attend Continuing Education courses at Iowa State University, University of Northern Iowa, Drake University, and Heartland Area Education Agency.

Organizations

Atherton Community Education Association (ACEA), 1970 – present
- Served two terms as president.
- Streamlined meeting procedures to effectively utilize time.
- Represented teachers on negotiations team; negotiated contract for certified staff.

P.E.O., Atherton, IA, 1985 – present
- Current president of 50-member organization; served two previous terms as president.
- Increased attendance at meetings through positive one-on-one communications.
- Sponsored International Peace Scholar through fund-raisers.
- Donated to ACCESS and sponsored a team in the 8-Hour Run for Life (cancer).

EMILY RAPPAPORT

111 River Drive ■ Park Ridge, NJ 07656 ■ (201) 695-2498 ■ erap@aol.com

EDUCATIONAL PUBLISHING/MATERIALS DEVELOPMENT

Highly qualified reading specialist offers accomplishments in publishing instructional reading materials.... Possess a strong background in classroom/remedial instruction.... Author of children's stories.

—— *Areas of Expertise* ——

Children's Literature — Curriculum Development — Staff Training
Print Production — Copyright Negotiations — Contracts

EDUCATION/PROFESSIONAL:

Montclair University, Upper Montclair, NJ — **MA DEGREE**/Certified Reading Specialist
William Paterson University, Wayne, NJ — **BA DEGREE**/Elementary Education
Education Association, New York, NY — Programs in Self Development & Communication

    Self Expression & Leadership Program   Communication-Access to Power I & II
    The Forum   Advanced Course in Communication

Beta Chi Chapter of Pi Lambda Theta, National Honor Professional Association in Education

State of New Jersey Certification: Reading Specialist/Reading Teacher (K-12)/Elementary Education

PUBLISHING EXPERIENCE:

NATIONAL STUDY SKILLS, INC., Paramus, NJ   1996-2000
A national supplemental learning program that emphasizes self-learning through repeated practice.

Coordinator/Materials Development & Instruction

Designed and developed instructional reading materials along with instructor's manual for use in over 900 math and reading centers in North America.

- Recruited to set up new reading department at US headquarters, servicing both advanced and remedial levels from preschool through high school.

- Produced three anthologies and four workbooks, including skills exercises and supporting literature — first-of-their-kind materials for this organization.

- Conducted extensive research to locate appropriate literature. Successfully negotiated contracts with publishers for rights to reproduce.

- Directed production of anthologies, coordinating with printers, illustrators and typesetters. Ensured that drawings conveyed a multicultural image and set a tone of egalitarianism.

- Authored original stories designed to accommodate Kumon instructional methodologies.

- Developed the corporation's recommended reading list for elementary school level.

- Spearheaded implementation of new reading materials by conducting training programs for regional managers and instructional staff. Presented an overview at national conference.

- Evaluated effectiveness of materials through on-site observations at several centers. Received excellent feedback from senior instructors.

Continued.....

Note how this individual's educational publishing qualifications—her primary area of expertise—are enhanced by extensive teaching experience, detailed on page 2.

RESUME 86, CONTINUED

EMILY RAPPAPORT   Page 2
(201) 695-2498

TEACHING EXPERIENCE:

LANGUAGE GROUP, Fort Lee, NJ   1987-1996
ESL Teacher (Part-Time)

- Assignments included accent reduction classes at Kean College as well as one-on-one training with international corporate clients.
- Made presentations to executive management of corporations to assess needs and develop English language training programs for their staff.

EAST ORANGE BOARD OF EDUCATION, East Orange, NJ   1994-1995
Developmental Reading Teacher

- Incorporated Bloom's Taxonomy of Higher Order Thinking (HOTS) into reading curriculum. Increased students' critical thinking skills.
- Initiated cooperative learning skills to enhance listening, verbal, thinking and writing skills. Facilitated improved group interaction.

PARAMUS BOARD OF EDUCATION, Paramus, NJ   1992-1994
Reading Teacher/Supplemental Reading Teacher

- Participated in pilot program to provide support to a classified student within a self-contained classroom. Trained classroom teachers in whole language approach to reading instruction.
- Implemented literature-based reading program for both remedial and developmental students. Included journal writing as means to assess that "what is said is clearly understood."

RIDGEWOOD BOARD OF EDUCATION, Ridgewood, NJ   1988-1991
Supplemental Teacher

- Spearheaded a special project based on creating books from inception – writing and illustration through binding. Led "Book Talks" program for student body and parents.

ST. ANTHONY'S SCHOOL, Fairview, NJ   1985-1988
Second Grade Teacher

- Taught self-contained class. Integrated many creative extended activities, enhancing reading instruction. Worked with local environmental center to create educational materials.

COMPUTER SKILLS:

Windows 95 — Office 97 — MS Word — Excel — Internet Research

RELATED EXPERIENCE/ACCOMPLISHMENTS:

- Active member of *Search Committee* for President of William Paterson College. Worked closely with Department Chairpersons to screen resumes and interview candidates.
- Selected *Member of the Year* by Women's Club of Park Ridge. Instrumental in planning for the transition to new countywide library lending system.
- *PTA President* for local school. Raised record amount of money to outfit school classrooms with ceiling fans.

Reference available on request.

MIRA SAHMANI

2001 Pinehurst Avenue, Suite 22
Toronto, Ontario A2B 3C3
Home: 416-555-6677 ◆ Pager: 416-555-7788

Objective: DAYCARE LICENSING ADMINISTRATOR

QUALIFICATIONS

BACKGROUND:
ECE with 21 years experience in child and daycare settings, including 12 years as an Executive Director responsible for the effective programming, operation, and compliance of community-based daycare facilities.

LEGISLATIVE KNOWLEDGE:
- Comprehensive knowledge and understanding of Day Nurseries Act, with the proven ability to interpret its standards and apply its guidelines to the successful operation of a daycare environment.
- Operational familiarity with Child & Family Services Act, in particular relating to Children's Aid responsibilities and guidelines.
- Comprehensive experience interpreting and applying standards set forth in appropriate Health & Fire regulations.
- Operational familiarity with Freedom of Information and Protection of Privacy Act, specifically as it relates to all criminal reference checking of daycare applicants and volunteers.

SPECIFIC STRENGTHS / SKILLS:
- Outstanding communication skills, with particular strength liaising with staff, parents, community members, Board of Directors, host school officials, professionals, municipal and government officials.
- Shrewd financial management and budgeting skills, with experience managing all fees, accounting, pay equity, and Operating/Wage Enhancement grants.
- Ability to thrive in complex and challenging situations.
- Excellent organizational and analytical skills as demonstrated by exemplary daycare management record.

EMPLOYMENT EXPERIENCE

EXECUTIVE DIRECTOR   1990 – Present
Glendale Centre for Kids   Toronto, Ontario
- Ensured compliance with all Ontario and Municipal laws and regulations concerning the operation, practice, and programming of the daycare.
- Created centre's Operational Philosophy and Mission Statement, and monitored compliance at all times.
- Developed centre's Policy & Procedures Manual to comply with and exceed all government guidelines.
- Chairperson for all monthly Ward 10 meetings, organizing agenda and speakers, and ensuring effective sharing of information and ideas.
- Managed a staff of 10 childcare professionals, including Assistant Director, Early Childhood Educators, and Assistant Teachers – evaluated performance, hired new staff, and resolved staff issues as required.
- Ensured open lines of communication between centre and all concerned parties, including parents, staff, Board of Directors, and government officials.

An expansive Qualifications summary leads off this chronological resume for a child-care administrator seeking a position as a Daycare Licensing Administrator.

MIRA SAHMANI   Home: 416-555-6677   Pager: 416-555-7788   2

EXECUTIVE DIRECTOR
Clearwood Community Childcare   1988 – 1990   North York, Ontario

- Coordinated creation and implementation of all policies and procedures for operation of new daycare facility.
- Created highly respected daycare centre within culturally diverse community, demonstrating excellent communication and listening skills, compassion, and creativity.
- Negotiated with host school, PCTA, and school board to secure daycare interests and develop mutually beneficial relationship.
- Provided consultative advice and training to new Board of Directors regarding roles and responsibilities.
- Managed a staff of 8 childcare professionals, overseeing all hiring, performance evaluations, and staff development.
- Successfully balanced Director role with additional teaching responsibilities.

INFANT HEAD TEACHER
Lilliput Childcare   1987 – 1988   Toronto, Ontario

- Created and implemented play activities to develop infant sensory acuity and ensured all basic daily needs were met.
- Implemented innovative program to teach parenting skills to teenage parents in host school.
- Implemented cooperative opportunities for high school students to volunteer in daycare to support Home Economics curriculum.
- Provided consultative advice for young parents, coordinating suitable community resources as required.

ASSISTANT SUPERVISOR
Rodale Community Daycare   1986 – 1987   Oshawa, Ontario

- Balanced administrative and teaching responsibilities in 70-child for-profit daycare.
- Created comprehensive program for preschool kindergarten children.
- Assisted in hiring, staff development, enrollment, policy-making, and marketing activities.

PRESCHOOL HEAD TEACHER
Von Trappe Daycare   1985 – 1986   North York, Ontario

- Created and implemented play and learning activities for toddler/preschool children.
- Modified program components as necessary to provide maximum benefit and enjoyment for children.

EDUCATION / PROFESSIONAL DEVELOPMENT

Practical Parenting Training Program   City of North York, 1999
True Colours   City of Toronto, 1999
Child Abuse Prevention Training Program   City of Toronto, 1997

Degree – Early Childhood Education   University of Toronto, 1984

Personal and professional references provided upon request.

CHAPTER 12

Resumes for Corporate Training and Development Professionals

- Corporate Training Managers
- Training and Development Professionals
- Corporate Trainers
- Training Consultants
- Executive Training and Development Professionals
- Technical Trainers/Training Managers
- Sales Trainers
- Performance Technologists
- Coaches/Mentors
- Software Trainers

Tim Wilson

6413 Chesapeake Lane
Atlanta, GA 30092

Home Phone   (404) 444-1234
E-mail   twilson25@aol.com

Corporate Training Manager
*Expertise in the Design, Development, Delivery and Administration
of National Corporate Training Programs*

- Organizational Needs Assessment
- Performance & Productivity Improvement
- Staff Training & Team Leadership
- Vendor Selection & Management
- Training Reporting & Tracking

- Training Program Design & Instruction
- Training Coordination & Scheduling
- Training Budgets & Cost Reduction
- Instructor Certification Implementation
- Meeting Planning & Logistics

Equally extensive experience in Project Management and Call Center Operations Management. Supervisory responsibilities for teams of up to 30 professionals and support staff. PC and Mac proficient in Microsoft Word, Excel, PowerPoint, WordPerfect, WordPro, and Pagemaker.

Professional Experience

VISA International – Atlanta, GA   **1997 to present**
National Training Implementation Manager

Recruited to lead training implementation across 9 regional credit card centers for large retail and credit card company. Manage issues between curriculum development division and training delivery function. Supervise and coach group of 5 national trainers. Select and manage vendor relationships and contracts. Responsible for all logistics for large-scale training programs including space allocation, materials, room set-up, catering, and meeting planning.

Training Programs

- Orchestrated design, development, and delivery of new training program for front-line managers. Planned all logistics for delivery of 48 hours of classroom training in 9 credit card centers within 12 months.
- Coordinated and implemented offerings of instructor certification program in 9 credit card centers nationwide.

Organizational Improvements

- Designed and implemented course evaluation forms for all areas of training resulting in measurements on course and trainer effectiveness.
- Developed administrative checklists for existing courseware to track materials, course registration, and attendance.

MasterCard International – Jacksonville, FL   **1990 to 1997**
Instructor / Course Developer / Registrar Manager (1993 to 1997)

Recruited to maintain and deliver series of management development courses for large credit card company with over $13 billion in annual receivables. Supervised team of managers and associates. Managed all vendor relationships and contracts and the entire registrar function.

Training Programs

- Delivered courses including *Passport to Excellence, The Business of UCS, Time Management, Performance Management, Managing Conflict,* and *Policy Deployment* to audiences in three operation center locations.

Note how the bullet points in the Professional Experience section are broken down into "Training Programs" and "Organizational Improvements," making the accomplishments in these two important areas easy to absorb in a quick read of the resume.

Tim Wilson

Organizational Improvements

- Reduced backlog of associates needing required orientation course by 78% in 12 months.
- Planned all course offerings and assisted in design and production of annual course catalogue.
- Scheduled all aspects of Universal Leadership Program for three operation centers.
- Reduced company expenses by $50,000 annually by redesigning course registration and cost allocation procedures.
- Analyzed registrar software needs and recommended improvements.

Recognition and Rewards

- Team Award, 1995
- Human Resource Spirit Award, 1994
- Team Leader Award, 1993

Team Manager – Call Center Operations (1990 to 1993)

Recruited to manage group of 30 customer service call center associates in bankcard processing environment. Managed call flow between two national call centers to meet and exceed customer service quality indicators. Hired, trained, and coached associates. Managed all aspects of call escalation to handle customer inquiries and concerns.

- Created functional team for weekend shift to enhance management of call volume and meet staffing requirements. Result was improved customer service and reduced need for hiring additional headcount.
- Suggested improved electronic communication vehicle which positively affected daily task management of over 2,000 associates.
- Spearheaded logistics for high-profile community project including staffing, scheduling, and ticket sales and production.
- Selected to deliver training for credit card application system for 700+ associates within 2 weeks.

Previous Professional Experience

Vice President / CFO - Launched entrepreneurial venture offering high-end sportfishing charter excursions to an exclusive clientele. Independently managed all financial planning, general accounting, banking, sales, customer service, advertising, and public relations functions.

Sales Executive – Top-producing sales associate of both residential and commercial properties throughout the Jacksonville, Florida, metro market. Managed the entire sales cycle, including market analysis to determine fair market pricing, property presentations, price/contract negotiations, mortgage consultations, and final property settlement/owner transfer.

Customer/Account Manager/Accountant - Several progressively responsible accounting and office management positions in the telecommunications and national retail chain industries. Demonstrated excellent communication, organizational, analytical and project management skills.

Education / Professional Development

Certificate in Training & Human Resource Development, 1999 - University of GA, Atlanta, GA
Coursework in Instructional Systems Design, Adult Learning, Consulting, and Testing & Evaluation

University of Virginia / Tidewater Community College / Florida Community College, 1998
Coursework in Business Management

Myers-Briggs Type Indicator (MBTI) Certified, 1996 - Type Resources, Inc.
American Society for Training & Development (ASTD), National Member, 1990 to Present

ALEXANDER G. HELM

1991 East 8260 South   (801) 495-4981
Sandy, Utah 84092   alexhelm@qwest.net

PROFILE

TRAINING AND DEVELOPMENT PROFESSIONAL with extensive experience in the design, delivery, evaluation, and enhancement of effective hands-on instructional programs that *improve efficiency, increase productivity, enhance quality,* and *strengthen financial results.*

Combine strong analysis, planning, organization, and consensus-building abilities with effective problem resolution, negotiation, and relationship management skills. Proven expertise in mechanical engineering, insurance risk assessment/loss prevention, and computer software.

Organized, take-charge professional with exceptional follow-through abilities and detail orientation; able to oversee projects from concept to successful conclusion. Efficiently and effectively prioritize a broad range of responsibilities to consistently meet tight deadlines. Demonstrated success in *surpassing productivity and performance objectives.*

Highly articulate and effective communicator. Excellent team building and interpersonal skills; work well with individuals on all levels. Recognized as a resource person, problem solver, and creative leader. Consistently receive highest possible ratings for technical expertise and training program excellence.

QUALIFICATIONS SUMMARY

Training Programs Management

- Conducted technical training programs for 1200 engineers operating worldwide.
- Administered $400,000 annual training budget for curriculum development and course materials.
- Implemented corporate training initiatives, including specialty software, e-mail, and MS Outlook.
- Coordinated training requirements and scheduling with field engineers and area supervisors.
- Managed course instructors, matching technical skill sets with appropriate courses and students.
- Arranged conference center accommodations, lodging, and training material production.

Technical Training Experience

- Presented 2- and 3-week training seminars with 25-40 students each (10 sessions per year).
- Engaged and challenged all course participants, accommodating varied levels of expertise.
- Bridged the gap between management/business objectives and technical/field experience.
- Provided post-training technical support to field engineers.
- Delivered intensive hands-on training programs in conference centers and in field locations.

Employee Development / Leadership

- Ensured that engineering staff had sufficient materials to complete 10+ days of training annually.
- Trained newly hired engineers in technical skill sets, company policy, and procedures.
- Coached training specialists to increase knowledge base and improve classroom presentations.

To de-emphasize career experience in loss prevention rather than a broader corporate training role, this resume creates a strong first page summarizing all relevant experience, then details career history on page 2.

ALEXANDER G. HELM   *Page Two*

Instructional Design / Assessment

- Developed CBT and multimedia tools, including PowerPoint presentations, slides, and videos.
- Reviewed student evaluations and consulted with training specialists to assess course effectiveness.
- Continuously refined curriculum, incorporating technology updates and quality improvements.
- Compiled and tested hands-on instructional materials and samples for presentations.
- Supervised instructional design specialists, providing expert technical review of course materials.

PROFESSIONAL EXPERIENCE

FM Global   1985 to Present
Commercial property insurance carrier — world's largest insurer of "highly protected risk"
insuring 45% of Fortune 500 companies.

Senior Loss Prevention Specialist, Salt Lake City, Utah — 1998 to Present

Conduct inspections and provide consulting services for regional insured client companies. Compile engineering reports according to procedural and technical quality standards, including specific recommendations for prevention or control of loss to property. Discuss engineering findings with insured clients, and assist with implementation of improvements to insured policies and procedures. Train and mentor less-experienced engineers and loss prevention specialists.

- Selected for 8-member engineering team to develop 2-day seminar to identify and quantify construction materials to evaluate insurance exposure.
- Trained 1200 engineers in 2-month window. Engineers subsequently identified $1 billion in loss potential and took corrective action to reduce insurance exposure.
- Received *Reward for Outstanding Contribution*. Training rated higher than any other program delivered in company history.

Senior Engineering Training Specialist, Norwood, Massachusetts — 1995 to 1997

- Directed company-wide engineering training programs for technical proficiency and loss prevention inspection/consulting procedures.
- Traveled frequently to deliver training programs to field engineers and evaluate effectiveness of training initiatives.

Loss Prevention and Engineering Training Specialist, Rochester, New York — 1987 to 1995

- Evaluated and assessed up to $10 billion of property for highly valued client, Eastman Kodak.
- Developed effective working relationships with executives and upper management, persuading adoption of improved loss prevention measures.
- Created and delivered successful 2-day training program for 40 Kodak staff members.

Loss Prevention Consultant, Pittsburgh, Pennsylvania — 1985 to 1987

EDUCATION

Bachelor's Degree in Mechanical Engineering, Rochester Institute of Technology, New York — 1985

Parker Martine

950 Douglas Avenue, Charlotte, NC 26547
(910) 634-5788 • ptine@spice.net

Corporate Trainer / Professor / Consultant
HUMAN RESOURCES and ORGANIZATIONAL DEVELOPMENT (OD)

Organizational Change Agent with 15 years expertise in building and developing training solutions for corporate performance optimization. Emphasis on aligning human resource functions with corporate initiatives to deliver world-class standards of productivity, efficiency, and quality. Excel in developing and presenting subject-appropriate curriculum for corporate training and college instruction. Key areas of experience include:

• Training & Development	• HR System Design	• Curriculum Development
• Organizational Learning	• Capability Assessment	• Change Management
• HR System Design	• Gap Analysis	• Instructional Systems Design
• Needs Assessment	• Training Facilitation	• Intervention Strategies
• Workshop Presentation	• Diagnostic Instruments	• Focus Sessions
• Curriculum Design	• Group Dynamics	• Career Development

EDUCATION and CERTIFICATION

- **MA, Human Resource Administration**, University of North Carolina, Chapel Hill, NC
- **BSe, Instructional Systems Design**, University of Central Florida, Orlando, FL
- **Instructional Design Certification**, The 4MAT System, Chicago, IL

PRESENTATIONS and PUBLICATIONS

- *"ISD in the DoD"* – Presented at the National Conference, American Society for Training and Development (ASTD), Orlando, FL – 1997
- *"An Analysis of Theogi's Group Methodology as Applied to the Workplace"* – Published in *The Journal of Human Resource Management*, Vol. I - 1999

PROFESSIONAL EXPERIENCE

PROFESSOR / HR PROGRAM DIRECTOR   1990 to Present
DEPARTMENT OF BUSINESS, WAKE FOREST UNIVERSITY, Raleigh, NC
Directed satellite campus Human Resource Development program, teaching courses at both satellite and main campus.
- **Program Management:** Managed the human resource development curriculum and faculty with responsibility for selection and development of elective courses and faculty recruitment.
- **Instruction & Curriculum Design:** Developed and taught courses including: ... Human Resource Development: An Introduction ... Instructional Systems Design ... Utilizing the 4MAT System ... Organizational Development ... Human Relations in Organizations ... Group Dynamics I & II ... Career Development in the New Economy ... Organizational Design Systems I ... Trainer's Toolbox.

The extensive list of "key areas of experience" can serve as a key-word summary for this experienced corporate trainer and university educator.

Parker Martine

PROFESSIONAL EXPERIENCE continued

INSTRUCTIONAL DESIGNER   1987 to 1990
THE CORPORATE SOLUTION, Jonesboro, NC
Developed corporate training programs and organizational training solutions for numerous Fortune 500 companies.

- **Curriculum Development:** Utilized Instructional Systems Design (ISD) Model to design curriculum and adjust programs according to feedback from human resource personnel.
- **Course Validation:** Validated all components of instructional programs to determine compliance with desired competencies.

SENIOR CORPORATE TRAINER   1984 to 1988
TERRAN INSTITUTE OF JUSTICE, Beacon Hill, NC
Recruited to develop and manage corporate training program.

- **Program Management:** Coordinated professional development of staff and faculty. Performed training, coordination, and implementation functions. Organized and coordinated in-house and external training functions.
- **Diversity Programming:** Identified corporate requirements to integrate programming in EEO, multiculturalism in the workplace, and cultural communications.
- **Curriculum Integration:** Worked with external consulting firm to adapt existing training program into an in-house function, reducing training costs by over 40% annually.
- **Instruction & Training:** Developed and taught programs for management training, personnel orientation, and thinking outside of the box.

REFERENCES

Personal and professional references available upon request.

C. Rudy Johnston

777 Corporate Drive
Irving, Texas 71111

Home: 972-333-2222
Fax: 972-999-5555

PERSONAL PROFILE

Creative, results-driven professional in design, development, and delivery of business solutions and instructional training. Client-oriented, flexible, and focused, with demonstrated ability to evaluate and adjust training to meet client needs. Extensive training and experience in instructional design, learning strategies, and motivational techniques. Project lead experience. Team-building and mentoring.

CAREER HIGHLIGHTS

Senior Consultant, DAGD – Dallas, Texas (1997-Present)

- Presented **Train the Trainer** to subject matter experts.
- Delivered **Training courses** on **SAP** Basic Navigation, Materials Management Purchasing, Sales and Distribution, and **Online Reference Documentation**.
- Exceptional knowledge of and experience with **SAP R/3 modules**, specifically Sales and Distribution, MM Purchasing and Materials Management, FI G/L, A/P, and A/R.
- Successfully presented training courses to numerous audiences from **diverse cultures** for whom **English** was a **second language**.
- Personally **requested by clients** as trainer due to outstanding job performance in prior training sessions, resulting in higher fee and increased revenues for the company.

Analyzed client needs and developed business-training solutions to fulfill requirements for companies undergoing computerized restructuring. Conducted individualized task analysis procedures to document business processes and determine training needs by subject matter and department. Presented proposed training projects to end-users and management in easy-to-understand format. Provided ongoing curriculum adjustment and design to correct for company and individual circumstances. Provided on-site end-user training to facilitate use and understanding of SAP software. Mentored new trainers and developed teams.

Previous Work Experience

Gifted / Talented and English Teacher, Irving Independent School District, Texas, 1991-1997; **Contributing Editor,** <u>News Times</u>, Irving, Texas, 1990-1991; **Secondary English Teacher,** Platfield Board of Education, New Jersey, 1987-1990; **Lecturing Docent,** Chicago Ballet, Illinois, 1985-1986; **Secondary English Teacher,** Alpine Independent School District, Chicago, Illinois, 1978-1985

EDUCATION / PROFESSIONAL DEVELOPMENT

Master of Liberal Arts – Humanities; GPA 3.8   Baptist University, Dallas, Texas 1997
Bachelor of Arts – English; Magna Cum Laude   Illinois Southern University, Chicago, Illinois 1977
Train the Trainer
English as a Second Language for Business
Change Management
SAP Basic Navigation

COMPUTER SKILLS

PowerPoint	Visio Flowchart	MS Word	MS Outlook
SAP	MS Paint	MS Excel	Paint Shop Pro
Mac Claris Works	Internet Savvy	Electronic Purchasing	E-Mail

This well-written resume packs a lot of information into a readable, one-page format. Note how previous work experience is given without detail because the most relevant experience is the current training consulting role.

Roberta T. Juarez

3482 Homestead Court ◆ Rochester, MI 48309 ◆ 248-555-6308

Profile

"Roberta was extremely knowledgeable . . ."
—Medical Records Technician

◆ Possess many traits of an effective communicator:

- Dynamic presence	- Humor
- Engaging demeanor	- Instinct
- Outgoing personality	- Proven platform skills

◆ Technical areas of expertise:

"Great info . . . you explain complex issues very well!"
—Case Manager

- Coordination of benefits	- Litigation
- Eligibility investigation	- Tort law
- Subrogation	- No-Fault insurance
- Fraud	- Workers Compensation
- Arbitration	- Benefit provision language

◆ Entrepreneurial spirit—identified niche and created company to fill it; over 15 years of experience as business owner with responsibility for all aspects of operations.

"Ms. Juarez presented the information in several different formats, using language that could be understood by everyone, and in a way that we could all apply to our own lives."
—Medical Records Manager

◆ A visionary who sees the big picture. Not afraid to take risks.

Highlights of Experience

Training/Public Presentation

◆ Developed corporate training program for newly created department and off-site support personnel.

◆ Presented over 125 training and informational sessions to all levels of employees, from management to caregivers; adapted presentation style based on setting and audience's level of expertise.

"Nice, because [it was] very informal and to the point—questions could be asked spontaneously."
—Claims Manager

◆ Created customized program as featured speaker at National Third Party Liability Group seminar (400+ audience over 3 days). Developed supporting literature for inclusion in educational packets; utilized appropriate speaker tools to enhance presentation.

◆ Addressed Eastern Michigan University's Adult Learning Seminar/Extended Degree program as a successful graduate of the program.

◆ Provided testimony in legal hearings and court cases.

Program Administration

◆ Developed corporate understanding of previously neglected area of Coordination of Benefits (COB) and cost avoidance; during one year alone saved or recouped $2.8 million for client organization.

"Thank you! Your seminar gave me a whole new perspective on how and why . . ."
—Surgical Staff

◆ Drafted policy and procedural documents on wide range of topics.

◆ Developed first-ever COB procedure manual utilized by employees in corporate and satellite locations.

◆ Collaborated with client corporation to expand and empower internal department, lessening need for contractor. Continued to provide consultative support on as-needed basis.

Professional Experience

"Examples given of different scenarios broadened understanding."
—Finance Department Manager

JUAREZ RESEARCH • Rochester, MI	1986-Present

Under exclusive contract with Health Care Network of SE Michigan
Founder/President

HEALTH CARE NETWORK OF SE MICHIGAN • Detroit, MI	1980-1986

Contract Enrollment Entry Specialist
Marketing Representative
Medicaid Sales Representative

Education

"Roberta enlightened me to issues I never knew about!"
—Support Staff Coordinator

SAGINAW VALLEY STATE UNIVERSITY • Saginaw, MI
Bachelor of Science in Business Administration   1996

MOTT COMMUNITY COLLEGE • Flint, MI
Associate of Business   1992

A functional format allows the grouping of training and program-administration experience for greatest impact. Note the seven short, powerful testimonials.

RAMONA GOMEZ-ROSARIO

7000 Prairie View Lane, Laredo, Texas 89534
(956) 256-0979 ➤ E-mail: meparler@msn.com

EXECUTIVE TRAINING AND DEVELOPMENT

PROFILE ➤ **Career interest in International Business Services** using fluency in Spanish and French language at near-native speaking level (translate, read, and interpret) and over 10 years' experience as a trilingual educator. Seeking opportunities in:

~~ training senior staff in cultural protocols, cultural nuances, and social / business etiquette

~~ facilitating an executive language-immersion program for overseas assignments

~~ conducting bilingual technology application training courses

~~ developing bilingual training manuals for Standard Operating Procedures

~~ serving as translator / interpreter during strategic negotiations

➤ **Comfortable relating to people of diverse cultures and ages.** U.S. citizen who has traveled extensively throughout Europe, Mexico, South America, and Canada. Willing to relocate and travel (internationally or domestically). Professional demeanor.

➤ **Technology:** Trilingual keyboarding fluency in word processing, database development, spreadsheet applications, and PowerPoint presentations. Proficient in delivery of online "webinars."

EDUCATION ➤ **Master of Arts – Spanish Language and Literature,** 1990
Bachelor of Arts – Spanish (Minor: Education), 1988
Texas State University

HONORS: Sigma Delta Pi Spanish Honorary Society, GPA: 4.0

➤ **International Study,** 1987-1988
Instituto Internacional, Madrid, Spain

Study area: Spanish history, language, culture, literature

Classes taught in Spanish by professors from the Universidad Complutense and Universidad Autonoma of Madrid

Completed entire coursework for major in Spanish, while living in Spain

➤ **Teaching Licenses:** States of Texas and Florida

EMPLOYMENT HISTORY

➤ **SPANISH / FRENCH PROFESSOR**
Rio Vista University, Laredo, Texas (1995-present)

➤ **SPANISH INSTRUCTOR:** CLASS TAUGHT ENTIRELY IN SPANISH
University of Miami, Miami, Florida (1990-1995)

This resume was created to help a trilingual language professor transition from academia to the international business world in a training and development capacity for executives.

RAMONA GOMEZ-ROSARIO   **PAGE TWO**

LEADERSHIP ACHIEVEMENTS

➤ AS SOUTHERN ASSOCIATION OF COLLEGES COMMITTEE MEMBER: Proposed
   new methods to improve business processes related to academic instruction.
   Identified trends that could affect enrollment ratios.

➤ AS TECHNOLOGY COMMITTEE MEMBER: Assessed classroom needs for
   technology equipment (computers, scanners, peripherals) benchmarking against
   $90,000 annual budget.

➤ AS TEXTBOOK COMMITTEE CHAIR: Reviewed and evaluated scope, sequence, and
   content of topic-specific textbooks to determine instructional viability. Justified the
   cost / benefit of adjunct materials (CD-ROM, audio visual, and others).

➤ AS SPANISH AND FRENCH LANGUAGE INSTRUCTOR: Created student-centered
   learning environment through use of innovative techniques including positive
   reinforcement and performance incentives, as well as curriculum design and
   implementation.

AFFILIATIONS (ACTIVE)

➤ American Council of Teachers of Foreign Languages
➤ National Educators Association
➤ Texas Educators Association
➤ Laredo Educators Association
➤ American Association of Teachers of Spanish and Portuguese

FAVORITE QUOTE APPLICABLE TO BUSINESS COMMUNICATIONS

*"Usted puede tener las ideas brillantes, pero si usted no los puede obtener a traves
de, sus ideas no lo obtendrian dondequiera."* (Spanish)

*"Vous pouvez avoir des idees brilliants, mais si vous ne pouvez pas les recevoir a
travers, vos idees ne vous recevront nullepart."* (French)

"You can have brilliant ideas, but if you can't get them across, your ideas won't get
you anywhere." (English)

— Lee Iacocca

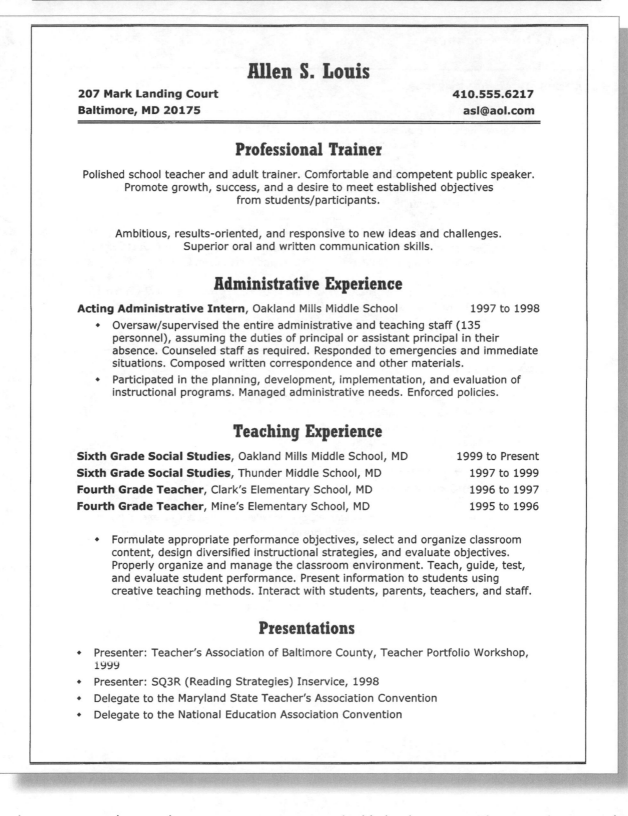

Allen S. Louis

207 Mark Landing Court   410.555.6217
Baltimore, MD 20175   asl@aol.com

Professional Trainer

Polished school teacher and adult trainer. Comfortable and competent public speaker.
Promote growth, success, and a desire to meet established objectives
from students/participants.

Ambitious, results-oriented, and responsive to new ideas and challenges.
Superior oral and written communication skills.

Administrative Experience

Acting Administrative Intern, Oakland Mills Middle School   1997 to 1998
- Oversaw/supervised the entire administrative and teaching staff (135 personnel), assuming the duties of principal or assistant principal in their absence. Counseled staff as required. Responded to emergencies and immediate situations. Composed written correspondence and other materials.
- Participated in the planning, development, implementation, and evaluation of instructional programs. Managed administrative needs. Enforced policies.

Teaching Experience

Sixth Grade Social Studies, Oakland Mills Middle School, MD   1999 to Present
Sixth Grade Social Studies, Thunder Middle School, MD   1997 to 1999
Fourth Grade Teacher, Clark's Elementary School, MD   1996 to 1997
Fourth Grade Teacher, Mine's Elementary School, MD   1995 to 1996

- Formulate appropriate performance objectives, select and organize classroom content, design diversified instructional strategies, and evaluate objectives. Properly organize and manage the classroom environment. Teach, guide, test, and evaluate student performance. Present information to students using creative teaching methods. Interact with students, parents, teachers, and staff.

Presentations

- Presenter: Teacher's Association of Baltimore County, Teacher Portfolio Workshop, 1999
- Presenter: SQ3R (Reading Strategies) Inservice, 1998
- Delegate to the Maryland State Teacher's Association Convention
- Delegate to the National Education Association Convention

In this resume, teaching and presenting experience are highlighted. It's not until you reach page 2 that you realize this individual is in the military. And even in that role, human resource experiences are emphasized.

Education & Certifications

Arizona State University
Master of Science in Teaching, 1994 (GPA: 4.0)
Major: Elementary Education with a specialization in Social Studies

University of Maryland
Bachelor of Arts in Political Science, 1991

Maryland Teaching Certificate, Advanced Professional 1-6 & Middle School, 1995
Arizona Teaching Certificate, K-6, 1995

**Completed 12 semester hours towards certification as Administrator I
Arizona State University and University of Maryland, 1996 to present

Inservice / Staff Development

- Computer Technology: ClarisWorks
- Computer Technology: Hyperstudio, ClarisWorks, Power Point and Internet
- Initiative and Confidence Course Certification
- *Baltimore Sun,* Newspaper in Education (NIE) Workshops
- Strategic Reading Instruction
- Previewing the Principalship
- Funding for Environmental Service Projects: Grant Writing

Military Experience

United States Navy Reserves, Commander (Administrative Manager)
SECRET Clearance   1989 to Present
Completed Signal Officer Basic Course (Academic Average: 90%)
Commended for above-average performance as a group leader, demonstrating decisiveness and ability to delegate.

- Plan, develop, and direct personnel systems to support the implementation of programs, i.e., personnel actions, assignments, awards, classifications, decorations, reenlistments, strength accounting/staffing, records maintenance, and pay management.
- Supervise a staff of 20 in the Personnel Actions Center supporting administrative actions for 200 personnel.
- Assisted a primary instructor in a specialized presentation. Formulated and developed communications-electronics class formats and curriculum.

Allen S. Louis, Page 2

Kelly Rene Pedersen

2390 High Street Sidney Avenue, Apt. B-216 ◆ Port Angeles, WA 98358 ◆ 360-457-6440 ◆ ITtrainer@sunlink.com

"As a Training Manager for almost two years, Kelly installed, trained, and consulted at hotels and conference centers all over the country, training 5 – 25 people each week, troubleshooting technical and networking issues, loading programs and client databases, and customizing our clients' reporting needs...she had to fully understand and professionally present our products and, many times, the concept of automation to our clients.

"During her tenure as Training Manager, Kelly predominately worked with our corporate clients — organizations such as Starwood, Wyndham, and Marriott. Her involvement in the rollout of our products was invaluable. She not only took care of our clients, but also provided feedback to our department on where we excelled as well as solutions for our growth areas.

"She was well received by our clients... The most consistent feedback was that Kelly was personable, patient, and knowledgeable about both the product and the industry. She is well organized, independent, and will always work to provide solutions to clients' needs..."
Marie R. Wells
Products & Services Mgr.
Software Solutions, Intl.

CAREER PROFILE

Goal-oriented self-starter with documented success in corporate training, account management, sales, and marketing. Reputation as outstanding trainer who holds student interest while keeping class "on track." Professional in performance and demeanor. Committed to providing outstanding customer service and support.

EDUCATION

1998 – B.A., Communication/International Affairs
University of Washington, Seattle, WA

~ Minor in Spanish, semester abroad in Mexico
~ Scholarship athlete for Women's Varsity Crew

QUALIFICATION SUMMARY

TRAINING
❑ Develop and facilitate hands-on, interactive training classes in use of proprietary software, ensuring development of clients' technical and product knowledge.
❑ Monitor students' progress and administer tests.
❑ Coordinate arrangements and set-up for training sites worldwide.
❑ Summarize training session feedback and develop proposals for course enhancements.

SALES & MARKETING
❑ Continually market training services and software products to encourage add-on sales.
❑ Provide support and follow-up to multiple accounts concurrently.
❑ Developed ideas and promotions to increase ratings and listener base for Southern New Hampshire radio station.
❑ Conducted demographic research to facilitate development of advertising programs.

TECHNICAL SKILLS
❑ Test and troubleshoot technical problems relating to proprietary and third-party software on both Quadbase and SQL Server 6.5 and 7.0 platforms.
❑ Comprehensive experience with Windows 95/98/NT operating systems and Microsoft Office 95/97/2000 including Word and Excel, as well as Lotus Notes and Clarify.
❑ Customize reports and create documents in Crystal 5.0 and 6.0.
❑ Load programs and databases.
❑ General understanding of network protocols, topology, and methodology.

COMMUNICATIONS
❑ Personable and professional public speaker.
❑ Project genuine understanding of and concern for interests of both client and company.
❑ Clear, concise, and accurate in written communications.
❑ Recognized ability to defuse potential problems and achieve group consensus.
❑ Extensive experience working successfully with people from diverse cultural, economic, and social backgrounds.
❑ Proficient in Spanish; teach classes and support customers in Latin America.

The multiple testimonials in this resume are carefully positioned so that the reader can still quickly skim this training professional's career history and accomplishments. Note the functional grouping of qualifications on page 1.

Kelly Rene Pedersen **Page 2**

> *"Kelly was an asset to the Install Support Team and the company.*
>
> *"Kelly is great at self-management. She was one of only a few people that we allowed to work remotely. She constantly reviews her workload based on level of severity and resources needed. She is able to handle multiple problems with ease and always uses her resources well to research issues and gather information.*
>
> *"Kelly is well respected and well liked by the team. She is continually working on her own or with others to expand her knowledge base and is always one of the first to take on new projects...."*
> Joan Selvern
> Install Support
> & Interface Manager
> Software Services, Intl.
>
> *"Over the last six years I have worked with many outstanding technical support representatives. Without a doubt, Kelly is one of the finest. I make this judgment based on the unique way she blends the elements of her broad technical knowledge and her outstanding people skills. Kelly is very personable; this has been key in establishing trust and open communication with the trainers as well as clients who depend on her daily. She is faced with very serious problems and is able to keep a cool, clear head as well as calming the person she is working with...."*
> Winston Roberts
> Senior Tech. Support Rep.
> Software Solutions, Intl.

PROFESSIONAL HISTORY

Software Solutions, International, Seattle, WA   1998 to Present
Installations Training Manager, *1999 – 2001*
Manage all aspects of staff and client training for this international company that provides software and e-commerce solutions to automate sales and operations for hospitality services. A Microsoft Certified Solutions Provider (MCSP), Software Solutions engineers sales automation and Web-enabled products on Windows platform technologies. All products are engineered and tested to be compatible with leading hardware and software systems.

- Install software and train Sales and Catering staff in its use.
- Develop and present on- and off-site product training. Assess customer needs and tailor training programs to meet individual requirements.
- Work closely with staff at training site to circumvent potential problems and ensure agenda, set-up, etc., are effective for productive training sessions.
- Provide consultant services for existing customers migrating from company's DOS product to company's Windows product.
- Conduct in-depth information and data gathering interviews to identify training strengths and areas for improvement. Develop comprehensive and timely reports for management.
- Assist hotel management with standardization of documentation. Assess working environment and created new standards and procedures.
- Assess and critique new trainer performance and develop written evaluations.

Installations Technical Support Representative, *1998 – 1999*
One of only three remotely based support representatives.
One of forty Support Representatives testing and troubleshooting technical and networking problems for over 1,000 clients worldwide.

- Independently supported Singapore and London offices during off-hours, concurrent with providing support throughout U.S. and Latin American countries.
- Acted as systems liaison in absence of on-site technical representative.
- Member of Installations and Interfaces Specialty Groups and Business Reporting Team.

KIRO FM, Seattle, WA   Summer 1997
Promotions Intern

- Originated ideas and developed promotions to increase ratings and listener base. Supervised promotional aspects of remote broadcast shows. Developed promotional database to track listener response.

Net-Works, Inc., Seattle, WA   Summer 1996
Marketing Intern

- Developed customer workshops for use of proprietary software. Assisted in development of web site for "sister corporation." Conducted market research.

COMMUNITY AFFILIATIONS

- Volunteer, academic tutoring for special populations, Seattle, WA
- Volunteer, Pacific Northwest Central American Network, Tacoma, WA
- Volunteer, Soup Kitchen, Seattle, WA

ADDITIONAL REFERENCES AVAILABLE UPON REQUEST

Jordan L. Baker

3489 Vista Boulevard
Home 415.854.2377

San Francisco, CA 91204
415.554.7201 **Work**

Profile

Highly motivated corporate manager with extensive experience in training and operations. Responsible for the development of training programs designed to address critical business needs such as:

- New hire orientation
- Core competencies relating to customer service, teambuilding, and software applications
- Performance planning and goal development

Committed to personal excellence as it supports the organization's culture and values, as evidenced by ongoing professional development coursework. Certified and trained in such topics as customer service, meeting management, instructional design and proprietary systems. Instrumental in innovative website creation and content management. Promoted three times within five years and winner of various awards at a leading financial institution.

Experience

2/99-Present: Senior Manager, Online Training
Merrill Lynch & Co., Inc., San Francisco, CA
Training Management functions encompass:

- Design and delivery of a three-day "New Hire Training" program complete with leader guide and participant handouts. Modules include Windows NT, Exchange, and Schedule+, team building, departmental overviews, industry basics and related vocabulary, internal systems and products, compliance, and corporate culture.
- The creation and facilitation of customer service, technical, and Merrill products and systems classes.
- The planning, creation, and delivery of courses and training as defined by extensive needs analyses with client groups.
- The design of program guides for core offerings, including leader and participant guides and materials, instructor prep and checklists, and class evaluations.

Project Management functions encompass:

- The coordination of new systems and product rollouts.
- The key point of contact in partnership with technical experts for determining product functionality, including usability testing and training.
- The introduction of Education Management System to over 2500 employees, plus all associated back-end development and data organization and input. Rollout includes all training, documentation, and communications pertaining to projects.
- The continuous administration, facilitation, and content revision of the aforementioned New Hire Training.
- The update and redesign, including the organization and facilitation of focus groups to determine the goal(s), of the intranet.
- The manufacture of a departmental standards manual which includes templates and guidelines on instructional design, content, writing, and style.

1997-1999: Senior Training Specialist, Mutual Funds Training
Merrill Lynch & Co., Inc., San Francisco, CA
Responsible for assessing training needs within the department and implementing programs to fulfill those needs. Major outcomes and deliverables included:

This resume presents a clean, sharp appearance. In the Experience section, note how training management functions are placed first to give them the most emphasis.

Jordan L. Baker **Page 2**

Experience, continued

- Management of departmental intranet site from conception through delivery and continuous maintenance
- Design and writing of various procedures workbooks
- Certification in and delivery of Customer Service classes
- Creation and delivery of customized team building workshops
- Authoring of a goal-setting workbook and delivering workshops
- Specialized department and procedurally specific job aids
- Consultations with staff members on departmentally related issues
- Inception of a departmental Toastmasters group
- Conducting individual training sessions with employees experiencing specific problems
- Producing a comprehensive training catalogue and scheduling of internal and external classes
- Certification in various courses that addressed performance planning and enhanced individual and team performance
- Creation of a monthly electronic departmental communication/bulletin

1995-1997: Mutual Fund Specialist, Mutual Fund Operations
Merrill Lynch & Co., Inc., San Francisco, CA
A very detailed and technical position accountable to various regulatory bodies. Worked within an exception-driven system to minimize risk to the firm, while maximizing the efficiency of our procedures and raising the level of customer service. Position required strong customer service, problem solving, and troubleshooting skills, and customers included actual clients as well as fund companies and financial institutions.

1993-1995: Nationwide Sales and Marketing Representative
Royal Trout, South San Francisco, CA
Accountable for building a nationwide customer base for a start-up company. Promoted and sold imported products from New Zealand, attended trade shows, and designed and disseminated marketing materials aimed at educating the customer as well as at selling the product. Tasks included the creation and implementation of a direct mail program.

1992-1993: Sales and Marketing Representative
Polarica Inc., San Francisco, CA
Responsible for the sale of wild game and other specialty items to foodservice and retail customers. Generated and serviced new accounts, and created and distributed all marketing and promotional materials in the SF branch. Additional responsibilities included light buying and inventory control.

Education, Etc.
BS Political Science
University of Rochester, New York

Training Coursework
Darryl Sink "Course Developer Workshop"
Langevin "Writing Skills for Trainers"
Langevin "Successful Training Manager; Achieving Organizational Impact"
Xerox Learning "Facilitating Teamwork"

Awards
Excellence in Service: 1998, two in 1999
Employee of the Quarter: Q2 1999, Q3 2000

Jennifer A. Barbaro

1616 Eagle Pointe Drive, Clearwater, FL 33764 — (727) 572-9088 — Mobile (727) 572-6636

QUICK PROFILE:
Effective combination of strengths: Technical expertise in training and corporate education, business acumen, and organization. Experience in needs assessment; design, implementation, and evaluation of employee training, management development programs, and customer/client training. Have trained all subjects, but specialties are management training, technical training, sales and customer service training, and course customization with real-life scenarios, quality program training, and public speaking. Computer skilled with instructional technology packages as well as popular software, i.e., Windows, Excel, MS Word, PowerPoint, and Access.

RELEVANT TASKS/ACHIEVEMENTS/AWARDS:

♦ Travel to nationwide field sites 75% to 100% of the time to conduct classroom training of retail sales associates and store management personnel. Essence of training consists of hands-on computer familiarization pertaining to billing, reports, inventory control, cash, and financial management, as GTE converts from 14 independent systems to 3 centralized software systems.

♦ Since training is in-depth, 5 days per week, pre-classroom set-ups and testing are done each Sunday in order to ensure equipment is up and running, with manuals, pictorials, flip-charts, and other peripherals in place.

♦ Ongoing troubleshooting of systems and/or PC problems at site locations.

♦ **Special Challenge:** Developing concurrent training and appropriate instructional methods for disparate groups of non-computer oriented end-users, each with a different level of knowledge, and orienting them to a software/hardware information processing environment to ensure product acceptance. Instrumental in bringing about attitudinal changes by designing game-playing and team-activity techniques.

♦ Provide positive reinforcement, motivational incentives, and give-aways to keep learners on track.

♦ Achieved company standard by meeting required platform time of 75%; also met required competency for instruction assessment resulting in a **4.90 rating out of a possible 5.0 or 98%.**

♦ Subsequent to training, provide 1-2 weeks of on-site technical support.

♦ While serving 3 years in the Customer Service/Call Center Department, interviewed and screened applicants and held final hiring authority. Trained new customer care representatives and supervisors in handling customer inquiries. Additionally, educated customers about cellular usage and market idiosyncrasies.

♦ Monitored more than 45 Customer Service and Financial Service personnel in the Call Center and provided one-on-one coaching and feedback as a QA Associate. **Achieved a 96% success rate, exceeding the goal by 6%.** Assisted in the design of curriculum for GTE University.

♦ Telemarketing sales to corporations selling COBRA compliance services. Leading revenue generator in department.

OTHER COMPETENCIES:
Customer Service and Sales programs such as Virtuoso, Mobiltrack, CAS, CACS, MNMS, OCTEL, POS, and COMS. Knowledge of Basic Spanish.

EMPLOYMENT HISTORY:

♦ GTE Wireless, Clearwater, FL	12/97-Present	Administrator/Sales Systems Training
♦ GTE Wireless, Tampa, FL	~ 4/96-12/97	Quality Assurance Associate
♦ GTE Wireless, Tampa, FL	~ 9/94-4/96	Customer Care Representative
♦ Applied Benefits Research, Palm Harbor, FL	~ 2/94-9/94	New Business Admin/Marketing Rep.

EDUCATION:
Florida State University, Tallahassee, FL ~ **B.A.,** Interpersonal Communication, 1993 ~ Major GPA 3.7~ Minor: Spanish
Spanish Honors Society & Communications Honor Society

PROFESSIONAL AFFILIATIONS:
Member, Women in Communications

A pure functional style was used to de-emphasize the fact that most of this individual's job titles were not clearly training related. Attention is drawn to important and measurable results by using bold, underlined type.

Janene Connolly

4208 Nottingham
Livonia, Michigan 48135
(555) 217-5313
jancon217@aol.com

Performance Technologist with nine years' experience in training and instructional design. Expert in facilitating adult groups through complex problem-solving to action and improvement. Implemented programs for total financial conversions at several banking institutions. Worked with organizations to create industry-leading training processes to meet the dynamic needs of the organization and, as new technology emerges, to strengthen the overall performance of employees to meet competitive market demands. Core competencies include:

- Organization Needs Assessment
- HR Policies & Procedures
- Technology Conversions
- Seminar/Workshop Design
- Executive Training & Leadership
- Customer Service Training

EDUCATION

Master's Degree, *Adult Instruction & Performance Technology*, UNIVERSITY OF MICHIGAN-DEARBORN, Dearborn, MI — Expected graduation — December 2001
Bachelor of Arts, *Art*, UNIVERSITY OF DETROIT/MERCY, Detroit, MI — graduated Magna cum Laude
Certified — Business as Unusual Trainer
Certified — Business Sales Development Trainer

PERFORMANCE TECHNOLOGY PROJECTS

- Designed a sales training program for Mail Boxes Etc. sales staff.
- Designed and developed a job aid and a focus group process for the Livonia Ford Transmission Plant to facilitate an employee move process.
- Wrote paper published on the University of Michigan web site: *"Making the Transition from Classroom Training to Distance Learning."*

PROFESSIONAL HISTORY

DEARBORN FEDERAL CREDIT UNION, Dearborn, MI
A full-financial institution
INSTRUCTOR 1999 – Present

Facilitate training, employee development, orientation and technology conversion classes for a 450-employee financial institution. Develop "on-the-job" training techniques and deliver instruction for various departments, to include tellers, member services, call center, loans and collections. Noted for resourcefulness, ability to handle diverse situations with ease, and talent for explaining material in an interesting and clear manner.

- Designed and developed training programs to meet company service standards.
- Conducted training needs assessments to determine employee performance gaps.
- Facilitated soft skills and technical instruction for all levels of employees.
- Created training manuals to enhance the employee learning process.
- Designed effective job aids to enhance employee on-the-job performance.
- Developed evaluation processes to judge performance results and to adjust future training sessions.
- Mentored training staff in adult learning techniques and instructional design concepts.

A strong summary and a separate section for important projects are used to enhance the impact of this chronological resume.

Janene Connolly

PAGE TWO

FIRST OF AMERICA BANK, Royal Oak, MI
Financial Institution
LEARNING SPECIALIST (1995 – 1999)

1984 – 1999

Provided stand-up training and verbal and written presentations for retail branch software conversions, new hire training, sales skills, supervisory, and procedural training. Worked with corporate department heads to evaluate training needs, and presented classes to assure all employees performed their jobs effectively.

- Applied adult learning concepts as facilitator of employee training programs.
- Exercised effective communication skills in working with all levels of employees.
- Acted as facilitator manager for all Michigan and Illinois platform trainers during the 1998 First of America/National City Bank conversion.
- Assisted instructional designers in the development of conversion training agendas, manuals, and job aids for all branch employees in Michigan and Illinois.
- Conducted stand-up training and train-the-trainer sessions for three major software conversions. Training encompassed employees in four states.

TRAINER / RETAIL BRANCH SUPPORT (1992 – 1995)

Trained employees in various training modules to include telephone help desk support, error resolution, written communications, and software testing.

- Traveled to Florida for three weeks, as the only new accounts facilitator, to provide training for the East Coast Florida Branch Conversion.
- Developed and distributed training manuals and job aids to be used at Michigan training sites for all Michigan branch employees.
- Trained over 200 branch "new accounts" staff on multiple on-line applications within a one-month time frame.

CUSTOMER SERVICE / BANKING (1984 – 1992)

Opened new customer accounts, cross-sold various financial products, and provided customer service.

- Sold bank products and provided high-quality service to bank customers.
- Performed manager / supervisor functions in the absence of the branch and assistant managers.
- One of the first employees to initiate micro-marketing (phone sales, mailings) techniques that resulted in personal sales increases of 150%.
- Played a vital role toward the branch consistently meeting, or exceeding, loan goals for specified time periods.

PROFESSIONAL AFFILIATIONS

American Society for Training and Development
International Society for Performance Improvement
Pi Lambda Theta, International Honor Society in Education

COMPUTER SKILLS

MS Word • Excel • Project • PowerPoint • Lotus Notes

CARLOS MENDEZ

15243 South Drive ◆ Olathe, Kansas 66066
913-555-1212 ◆ cmendez@email.com

TECHNOLOGY PROFILE
Trainer ◆ Leader ◆ Coach ◆ Mentor

Technical Trainer and Team Leader with 18-year career delivering world-class customer support training programs in networked multi-function printer market. Change agent advancing technology in the workplace. Proven negotiation skills contributing to successful goal- and task-oriented problem-solving. Strong work ethic demonstrated through commitment to company growth and productivity.

Certification: Microsoft Certified System Engineer (MCSE), 1998

Operating Systems: Windows 2000, Windows NT 4.0, Windows 95/98, Novell NetWare 3.12/4.x

Software: Microsoft Office Suite

PROFESSIONAL EXPERIENCE

UNIVERSAL COPIER CORPORATION, Kansas City, Missouri   1982 to Present
Global company offering customized solutions for simplifying document life cycles

Senior Technical Trainer, 6/97 to Present

Hire and train permanent customer support analysts sourced from pool of sub-contractors. Monitor on-phone performance of support analysts, providing ongoing feedback to management and analysts. Develop and present training programs on products and network connectivity based upon personal research and testing. Edit user documentation that is incorporated into training curriculum. Organize, facilitate, and moderate bimonthly national conference calls for field analysts. Conduct periodic workshops to update all telephone analysts on software changes. Present focused training classes to non-technical managers on new technology and product advancements.

❖ Initiated and led start-up of focal training team to centralize generic training and eliminate redundancies in customer support center, thus improving productivity and reducing average class cost by $5000.

❖ Earned multiple annual achievement awards, including one in 1999 for moderating live talk show that provided critical solutions for hundreds of field analysts.

❖ Created training strategy that increased service level of support center from 15% to 85% within four months.

❖ Supervised launch of easy-access problem solving web site for offering valuable resources to all field personnel.

❖ Designed step-by-step job aids for telephone analysts that reduced research and telephone time.

❖ Increased customer satisfaction by facilitating communication between engineering department and customer support communities.

Continues on page 2

As with most technology resumes, this resume includes specific mention of technology expertise. Bullet-point accomplishment statements are clearly distinguishable from the summary of position activities.

Page 2, Resume of Carlos Mendez   913-555-1212

Technical Trainer, 3/91 to 6/97

Devised and presented stand-alone, multi-function desktop training for customer support analysts. Assisted with selection, testing and hiring of new staff. Monitored telephone performance of analysts. Facilitated workgroup startup and meetings. Coached team of 15 in absence of manager.

❖ Developed and delivered state-of-the-art training to support centers in New York and London that achieved worldwide company recognition and generated $11,000 in revenue. Earned annual company achievement award in 1995.

❖ Designed first training and support Web site for support center, receiving company-wide recognition when showcased at annual Teamwork Day in Las Vegas, Nevada, in 1993.

❖ Led team effort to create the SOS (Help) Office that served as an escalation point for customer support analysts.

❖ Created company-wide troubleshooting guide for multi-function copier products.

❖ Earned President's Award for demonstrating new LAN/FAX product at NetWorld show in Washington, DC, 1991.

Additional Relative Experience:

Facsimile Customer Support Analyst, 1/89 to 3/91

Data Communications Analyst, 4/87 to 1/89

Personal Computer Support Representative, 6/86 to 4/87

Customer Support Representative/Word Processor, 11/84 to 6/86

Senior Administrative Aide, 6/83 to 11/84

Administrative Assistant, 1/82 to 6/83

CITY OF OLATHE, KANSAS   1978 to 1982

Mediator/Intake Specialist
Resolved disputes for walk-ins and referrals from the Olathe Police Department.

EDUCATION

Networking Technologies Certificate, Sunflower College, Avery, Kansas, 1997

AAS Degree in Mid-Management, State Community College, Stanley, Kansas, 1990

Company Sponsored Professional Development

- Management Development, 2000
- Leadership through Quality, 1999
- Train the Trainer, 1992
- Preparing for Leadership, 1999
- Network Printing Core, 1998
- Sales Training, 1990

CHRISTOPHER SAMPSON

1019 Swan Road
Detroit, Michigan 48823

547-503-4521
E-mail: cbrown_101@hotmail.com

OBJECTIVE

To obtain a position as a Curriculum Software Trainer

HIGHLIGHTS OF QUALIFICATIONS

✓ Over 14 years progressive experience as a Consultant, Trainer, Project Manager, and System Analyst.
✓ Extensive experience writing curriculum, training manuals, and training scripts and recommending design changes for multimedia applications.
✓ Highly effective liaison between widely diverse levels of staff and users to problem solve technical and functional issues.
✓ Adept at tailoring training presentations to meet the consumers' needs.
✓ Critical evaluation and resolution of training issues from prototype testing to full production to increase software marketability for all levels of users on a national basis.
✓ Ability to work with diverse customers and maintain a high level of customer service.

EXPERIENCE

T. ROWE PRICE, Detroit, Michigan

1997 to Present

Senior Programmer/Analyst
Led team and managed project to certify that all facets of computer interfacing between client companies and T. Rowe Price's Retirement Plan Service and Information Technology Department were Y2K compliant.
✓ Completed project ahead of time by serving as a liaison and selling the importance of the project and obtaining the cooperation of departments.
✓ Facilitated design meetings between consultants, business analysts, and technicians.
✓ Determined priority and format for testing 6 Retirement Plan Systems and 75 programs.

UNITED GUARANTY INSURANCE COMPANY, INC., Detroit, Michigan

1995 to 1997

Consultant
Coded and tested programs for Information Warehouse System to enhance systems for acquired companies.
Developed design specification and project estimates for completion of enhancement.

ANALYSTS INTERNATIONAL CORPORATION (AIC), Macon, GA

1993 to 1995

Trainer/Business Analyst 1994 - 1995 (SYSTEMATIC TELECOMMUNICATIONS SERVICE, INC.)
Created training database with 200+ files for training exercises.
✓ Wrote and tested training scripts on multiple databases.
✓ Developed curriculum and generated graphics for training materials.
✓ Recommended design changes on a multimedia application of a nationally utilized billing and sales software package.
✓ Developed curriculum and conducted Train-the Trainer classes on a Cellular Billing and Sales software package used within a client/server environment.

The Highlights of Qualifications section combines strong qualifications that "sell" this technical individual for the pure training positions he's seeking.

CHRISTOPHER SAMPSON   Page Two

EXPERIENCE (Continued)

Consultant (ALANTIC GAS AND LIGHT) 1993
Programmed and tested complex developmental programs for appliance warranty project. Modified loan program, audit program and financial accounting control software.

FLORIDA GAS & LIGHT COMPANY, Miami, Florida   1987 to 1993

Systems/Data Analyst 1991 - 1993
Re-engineered a Customer Information System of 1.8 million customers into a "Real-time" payment and billing system for 35 work groups in one implementation.
- ✓ Led team of 10 analysts and resolved the technical and functional problems to increase user confidence.
- ✓ Interviewed users and wrote over 20 functional requirement documents.
- ✓ Wrote design specifications for over 50 enhancements.
- ✓ Served as a highly visible liaison between all levels of users and programmers to problem-solve 100+ technical and functional issues both pre- and post-implementation of system.
- ✓ Created and marketed prototypes to all levels of users through User Acceptance Testing.
- ✓ Consulted with Cleveland Gas and Light on the design, implementation and administration of system.

Training/Planning Analyst 1987 - 1991
Analyzed, updated, and designed computer-based training in conjunction with computer programmers.
- ✓ Wrote 50+ User Procedures, Participant and Instructor Guides, and Online Help Procedures (materials used nationally by numerous utility companies).
- ✓ Conducted presentations, demonstrations, and in-depth training classes for diverse audiences from senior managers to clerical staff.
- ✓ Customized training programs to meet the needs of the customers.

EDUCATION

MBA, Computer Information Systems 1987
MICHIGAN STATE UNIVERSITY, East Lansing, Michigan, *cum laude*

BS in Business Administration, Computer Information Systems 1985
MARYGROVE COLLEGE, Detroit, Michigan, *cum laude*

References Available Upon Request

APPENDIX

Internet Career Resources for Education Professionals

With the emergence of the Internet has come a huge collection of job search resources for education professionals. Here are just a few of our favorites.

Dictionaries and Glossaries

Outstanding information on key words and acronyms.

Acronyms	http://acronymfinder.com
Key words	http:/www.keywordcity.com/DirGC.html

Job Search Sites

You'll find thousands and thousands of current professional employment opportunities on these sites.

GENERAL SITES

4Work	www.4work.com
6FigureJobs	www.6figurejobs.com
America's Job Bank	www.ajb.dni.us
Best Jobs USA	www.bestjobsusa.com
Career Atlas for the Road	www.jobmag.com/guide/c047/c047262.htm
CareerBuilder	www.careerbuilder.com
CareerCity	www.careercity.com
Career.com	www.career.com
CareerEngine	www.careerengine.com

CareerExchange	www.careerexchange.com
Career Exposure	www.careerexposure.com
Career Magazine	www.careermag.com
Career Mosaic	www.careermosaic.com
CareerShop	www.careershop.com
CareerSite	www.careersite.com
CareerWeb	www.careerweb.com
Cruel World	www.cruelworld.com
Digital City (jobs by location)	home.digitalcity.com
Excite	www.excite.com/careers
FlipDog	www.flipdog.com
Futurestep	www.futurestep.com
GETAJOB!	www.getajob.com
Headhunter.net	www.headhunter.net
HotJobs.com	www.hotjobs.com
Internet Job Locator	www.joblocator.com
Internet's Help Wanted	www.helpwanted.com
It's Your Job Now	www.ItsYourJobNow.com
JobBankUSA	www.jobbankusa.com
Job Center	www.jobcenter.com
JOBNET.com	www.jobnet.com
JobOptions	www.joboptions.com
JOBTRAK.COM	www.jobtrak.com
JobWeb	www.jobweb.com
Monster.com	www.monster.com
NationJob Network	www.nationjob.com
Net Temps	www.net-temps.com
Online-Jobs.Com	www.online-jobs.com
Shawn's Internet Resume Center	www.inpursuit.com/sirc
The Job Market Recruiting	www.thejobmarket.com
TopJobs USA	www.topjobsusa.com
WorkTree	www.worktree.com
Yahoo! Careers	http://careers.yahoo.com/

EDUCATION CAREER SITES

Academic360.com: Jobs in Higher Education	www.academic360.com
CareerAge	www.careerage.com
Chronicle of Higher Education	http://chronicle.com/jobs
Digital Education Network	www.jobs.edunet.com
Education Jobs	www.educationjobs.com
Education Week: Job Search	www.edweek.org/jobs.cfm
Education World Employment Center	www.education-world.com/jobs
Hire-Ed	www.hire-ed.org
IQ Education	www.iqmedia.co.uk
Iteachnet's International Education Jobs List	www.iteachnet.com/jobsb.html
K-12 Jobs	http://K-12jobs.com
Teaching Jobs	www.teaching-jobs.org/index.htm
University Job Bank	www.ujobbank.com

CAREERS FOR MINORITIES AND WOMEN

Blackworld.com	www.blackworld.com
Careers For Women	www.womenconnect.com/info/career/index.htm
ClassifiedsForWomen	www.classifiedsforwomen.com
IMDiversity.com	www.minorities-jb.com

PROFESSIONAL CAREERS

Contract Employment Weekly	www.ceweekly.com
ProfessionalCareer	www.professionalcareer.com
Vault.com	www.vault.com

GOVERNMENT CAREERS

Federal Jobs Central	www.fedjobs.com
Government Careers	www.getagovjob.com
Jobs in Government	www.jobsingovernment.com

CAREERS FOR SENIORS

MaturityWorks   www.maturityworks.org
(careers for seniors)

ENTRY-LEVEL CAREERS

CampusCareerCenter   www.campuscareercenter.com

College Grad Job Hunter   www.collegegrad.com

Jobsource   www.jobsource.com

JOBTRAK   www.jobtrak.com

Company Information

Outstanding resources for researching specific companies and schools.

555-1212.com   www.555-1212.com
(directory information)

AllBusiness.com   www.comfind.com

Chambers of Commerce   www.uschamber.com/Chambers/
                                     Chamber+Directory/default.htm

Experience Network   www.experiencenetwork.com

Fortune 500 Companies   www.fortune.com/fortune/fortune500

Hoover's Business Profiles   www.hoovers.com

infoUSA   www.infousa.com
(small-business information)

Intellifact.com   www.intellifact.com/company_research.htm

SuperPages.com   www.bigbook.com

Web66: International School   http://web66.coled.umn.edu/
Web Site Registry   schools.html

Interviewing Tips and Techniques

Expert guidance to sharpen and strengthen your interviewing skills.

About.com Interviewing   jobsearch.about.com/business/
                                     jobsearch/msubinterv.htm

Bradley CVs Introduction   www.bradleycvs.demon.co.uk/
to Job Interviews   interview/index.htm

Dress for Success   www.dressforsuccess.org

Job Interview.net   www.job-interview.net

Salary and Compensation Information

Learn from the experts to strengthen your negotiating skills and increase your salary.

Abbott, Langer & Associates	www.abbott-langer.com
America's Career InfoNet	www.acinet.org/acinet/default.htm?tab=wagesandtrends
Bureau of Labor Statistics *Occupational Outlook Handbook*	stats.bls.gov/ocohome.htm
CareerJournal	www.careerjournal.com/?content=cwc-salaries/index.html
Compensation Link	www.compensationlink.com
Crystal Report	www.crystalreport.com
Economic Research Institute	www.erieri.com
JobStar	jobsmart.org/tools/salary/index.htm
Management Consultant Salary Survey	www.cob.ohio-state.edu/~fin/jobs/mco/salary.htm
Monster.com: The Negotiation Coach	midcareer.monster.com/experts/negotiation
Salarysurvey.com	www.salarysurvey.com
Wageweb	www.wageweb.com
Working Woman	www.workingwoman.com/salary
WorldatWork (formerly American Compensation Association)	www.acaonline.org/
Yahoo! Salaries	http://careers.yahoo.com/careers/salaries.html

GEOGRAPHIC INDEX OF CONTRIBUTORS

The sample resumes in chapters 4 through 12 were written by professional resume writers. If you need help with your resume and job search correspondence, you can use the following list to locate the career professional in your area.

A note about credentials: Nearly all of the contributing writers have earned one or more professional credentials. These credentials are highly regarded in the careers and employment industry and are indicative of the writer's expertise and commitment to professional development. Here is an explication of each of these credentials:

Credential	Awarded by	Recognizes
CAC: California Accredited Consultant	California Staffing Professionals	Committment to the staffing industry and the laws that govern it
CCM: Credentialed Career Master	Career Masters Institute	Specific professional expertise, knowledge of current career trends, commitment to continuing education, and dedication through *pro bono* work
CEIP: Certified Employment Interview Professional	Professional Association of Résumé Writers	Expertise in interview preparation strategy
CPC: Certified Personnel Consultant	National Association of Personnel Services	Expertise in staffing and placement
CIPC: Certified International Personnel Consultant	International Confederation of Personnel Services	Expertise in staffing and placement
CPRW: Certified Professional Resume Writer	Professional Association of Résumé Writers	Knowledge of resume strategy development and writing

continues

Credential	Awarded by	Recognizes
JCTC: Job and Career Transition Coach IJCTC: International Job and Career Transition Coach	Career Planning and Adult Development Network	Training and expertise in job and career coaching strategies
LPC: Licensed Professional Counselor	Individual states	Master's in counseling plus three years of supervised counseling experience
MA: Master of Arts degree MS: Master of Science degree MBA: Master of Business Administration M.Ed.: Master of Education MFA: Master of Fine Arts	Accredited university	Graduate-level education
NCC: National Certified Counselor NCCC: National Certified Career Counselor	National Board for Certified Counselors (affiliated with the American Counseling Association and the American Psychological Association)	Qualification to provide career counseling
NCRW: Nationally Certified Resume Writer	National Résumé Writers' Association	Knowledge of resume strategy development and writing

United States

ALABAMA

Don Orlando, MBA, CPRW, JCTC, CCM
Executive Master Team—Career Masters Institute
President, The McLean Group
640 S. McDonough St.
Montgomery, AL 36104
Phone: (334) 264-2020
Fax: (334) 264-9227
E-mail: yourcareercoach@aol.com

Teresa L. Pearson, CPRW, JCTC
President, Pearson's Resume Output
16 Castle Way
Rucker, AL 36362
Phone: (334) 503-4314
E-mail: pearsonresume@snowhill.com

ARIZONA

Patricia S. Cash, CPRW
President, Resumes For Results
P.O. Box 2806
Prescott, AZ 86302
Phone: (520) 778-1578
Fax: (520) 771-1229
E-mail: pscash@goodnet.com

CALIFORNIA

Nita Busby, CPRW, CAC
Owner, Resumes, Etc.
438 E. Katella, Suite J
Orange, CA 92867
Phone: (714) 633-2783
Fax: (714) 633-2745
E-mail: resumes100@aol.com
URL: www.resumesetc.net

Leatha Jones
Write Connection Career Services
P.O. Box 351
Vallejo, CA 94590
Phone: (707) 649-1400
Fax: (707) 649-9141
E-mail: Leatha@writeconnection.net
URL: www.writeconnection.net

Nancy Karvonen, CPRW, CEIP, IJCTC, CCM
Executive Director, A Better Word & Resume
771 Adare Way
Galt, CA 95632
Phone: (209) 744-8203
Fax: (209) 745-7114
E-mail: careers@aresumecoach.com
URL: www.aresumecoach.com

Myriam-Rose Kohn, CPRW, JCTC, CCM
President, JEDA Enterprises
27201 Tourney Rd., Suite 201
Valencia, CA 91355-1857
Phone: (661) 253-0801
Fax: (661) 253-0744
E-mail: myriam-rose@jedaenterprises.com
URL: www.jedaenterprises.com

Denise Larkin, CPRW
President, ResumeRighter.com
P.O. Box 233, 536 Grand Ave.
Oakland, CA 94610
Phone: (510) 891-0200
Fax: (510) 891-0157
E-mail: denise@resumerighter.com
URL: www.resumerighter.com

Anita Radosevich, CPRW, JCTC
President, Anita's Business & Career Services
315 W. Pine St., Suite #5
Lodi, CA 95240
Phone: (209) 368-4444
Fax: (209) 368-2438
E-mail: anita@abcresumes.com
URL: www.abcresumes.com

Vivian Van Lier, CPRW, JCTC, CEIP
President, Advantage Resume & Career Services
6701 Murietta Ave.
Valley Glen (Los Angeles), CA 91405
Phone: (818) 994-6655
Fax: (818) 994-6620
E-mail: vvanlier@aol.com
URL: www.CuttingEdgeResumes.com

Roleta Fowler Vasquez, CPRW
Chief Writer, Wordbusters Resume & Writing
  Services
Fillmore, CA 93015-1137
Phone: (805) 524-3493
Fax: (805) 524-3470
E-mail: resumes@wbresumes.com
URL: www.wbresumes.com

CONNECTICUT

Jan Melnik, CPRW, CCM
President, Absolute Advantage
P.O. Box 718
Durham, CT 06422
Phone: (860) 349-0256
Fax: (860) 349-1343
E-mail: CompSPJan@aol.com
URL: www.janmelnik.com

FLORIDA

Laura A. DeCarlo, CCM, CPRW, JCTC
President, A Competitive Edge Career Service
1665 Clover Circle
Melbourne, FL 32935
Phone: (800) 715-3442
Fax: (321) 752-7513
E-mail: getanedge@aol.com
URL: www.acompetitiveedge.com

Art Frank, MBA
President, Resumes "R" Us
334 Eastlake Dr., Suite 200
Palm Harbor, FL 34685
Phone: (727) 787-6885
Fax: (727) 786-9228
E-mail: AF1134@aol.com

René Hart, CPRW
Executive Director, Resumes For Success!
5337 N. Socrum Loop Rd. #116
Lakeland, FL 33809
Phone: (863) 859-2439
Fax: (509) 277-0892
E-mail: renehart@resumesforsuccess.com
URL: www.ResumesForSuccess.com

Beverly Harvey, CPRW, JCTC, CCM
President, Beverly Harvey Resume & Career
  Service
P.O. Box 750
Pierson, FL 32180

Phone: (386) 749-3111
Fax: (386) 749-4881
E-mail: beverly@harveycareers.com
URL: www.harveycareers.com

Lisa LeVerrier Stein, MA, MS, CPRW, JCTC
President, Competitive Advantage Resumes &
  Career Coaching
433 Plaza Real, Suite 275
Boca Raton, FL 33432
Phone: (954) 571-7236
Toll-free: (800) 750-5690
Fax: (954) 481-2695 or (800) 656-2712
E-mail: gethired@earthlink.net
URL: www.jobcoaching.com, www.lawyerre-
sumes.com

ILLINOIS

Loretta Heck
All Word Services
924 E. Old Willow Rd., Suite 102
Prospect Heights, IL 60070
Phone: (847) 215-7517
Fax: (847) 215-7520
E-mail: siegfried@ameritech.net

INDIANA

Deloris J. Duff, CPRW, IJCTC
President, Document Developers
5030 Guion Rd.
Indianapolis, IN 46254
Phone: (317) 297-4661
Fax: (317) 290-0809
E-mail: deesdocs@earthlink.net

IOWA

Marcy Johnson, CPRW, CEIP
President, First Impression Resume & Job
  Readiness
11805 U.S. Hwy. 69
Story City, IA 50248
Phone: (515) 733-4998
Fax: (515) 733-4681
E-mail: firstimpression@storycity.net
URL: www.resume-job-readiness.com

KENTUCKY

Debbie Ellis, CPRW
President, Career Concepts
103 Patrick Henry Ct.
Danville, KY 40422
Phone: (859) 236-4001
Fax: (888) 329-5409
E-mail: info@resumeprofessional.com
URL: www.resumeprofessional.com

Andrea Peak
Envision Resume Services
P.O. Box 7523
Louisville, KY 40257
Phone: (888) 844-4348
Fax: (888) 844-4348
E-mail: apeak@envision-resumes.com
URL: info@envision-resumes.com

MAINE

Rolande L. LaPointe, CPC, CIPC, CPRW, IJCTC, CCM
President, RO-LAN Associates, Inc.
725 Sabattus St.
Lewiston, ME 04240
Phone: (207) 784-1010
Fax: (207) 782-3446
E-mail: RLapointe@aol.com

MARYLAND

Diane Burns, CPRW, IJCTC, CCM, CEIP
President, Career Marketing Techniques
5219 Thunder Hill Rd.
Columbia, MD 21045
Phone: (410) 884-0213
Fax: (410) 884-0213
E-mail: dianecprw@aol.com
URL: www.polishedresumes.com

Sherry Jean Kolbe, CPRW
President, Resume Consultants
212 Washington Ave.
Towson, MD 21204
Phone: (410) 823-9568
Fax: (410) 494-8434
E-mail: resumeconsult@hotmail.com

MASSACHUSETTS

Bernice Antifonario, MA
President, Antion Associates, Inc.
885 Main St. #10A
Tewksbury, MA 01876
Phone: (978) 858-0637
Fax: (978) 851-4528
E-mail: Antion1@aol.com
URL: www.antion-associates.com

Beate Hait, CPRW, NCRW
President, Word Processing Plus
80 Wingate Rd.
Holliston, MA 01746
Phone: (508) 429-1813
Fax: (508) 429-4299
E-mail: beateh1@aol.com
URL: www.ibssn.com/resumes

MICHIGAN

Janet L. Beckstrom
President, Word Crafter
1717 Montclair Ave.
Flint, MI 48503
Phone: (800) 351-9818
Fax: (810) 232-9257
E-mail: wordcrafter@voyager.net

Joyce L. Fortier, MBA, CPRW, JCTC, CCM
President, Create Your Career
23871 W. Lebost
Novi, MI 48375
Phone: (248) 478-5662
Fax: (248) 426-9974
E-mail: careerist@aol.com
URL: www.careerist.com

Deborah Schuster, CPRW
President, The Lettersmith
P.O. Box 202
Newport, MI 48166
Phone: (734) 586-3335
Fax: (734) 586-2766
E-mail: lettersmith@foxberry.net
URL: www.thelettersmith.com

MINNESOTA

Barb Poole, CPRW
President, Electronic Ink
1812 Red Fox Rd.
St. Cloud, MN 56301
Phone: (320) 253-0975
Fax: (320) 253-1790
E-mail: eink@astound.net

Linda Wunner, CPRW, IJCTC, CEIP
President, A+ Career & Resume Design
4516 Midway Rd.
Duluth, MN 55811
Phone: (218) 729-4551
Fax: (218) 729-8227
E-mail: linda@successfulresumes.com
URL: www.successfulresumes.com

MISSOURI

Meg Montford, CCM, CPRW
Director, Abilities Enhanced
P.O. Box 9667
Kansas City, MO 64134
Phone: (816) 767-1196
Fax: (801) 650-8529
E-mail: meg@abilitiesenhanced.com
URL: www.abilitiesenhanced.com

NEVADA

Cindy M. Fass
President, Comprehensive Resume Services
5300 Spring Mountain Rd., 212-D
Las Vegas, NV 89146
Phone: (702) 222-9411
Fax: (702) 222-9411
E-mail: crsinvegas@aol.com

NEW HAMPSHIRE

Michelle Dumas, NCRW, CPRW, CCM
Executive Director, Distinctive Documents
Somersworth, NH 03878
Phone: (800) 644-9694
Fax: (603) 947-2954
E-mail: resumes@distinctiveweb.com
URL: www.distinctiveweb.com

NEW JERSEY

Vivian Belen, NCRW, CPRW, JCTC
Managing Director, The Job Search Specialist
1102 Bellair Ave.
Fair Lawn, NJ 07410
Phone: (201) 797-2883
E-mail: vivian@jobsearchspecialist.com
URL: www.jobsearchspecialist.com

Nina K. Ebert, CPRW
President, A Word's Worth
808 Lowell Ave.
Toms River, NJ 08753
Phone: (732) 349-2225
Fax: (609) 758-7799
E-mail: wrdswrth@gbsias.com
URL: www.a-wordsworth.com

Susan Guarneri, NCC, NCCC, LPC, CPRW, IJCTC
President, Guarneri Associates/Resumagic
1101 Lawrence Rd.
Lawrenceville, NJ 08648
Phone: (609) 771-1669
Fax: (609) 637-0449
E-mail: Resumagic@aol.com
URL: www.resume-magic.com

Fran Kelley, MA, CPRW, JCTC, SPHR
President, The Resume Works
71 Highwood Ave.
Waldwick, NJ 07463
Phone: (201) 670-9643
E-mail: TwoFreeSpirits@worldnet.att.net
URL: www.careermuse.com

Rhoda Kopy, CPRW, JCTC, CEIP
President, A Hire Image
26 Main St., Suite E
Toms River, NJ 08753
Phone: (732) 505-9515
Fax: (732) 505-3125
E-mail: ahi@infi.net
URL: www.jobwinningresumes.com

Igor Shpudejko, CPRW, JCTC, MBA
President, Career Focus
842 Juniper Way
Mahwah, NJ 07430
Phone: (201) 825-2865
Fax: (201) 825-7711
E-mail: ishpudejko@aol.com
URL: www.careerinfocus.com

NEW YORK

Ann Baehr, CPRW
President, Best Resumes
122 Sheridan St.
Brentwood, NY 11717
Phone: (631) 435-1879
Fax: (631) 435-3655
E-mail: resumesbest@earthlink.net

Arnold G. Boldt, CPRW, JCTC
Arnold-Smith Associates
625 Panorama Trail, Building 1, Suite 120C
Rochester, NY 14625
Phone: (585) 383-0350
Fax: (585) 387-0516
E-mail: Arnie@ResumeSOS.com
URL www.ResumeSOS.com

Deborah Wile Dib, CCM, NCRW, CPRW, JCTC
President, Advantage Resumes of New York
77 Buffalo Ave.
Medford, NY 11763
Phone: (631) 475-8513
Fax: (501) 421-7790
E-mail: gethired@advantageresumes.com
URL: www.advantageresumes.com

Kirsten Dixson, CPRW, JCTC,
Certificate in Career Planning and Development
New Leaf Career Solutions
P.O. Box 991
Bronxville, NY 10708
Phone: (866) NEW-LEAF (toll free)
Fax: (888) 887-7166 (toll free)
E-mail: info@newleafcareer.com
URL: www.newleafcareer.com

Donna Farrise
President, Dynamic Resumes of Long Island, Inc.
300 Motor Pkwy., Suite 200
Hauppauge, NY 11788
Phone: (631) 951-4120
Toll-free: (800) 528-6796
Fax: (631) 952-1817
E-mail: donna@dynamicresumes.com
URL: www.dynamicresumes.com

Linda Matias, JCTC, CEIP
Executive Director, CareerStrides
34 E. Main St. #276

Smithtown, NY 11787
Phone: (631) 382-2425
Fax: (631) 382-2425
E-mail: careerstrides@bigfoot.com
URL: www.careerstrides.com

Salome Randall Tripi, CPRW
President, Careers TOO
3123 Moyer Rd.
Mount Morris, NY 14510
Phone: (716) 658-2480
Fax: (716) 658-2480
E-mail: srttoo@frontiernet.net
URL: www.careers-too.com

NORTH CAROLINA

Doug Morrison, CPRW
President, Career Planners
2915 Providence Rd., Suite 250
Charlotte, NC 28211
Phone: (704) 365-0773
Fax: (704) 365-3411
E-mail: dmpwresume@aol.com

OHIO

Deborah S. James
President, Leading Edge Resume & Career Services
1010 Schreier Rd.
Rossford, OH 43460
Phone: (419) 666-4518
Fax: (419) 791-3567
E-mail: djames@leadingedgeresumes.com
URL: www.leadingedgeresumes.com

Teena Rose, CPRW
President, Resume to Referral
P.O. Box 328
Dayton, OH 45322
Phone: (937) 264-3025
Fax: (937) 264-9930
E-mail: admin@resumetoreferral.com
URL: www.resumebycprw.com

PENNSYLVANIA

Jewel Bracy DeMaio, CPRW
President, A Perfect Resume.com
419 Valley Rd.
Elkins Park, PA 19027
Phone: (800) 227-5131
Fax: (215) 782-8278
E-mail: mail@aperfectresume.com
URL: www.aperfectresume.com

Jane Roqueplot, Certified Behavioral Consultant
President, JaneCo's Sensible Solutions
Jane D. Rae, Vocational Consultant
194 North Oakland Ave.
Sharon, PA 16146
Phone: (724) 342-0100
Fax: (724) 346-5263
E-mail: info@janecos.com
URL: www.janecos.com

TENNESSEE

Carolyn Braden, CPRW
President, Braden Resume Solutions
108 La Plaza Dr.
Hendersonville, TN 37075
Phone: (615) 822-3317
Fax: (615) 826-8611
E-mail: bradenresume@home.com

Marta L. Driesslein, CPRW
President, Cambridge Career Services, Inc.
300 Montvue Rd., Suite A
Knoxville, TN 37919
Phone: (865) 539-9538
Fax: (865) 453-3109
E-mail: careerhope@aol.com
URL: www.careerhope.com

TEXAS

Lynn Hughes, MA in Counseling and Personnel, CEIP
A Resume and Career Service, Inc.
P.O. Box 53932
Lubbock, TX 79453
Phone: (806) 785-9800
Fax: (806) 747-0868
E-mail: lynn@aresumeservice.com
URL: www.aresumeservice.com

Shanna Kemp, M.Ed., IJCTC, CPRW
President, Kemp Career Services
1801 E. Palm Valley Blvd. #1132
Round Rock, TX 78664
Phone: (512) 246-6434
Fax: (512) 246-8353
E-mail: respro@aresumepro.com
URL: www.aresumepro.com

Ann Klint, NCRW, CPRW
President, Ann's Professional Resume Service
2130 Kennebunk Ln.
Tyler, TX 75703
Phone: (903) 509-8333
Fax: (734) 448-1962
E-mail: Resumes-Ann@tyler.net

Kelley Smith, CPRW
President, Advantage Resume Services
P.O. Box 391
Sugar Land, TX 77487
Phone: (281) 494-3330
Fax: (281) 494-0173
E-mail: info@100kresumes.com
URL: www.100kresumes.com

UTAH

Lynn P. Andenoro, CPRW, JCTC, CCM
President, My Career Resource
1214 Fenway
Salt Lake City, UT 84102
Phone: (801) 883-2011
Fax: (801) 582-8862
E-mail: Lynn@MyCareerResource.com
URL: www.MyCareerResource.com

Diana C. LeGere
President, Executive Final Copy
P.O. Box 171311
Salt Lake City, UT 84117
Phone: (866) 754-5465
Fax: (626) 602-8715
E-mail: execfinalcopy@email.msn.com
URL: www.executivefinalcopy.com

VIRGINIA

Anne G. Kramer
President, Alpha Bits
4411 Trinity Ct.
Virginia Beach, VA 23455
Phone: (757) 464-1914
E-mail: akramer@kiscomputers.net

Becky Stokes, CPRW
President, The Advantage, Inc.
401 Mill Ln.
Lynchburg, VA 24503
Phone: (800) 922-5353
Fax: (804) 384-4700
E-mail: advanresume@earthlink.net
URL: www.advantageresume.com

WASHINGTON

Janice M. Shepherd, CPRW
Owner, Resumes by Write On
Bellingham, WA 98226
Phone: (360) 738-7958
Fax: (360) 738-1189
E-mail: resumesbywriteon@earthlink.net
URL: www.resumesbywriteon.com

Lonnie L. Swanson, CPRW, IJCTC
President, A Career Advantage
21590 Clear Creek Rd. NW
Poulsbo, WA 98370
Phone: (360) 779-2877
Fax: (360) 779-2877
E-mail: resumes@nwinet.com
URL: www.TheResumePros.com

WISCONSIN

Michele Haffner, CPRW, JCTC
Advanced Resume Services
1314 W. Paradise Ct.
Glendale, WI 53209
Phone: (877) 247-1677
Fax: (414) 228-7322
E-mail: michele@resumeservices.com
URL: www.resumeservices.com

Julie Walraven
President, Design Resumes
1202 Elm St.
Wausau, WI 54401
Phone: (715) 845-5664

Fax: (715) 845-8076
E-mail: design@dwave.net
URL: www.designresumes.com

Australia

Gayle Howard, CPRW
Founder/Owner, Top Margin Resumes Online
7 Commerford Pl.
Chirnside Park, Melbourne
3116 Australia
E-mail: getinterviews@topmargin.com
URL: www.topmargin.com

Canada

Ross Macpherson, MA, CPRW, JCTC, CEIP
President, Career Quest
1586 Major Oaks Rd.
Pickering, Ontario
L1X 2J6 Canada
Phone: (905) 877-8548
Phone: (877) 426-8548
Fax: (905) 426-4274
E-mail: ross@yourcareerquest.com
URL: www.yourcareerquest.com

Nicole Miller
Mil-Roy Consultants
1729 Hunter's Run Dr.
Orleans, Ontario
K1C 6W2 Canada
Phone: (613) 834-2160
E-mail: resumesbymilroy@hotmail.com

New Zealand

Paula Stenberg
President, CV Style Ltd.
Level 5B, Lister Bldg., 9 Victoria St. East
Auckland, New Zealand
E-mail: paula@cvstyle.co.nz
URL: www.cvstyle.com

INDEX

JIST's Teacher and Educator Library
Essential Advice for a Successful Teaching Career!

The Unauthorized Teacher's Survival Guide, Seco nd Edition
by Jack Warner and Clyde Bryan, with Diane Warner

From how to handle your first day on the job to dealing with burnout, this book covers all the things no one ever told you in your formal education courses. Written by two "old pros" who have survived more than 50 years of classroom teaching, The Unauthorized Teacher's Survival Guide is invaluable for new teachers and reassuring for more experienced educators. This new edition includes a thorough list of the most helpful Web sites for teachers, as well as information on how to recognize the potential for violence in your school.

Order code: LP-P1102
$14.95 • 224 pages • 6 x 9
ISBN: 1-57112-110-2 • Park Avenue

Expert Resumes for Teachers and Educators
by Wendy S. Enelow and Louise M. Kursmark

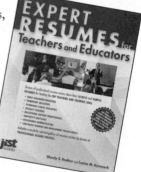

Professional resume writers share their step-by-step resume writing secrets, as well as samples of real job-getting resumes. This gallery of over 180 pages of carefully selected sample resumes is targeted to helping you land the top teaching and training jobs: Early Childhood Educators • Elementary Educators • Secondary-School Educators • Specialty Teachers • Educational Support Professionals • University Educators • Educational Administrators • Corporate Training and Development Professionals

Order code: LP-J7993
$16.95 • 272 pages • 8 x 11
ISBN: 1-56370-799-3 • JIST Works

Inside Secrets of Finding a Teaching Job, Second Edition
by Jack Warner and Clyde Bryan, with Diane Warner

Tap the experts to get the inside track on your job search! The authors combine their 50 years of teaching experience with advice from hundreds of teachers, administrators, and personnel professionals. The result: A powerful guide to landing the perfect teaching job. Includes real-world success tips; the most commonly asked teacher interview questions; help with creating attention-getting resumes, portfolios, demonstration videos, and mission statements; and ways to follow up that increase your visibility and highlight your strengths.

Order code: LP-J921X
$12.95 • 208 pages • 6 x 9
ISBN: 1-56370-921-X • JIST Works

Order today!
Call 800-648-JIST, fax us at 800-JIST-FAX,
or visit us online at www.jist.com.

JIST Ordering Information

JIST specializes in publishing the very best results-oriented career and self-directed job search material. Since 1981 we have been a leading publisher in career assessment devices, books, videos, and software. We continue to strive to make our materials the best there are, so that people can stay abreast of what's happening in the labor market, and so they can clarify and articulate their skills and experiences for themselves as well as for prospective employers. **Our products are widely available through your local bookstores, wholesalers, and distributors.**

The World Wide Web

For more occupational or book information, get online and see our Web site at **www.jist.com**. Advance information about new products, services, and training events is continually updated.

Quantity Discounts Available!

Quantity discounts are available for businesses, schools, and other organizations.

The JIST Guarantee

We want you to be happy with everything you buy from JIST. If you aren't satisfied with a product, return it to us within 30 days of purchase along with the reason for the return. Please include a copy of the packing list or invoice to guarantee quick credit to your order.

How to Order

For your convenience, the last page of this book contains an order form.

Consumer Order Line:
Call toll free 1-800-648-JIST.
Please have your credit card (VISA, MC, or AMEX) information ready!

Mail your order:
JIST Publishing, Inc.
8902 Otis Avenue
Indianapolis, IN 46216-1033

Fax your order:
Toll free 1-800-JIST-FAX

Order online:
www.jist.com

JIST Order and Catalog Request Form

Purchase Order #: _____ (Required by some organizations)

Billing Information

Organization Name: _____

Accounting Contact: _____

Street Address: _____

_____

_____

City, State, ZIP: _____

Phone Number: ( ) _____

Shipping Information with Street Address (If Different from Above)

Organization Name: _____

Contact: _____

Street Address: (We *cannot* ship to P.O. boxes) _____

_____

City, State, ZIP: _____

Phone Number: ( ) _____

Please copy this form if you
need more lines for your order.

Phone: 1-800-648-JIST
Fax: 1-800-JIST-FAX
World Wide Web Address:
http://www.jist.com

Credit Card Purchases:

VISA_____ MC_____ AMEX_____

Card Number: _____

Exp. Date: _____

Name As on Card: _____

Signature: _____

Quantity	Order Code	Product Title	Unit Price	Total
	—	**Free JIST Catalog**	**Free**	—

Subtotal	
+6% Sales Tax *Indiana Residents*	
+Shipping/ Handling/Ins. (See left)	
TOTAL	

jist
Publishing

8902 Otis Avenue
Indianapolis, IN 46216

Shipping / Handling / Insurance Fees

In the continental U.S. add 7% of subtotal:
- Minimum amount charged = $5.00
- FREE shipping and handling on any prepaid orders over $50.00

Above pricing is for regular ground shipment only. For rush or special delivery, call JIST Customer Service at 1-800-648-JIST for the correct shipping fee.

Outside the continental U.S. call JIST Customer Service at 1-800-648-JIST for an estimate of these fees.

Payment in U.S. funds only!

JIST thanks you for your order!